101
GREAT GAA
TEAMS

101 GREAT GAA TEAMS

JOHN SCALLY

BLACK & WHITE PUBLISHING

First published in the UK in 2021
This edition first published in 2022 by
Black & White Publishing Ltd
Nautical House, 104 Commercial Street, Edinburgh EH6 6NF

A division of Bonnier Books UK
4th Floor, Victoria House, Bloomsbury Square, London, WC1B 4DA
Owned by Bonnier Books
Sveavägen 56, Stockholm, Sweden

The publisher has made every reasonable effort to contact copyright holders
of images in the picture section. Any errors are inadvertent and anyone who
for any reason has not been contacted is invited to write to the publisher so
that a full acknowledgement can be made in subsequent editions of this work.

A CIP catalogue record for this book is available from the British Library.

ISBN: 978 1 78530 391 3

1 3 5 7 9 10 8 6 4 2

Typeset by Iolaire Typesetting, Newtonmore
Printed and bound in Great Britain by Clays Ltd, Elcograf S.p.A.

www.blackandwhitepublishing.com

They are our family, our friends, our people – we remember them all.

BRENDAN GLEESON
in Croke Park at the ceremony to mark the
Bloody Sunday Centenary commemoration

In Ireland, back through the centuries, the tribes were led by the chieftain. And Christy Ring was our chieftain.

DÓNAL O'GRADY

Pat Spillane said after the match he was speechless. That was the only good thing about it.

JOE BROLLY
after Dublin hammer Meath
in the 2020 Leinster final.

GER CANNING: *What would it mean to Offaly if they win the All-Ireland?*

JOHNNY PILKINGTON: *A lot of drinking, Ger.*

To John O'Mahony:

A man of honour, decency and integrity.
His voice like thunder spake
And he brought the West awake.

CONTENTS

Foreword by Anthony Daly   xv

Introduction   1

PART I: DESERT ISLAND TEAMS   5

  1. Heffo's Army: Dublin 1974–79   7

  2. Dancing at the Crossroads: Wexford 1996–97   11

  3. The Men Behind Dwyer: Kerry 1975   17

  4. Sweet Dreams Are Made of This: Cork 1990   21

  5. Top Cats: Kilkenny 2006–09   26

  6. We are Meath: Meath 1986–91   30

  7. Waterford Wizards: Waterford 1998–2010   33

  8. Players of the Faithful: Offaly 1980–82   39

  9. Shannon Waters Tears of Joy that Flow: Limerick 2018–21   43

10. Lilywhite Legends: Kildare 1997–2000   46

11. The Famine Days Are Over: Tipperary 1987–91   50

12. Laois Legends: Laois 1988–2001   55

13. People of Galway, We Love You: Galway 1980–88   58

14. King Size: Cavan 1997   62

15. The Rebel Yell: Cork 2002–18   66

16. No Fancy Dans: Galway 1998–2001   69

17. Keeping the Faithful: Offaly 1994–98   71

18. The Earley Years: Roscommon 1977–80   75

19. Dalo's Dubs: Dublin 2008–14   79

20. Thy Kingdom Go: Cork 1987–90   83

21. Five-in-a-Row: Kerry 2014–18   86

22. No Ordinary Joe: Galway 2008–21   89

23. Connacht Gold: Mayo 1987–89   92

PART II: THE GAMECHANGERS   95

24. Where We Sported and Played: Cork 1939–47   97

25. The Heather Blazing: Wexford 1955–56   108

26. Micko's Maestros: Kerry 1978–86   113

27. Raising the Banner: Clare 1995–97   116

28. Galway Boys Hurrah: Galway 1964–66   121

29. Mighty Mackey: Limerick 1934–40   124

30. Small Heads and Small Arses: Cork: 2004–16   127

31. The Black and Amber: Kilkenny 1969–75   130

32. The Kings of Ulster: Cavan 1947–52   133

33. Striking It Big: Cork 2003–06   135

34. Kings of the Kingdom: Kerry 1903–14   137

35. The Tipperary Trailblazers: Tipperary 1949–52   141

36. Mayo's Magnificence: Mayo 1950–51   144

37. The Strife of Brian: Kilkenny 2000–03   147

38. How the West was Won: Corofin 2018–20   150

39. The Premier Team: Tipperary 1960–71   153

40. The Terrible Twins: Galway 1956–59   157

41. Dublin's Camogie Queens: Dublin 1941–67   160

42. Down but Not Out: Down 1991–94   163

43. Corkers: Cork 1975–79   167

44. A Blue Christmas: Dublin 2017–21   170

45. Belfield Brilliance: UCD 1970s   173

46. The Happiest Days of Our Lives:
    St Kieran's College 2009–19   176

47. Blessed Are the Peacemakers: Kerry 1929–32   179

48. Christy of the Rovers: Glen Rovers 1941–67   181

49. Jimmy's Winning Matches: Donegal 2011–14   184

50. Hymn to Her: Kilkenny 1974–91   188

51. Six of the Best: Crossmaglen 1996–2003   191

PART III: THE FIRST CUT IS THE DEEPEST   195

52. The Boys in Blue: Dublin 2013–21   197

53. Offaly Proud: Offaly 1980–89   201

54. Up Down: Down 1960–68   204

55. Doyens of the Déise: Waterford 1938–48   207

56. Mighty Meath: Meath 1940–54   210

57. Shannonside Sensations: Limerick 1921–23   213

58. With God on Their Side: Tyrone 2003–08   216

59. Five out of Six Ain't Bad: Tipperary 1999–2004   218

60. O'er the Bright May Meadows of Shelmalier:
    Wexford 1912–18   221

61. Carlow's Crowning Glory: Carlow 1941–44 224

62. Donegal's Destiny: Donegal 1989–92 227

63. Come on the Rossies: Roscommon 1943–47 230

64. Kilkenny Kings: Kilkenny 1931–35 234

65. Antrim Arrive on the Big Stage: Antrim 1946 237

66. The Longford Leaders: Longford 1965–68 242

67. For Nudie Reason: Monaghan 1979–88 247

68. Westmeath's Wonderland: Westmeath 2004 250

69. Fields of Dreams: Armagh 2002 253

70. From Small Acorns: Derry 1993 257

71. The Offaly Rovers: Offaly 1959–72 261

72. The Wee County Hit the Big Time: Louth 1950–57 266

73. The Green and Red of Mayo: Mayo 1936 269

74. The Triple Crown: Sleacht Néill 2016 272

75. Team Thomond: Thomond College 1978 275

PART IV: TEAMS FOR ALL SEASONS 279

76. Mighty Men: Meath 1996–99 281

77. The Clare Champions: Clare 1974–78 284

78. The Wicklow Way: Wicklow 1952–55 289

79. Out of the West: Sligo 1997–2007 292

80. The Script of Hurt: Mayo 2012–21 295

81. The Cats are Back: Kilkenny 2011–15 298

82. The Edge of Glory: Laois 2003–05 302

83. Fermanagh Fly Sky High: Fermanagh 2004 305

84. From Clare to Here: Clare 1992 307

85. The Trip to Tipp: Tipperary 2010–19   310

86. Lovely Leitrim: Leitrim 1990–96   314

87. The Kingdom's Decade?: Kerry 2000–11   317

88. The Treaty's Title: Limerick 1973–74   320

89. Brain and Bawn: Kerry 1940–46   323

90. The Men Behind the Wire: Burke's Brigade 1916   326

91. The Purple and Gold: Wexford 1970–77   329

92. Simply the Best: Mayo 1999–2003   331

93. Lord of the Rings: Munster 1940–63   334

94. Observe the Sons of Ulster: Ulster 1984   337

95. So Far Away. So Close: Mayo 1996–2006   341

96. Pat on the Back: Dublin 2011   344

97. The Darkest Day: Tipperary 1920–22   347

98. What the Doctor Ordered: Kerry 1953–59   350

99. The Boxers: Ireland 2006–08   354

100. The Pride of the Parish: Feakle 1987–88   356

101. Graced by Michael Collins: Dublin 1921   361

Acknowledgements   363

FOREWORD

I played on a great team that went on a great journey.

I think that after the League final in 1995, ninety per cent of Clare followers felt that is it: we can't take any more trouncings. You couldn't blame them. Although we hadn't been trounced on the scoreboard, in hurling terms we had been. Coming out after the game one supporter said, 'Kilkenny were a different class.' This massacre came on the back of major defeats in the two previous years in Munster finals. When Ger Loughnane spoke about us winning the Munster final, none of the fans believed him.

There were less than 15,000 supporters at our first game in the Championship and most of them were from Cork. Even when we beat Cork and the Munster final was jammed, it was mostly filled with Limerick people.

Everybody in Clare was convinced we had no chance of winning that game because we'd played Galway in a challenge match in Shannon two weeks before and bombed.

The scenes when we won the Munster final in 1995 were something to treasure. Although there weren't that many Clare people there, they were absolutely fanatical.

Bringing home the cup was absolutely incredible. There was a wonderful feeling of achievement and togetherness. We came over the bridge in Limerick and that was fantastic, but we were on our own because there wasn't a Clare person in sight. We thought it would be just a bit of a celebration in Ennis.

When we got to Cratloe we couldn't get through with crowds. It was such a scene of celebration and sporting hysteria. We couldn't even get to Shannon because we were a mile late getting to Ennis, but they had bonfires for us and everything. Clare FM was well established and it was putting out bulletins of our progress, so everybody knew where we were.

In 1992, the Clare footballers had won the Munster title and that generated great celebrations, but hurling was the game that had produced all the disappointments. This was a real breakaway from all that. You have to remember that when people talked about winning in Clare all they meant was winning the Munster final. The All-Ireland final wasn't even contemplated because the Munster final had always been such a stumbling block.

For myself personally it was winning the Munster final and the satisfaction that came from that. The boys often talk about how unprepared the Clare people were for our win. We got back to Clarecastle and there was no podium. My mother was normally an avid bingo goer on Sunday nights, and all I said was it must be a very special night if she hadn't gone.

Then there was an All-Ireland to challenge for. No one will ever forget the night the training was bad and Stephen McNamara had complained of a stomach bug and Loughnane brought us all back into the dressing room because we were so lethargic in training. He gave a tyranny of a speech and began with me. 'It starts with the captain.' He lambasted me and then everybody else and eventually he came around to Stephen Mac. He hit him a kind of belt in the stomach and said: 'Sick, Mac? Sick is coming out of Croke Park beaten.' I think that was a turning point because we weren't going to settle for winning Munster – we were going to go all the way.

We were different people and there was a swagger in our steps going into work – we were nearly like new men.

The Sparrow (Ger O'Loughlin) and myself went for a swim the day before the final and I asked him what he thought, and he said he thought we were going to win. I said I felt the same. I had bought in to the theory that it was our year. There was a bit of magic in the air in Croke Park that day. It just seemed the way things fell into place. On the day Offaly got two fortunate goals, but we never dropped our heads. We came out and hurled away and got the break with the goal two minutes from the end. Offaly got the goal just before half-time and everyone says that's a great time to get a goal, but it's probably a better time to get one with two minutes to go. Clare were on the way to victory.

It was great going to the schools afterwards just to witness the magic, the awe and the wonder, but to me the most special part was meeting the older people. I remember meeting my brother's father-in-law crying in Thurles after we won. He could remember back to 1955 and all the catalogue of Clare's heartbreaks. At the time I was so wound up and drained from games that I didn't fully appreciate it until later. I do now.

That Clare team gave me and the county memories that will last a lifetime.

This book is a long overdue tribute to great GAA teams.

I hope you enjoy it.

Anthony Daly
September 2021

INTRODUCTION

'Ninety-nine per cent of the world's lovers are not with
their first choice. That's what makes the jukebox play.'

WILLIE NELSON

Willie Nelson's statistics do not hold up in the GAA. For many of
us, our team is our first love. It is also our last love.

They are our cups of blessings.

They are the chosen few who have drunk from the chalice of
immortality.

For GAA fans, our great teams refine the soul and bring colour
and richness into the dullest life. In barren years we become
blind to beauty and lose our sense of wonder, with a consequent
impoverishment of spirit – the spirit that only grows by winning
big games – like a flower opening to the sun. Winning introduces
us to the Italian concept of '*dolce far niente*' (sweet idleness) as we
bask in the reflected glory of our teams. When our team is on a
winning streak it imbues us with a deep feeling and solidarity and
a glow that uplifts the spirit.

Great teams have a special power. They touch a deep chord in
every fan's heart; they refine the spirit when we listen to the music

1

of life, the sound of the wind in the trees, the sound of laughter, the sounds of nature. The thunderous applause for our great teams is the sweetest sound of all. They enable us to tap into the core of life and become energised, to become in touch with our own deepest feelings and get in touch with others.

In this heightened emotional space, we begin to notice the small things with a keener eye, and marvel (for example) at the process by which the humble dandelion morphs into the exquisite delicacy of that white orb that captures the hearts of children. In that sense, we all become children again, for in the previous 'normal of losing regularly' we knew the truth of Francis Thompson's words: ''Tis ye, 'tis our estranged faces/That miss the many-splendoured thing'.

That's the particular thrill of great teams. They can liberate the body, the heart – even the spirit – from years or generations of heartbreak. They can so lift the soul that they give it a taste of heaven. The role of great teams is to arouse the music within us that the rough, hard life we lead so often puts to sleep. Like the eagle flying majestically or the brilliant ballet of the sparkling stars, the great teams proclaim the rhythm and harmony of our liberation from the mundane.

This book is a well-deserved and – as Anthony Daly notes in his foreword – long-overdue tribute to our great teams. Inevitably a collection such as this can only be a personal one. No two GAA fans would pick the identical hundred great teams. Which ones? If the answer is easy, it is generally wrong. Many of them are obvious and pick themselves. I am very happy to include these. However, I was determined to also include a few less obvious ones – which perhaps give an insight into the totality of the humanity, humour and history of the story of Gaelic games.

I could fill a book on great Kerry and Dublin football teams and of Kilkenny, Cork and Tipperary hurling teams alone. However, as the GAA is a national movement, I was determined that each county would be represented. This of course restricts the space to select teams that have achieved great things and were great in their own way.

We do not talk about great teams from an innocent place. All GAA fans see things through the prism of their own counties. Consequently, we audit greatness in different ways. When Dublin won the six-in-a-row in 2020, they were clearly a great team. However, when Leitrim won the Connacht title in 1994, their fans were entitled to label their side 'great' given the scale of that achievement. Each county has had its own brush with great teams even though they may not all attract equal acclaim on a national level.

I did not want to turn this book into a collection of match reports but rather give the reader an insight into the stories behind these teams through the eyes of the men and women who made them happen.

Play on.

PART I

Desert Island Teams

There is a moving scene in one of my favourite films, *The Shawshank Redemption*. The central character Andy is all alone in the warden's office. He plays an aria from *The Marriage of Figaro*, first for himself, and then through the public address system, at which point every last man in the prison looks up and stands still to listen to this beautiful piece. Then Andy's friend Red, played so brilliantly by Morgan Freeman, remarks that he had no idea what those women were singing about because some things are better left unsaid.

Great teams inspire us at a level so deep it can't be expressed in words and make our hearts beat faster because of it. They make us soar higher and farther than anybody in a grey place dares to dream.

Each fan of Gaelic games is an island. We bring different emotional responses to teams, through the blinkers of our own biases and prejudices. We love them for all their faults.

For this opening section I pick some of my own favourite teams.

1

HEFFO'S ARMY

Dublin 1974–79

My favourite film is *Gladiator*. The key scene is when Russell Crowe's enslaved former general, Maximus, takes off his mask and reveals his identity to Joaquin Phoenix's evil emperor in front of a Coliseum full of raucous Romans.

By accident rather than design, I attended Dublin's first match in the Leinster Championship in 1974. It was my first visit to Croke Park to see Roscommon lose the League final replay to Kerry. Most neutrals there would have laughed at the idea that this Dublin team would change the face of Gaelic football forever. Four months later they took off their mask and we gasped in wonder.

Over the last ten years, Dublin have become the superpower of football. However, this was not their first time in this role. By 1923, Dublin's footballers had won their fourteenth All-Ireland, but eventually they began to lag behind Kerry and never caught up – especially as they won only one All-Ireland in each of the 1940s, '50s and '60s. In 1973, their star forward from the 1958 All-Ireland winning team, Kevin Heffernan, was appointed team manager and he would not only transform the place of Gaelic football in the county but throughout the country. When he took the job though things looked bleak: 'There were four fundamental points: the team had won nothing, it had done nothing, morale was at a low ebb and confidence just was not there.'

A first Leinster title in nine years began the road to glory. Then they staged a stirring comeback against Galway in the 1974 All-Ireland final. Galway led 1-4 to 0-5 at half-time, but Liam Sammon, who had never missed a penalty for Galway, had his effort saved by Paddy Cullen in the second half, and Heffo's heroes won by 0-14 to 1-6.

This became arguably the GAA's most famous rivalry when Kerry beat them 2-12 to 0-11 in the 1975 All-Ireland final. The Dubs did gain revenge in '76 though, on a 3-8 to 0-10 score. In 1977 they clashed again, this time in the All-Ireland semi-final with Dublin emerging victorious, 3-12 to 1-13. The game has often been described as 'the greatest Gaelic football match ever'. The Jacks would go on to complete back-to-back All-Irelands by crushing Armagh, 5-12 to 3-6.

They played in six consecutive All-Ireland finals; losing to Kerry in '78 and '79. Their influence on Gaelic football cannot be understated. They brought unprecedented media attention and glamour to the game and encouraged a new generation of kids to play football. The late RTÉ commentator Mick Dunne is credited with their switch from white to navy shorts in 1974 because it would look better on television.

C'MON YE BOYS AND BLUE

'The Blue Panther' Anton O'Toole revealed some of the secrets of the team to me: 'Heffo turned us all into stars and the likes of Kevin Moran and Brian Mullins into superstars. He could spot a solution for every problem. He dragged Jimmy Keaveney from retirement. Without Jimmy and his brilliance over a dead ball, we would have won nothing. Equally, Heffo knew when a lad had passed his prime and needed to be retired.

'He had our games recorded. At that time video analysis was alien to the GAA, though now it has become nearly overkilled. Heffo was always ahead of the curve, before anyone else knew there was a curve. Even as a player he had that innovation. He is credited with introducing the third man midfielder. This isn't false modesty, but we were a fairly average and often disinterested group of players when he came on the scene. He kept things lean and mean and had only two selectors. He raised our fitness to a whole new level, though Mick O'Dwyer's Kerry lads quickly matched us. Our rivalry with Kerry fuelled his ambition and he pushed us even harder because of it.

'We were all very surprised when he walked away for a while when we were in our prime. In fairness to him, Tony Hanahoe stepped up and did a brilliant job leading us. I guess it's no secret that David Hickey was unhappy when Heffo came back. David was a brilliant forward but wasn't a man for hiding his feelings! He was like Heffo himself in that respect, and as we've seen, he's played a major role in Irish life through his career as a surgeon and his campaigning work about the situation in Cuba and is a man of strong opinions. No wonder Joe Brolly likes him!

'Heffo loved Dublin but he had such a huge love for St Vincent's. He was a great mentor to Pat Gilroy, and the St Vincent's connection was crucial in respect. In many ways Pat continued Kevin's legacy.'

The definitive epithet for Heffo's army came from the man best equipped to evaluate them, Jim Gavin: 'Nothing will ever match Kevin Heffernan's team and what he did for Dublin GAA. His spark and genius – we just stand on their shoulders really.'

DUAL STAR

Kevin Moran played under Kevin Heffernan with Dublin and under Alex Ferguson at Manchester United. What links them in his eyes? 'They were both absolute winners.'

Kevin Moran went for a two-day trial at Manchester United. After that, the then United manager Dave Sexton offered him a two-and-a-half-year contract on a salary of £100 a week. At the time, he was making £17 a week in his job as an accountant. Such was Moran's commitment to the Dubs though that he asked for three weeks to consider it. Why? 'I was so lucky to play with those bunch of lads. To this day we are still incredibly close.'

Moran is a man of absolute integrity. He was famously the first man ever sent off in an FA Cup Final in 1985. After the game finished, the United manager Ron Atkinson told him he couldn't get a medal because he'd been sent off but instructed him to walk up the steps nonetheless because of his contribution all season. The official presenting the medals was oblivious to the rule and was about to present Moran with the medal when Kevin said to him: 'No, you can't give me that.' He was given the medal a few months later.

2

DANCING AT THE CROSSROADS

Wexford 1996–97

> *'An hour with a wise man is better than a
> lifetime studying books.'*
>
> LIAM GRIFFIN

It was as if some beautiful bird flapped into their old cages and
made those walls dissolve away. And for that wonderful time,
every Wexford hurling fan felt free.

It has become part of hurling orthodoxy to refer to the mid-
1990s as hurling's 'revolution years' as Offaly, Clare and Wexford
prevented the three traditional hurling superpowers of Kilkenny,
Cork and Tipperary from winning the All-Ireland for five years.

The word change normally refers to new beginnings. But the
mystery of revolution more often happens not when something
new begins but when something old falls apart. The pain of something old falling apart – chaos – forces the established order to go
to a new place.

We will normally do anything to keep the old thing from falling
apart, yet this is when we need patience and guidance instead of

tightening our controls and certitudes. While a desire for change can force a revolution, such periods in history – such as French society in 1789 – always include a disconcerting reorientation. It can either help people to find new meaning or it can force them to close down and slowly turn bitter. Change happens, but revolution is always a process of letting go, living in the confusing, shadowy space for a while. Eventually, we are spit up on a new and unexpected shore. The problem in hurling is that from 1999–2012 we arrived back at the same shore we'd left behind in 1993 with the three old powers ruling the roost again and banishing the other counties from the top prize.

The mid-1990s did not generate an authentic revolution in hurling, but they did generate a unique magic – and Liam Griffin's Wexford were at the heart of it. Clare brought new colour to Croke Park when they won the All-Ireland in 1995, but Wexford added their own quota of colour. It helped that they had such great characters like 'the Maradona of the Slaney' Seán Óg Flood and 'the Brother' Larry O'Gorman.

TAKE CARE OF BUSINESS

It has been said that Jurgen Klopp could go on to become the chief executive of an FTSE top 100 company because of his intelligence, his management skills, his leadership qualities and his exceptional gifts as a communicator. Having built up a strong business of his own, Liam Griffin would bring a unique skill set to the job of managing Wexford.

Griffin also embraced what were innovative methods at the time. In 1996 he had a sports psychologist, Niamh Fitzpatrick, work with the panel, but he kept it under wraps. Such was the professionalism that he brought to the task, he had an interview process to select her. A master of misdirection, on the press night he instructed her to, 'Run out there and rub Larry Murphy's leg,' because he wanted the journalists to think she was a physiotherapist. He combined that innovation with an emphasis on traditional skills such as hooking and blocking.

Griffin promoted lateral thinking: 'My point in the dressing room was very simple. We don't have a D. J. Carey! We don't have a John Troy! But I tell you what – that doesn't mean we can't beat them – if we use our brains!'

He is keen not to take the credit for Wexford's triumph.

'I was lucky because of players of the calibre of Liam Dunne. If I didn't have him or a George [O'Connor] or a [Martin] Storey or all those fellas, there wouldn't be a Liam Griffin. I genuinely have a great love of all those guys. Because we joined arms and walked down the road together. No one broke the chain.'

Griffin led Wexford to glory despite a challenging background. His beloved wife Mary was diagnosed with Multiple Sclerosis the previous December. After the Christmas Eve diagnosis his immediate instinct was to resign but Mary persuaded him to stay on. He claims they probably wouldn't have won it in 1996 only for her. The focus she gave him, knowing that Wexford's Championship would be his last because he wanted to be available to care for her.

WALK TALL

Without wonder, the people perish. Wonder is a lovely quality that enables us to see into the freshness of things, to be able to look with a new eye on every day that dawns, on every sun that sets. Wonder is what sends a thrill through our being when spring sends the sap through the trees and makes the heart leap when it spots a rainbow in the sky.

In the summer of 1996, Liam Griffin's band of merry men created a purple-and-gold wonderland in Wexford. He did get inspiration from an unlikely source. RTÉ sent cameras down to Offaly before the Leinster final to capture the mood of the county, and former

Taoiseach Brian Cowen was prominent on the news when he was filmed singing the 'Offaly Rover' in a local pub. Liam Griffin was sitting at home in front of his television and saw Cowen singing 'A rover I have been and a rover I will stay'.

'They were singing the "Offaly Rover" and I suddenly thought, *"The Boys of Wexford" and "Kelly the Boy from Killane"*. That was me, to use a sports psychology term, finding an anchor. I decided that this was where we needed to make a stand. So I got up at five o'clock in the morning and I walked the beach in St Helen's up and down. I was saying to myself, "This is much more than a hurling match."

'This was way bigger than any game. I started to think, *We're actually fighting for a way of life here. This hurling is on the way out in this county. We haven't won an All-Ireland final since 1968. We're nobodies now. We're hurling for the actual saving of this game here.* And then I thought of my own dad. All the matches that my father brought me to as a kid.

'So I wrote a speech, and the speech was all about who we were and where we came from. I spoke to Niamh Fitzpatrick about what I was going to do, and I said, "Am I going to drive them mental?"

'She said, "No, I think it's brilliant." And I replied, "I want them to come back into Wexford with that cup. So, I'm going to stop the bus."

'Then she said, "Walk them out of Wexford then. And then let them walk back in again with it."'

He didn't tell anyone else about his plan, so when he asked the Wexford team bus driver to stop just before the Wexford–Wicklow border on the way to the Leinster final and then ordered everyone off, there were puzzled looks all around.

'We were going to walk out of Wexford, and we were going to walk back, and we were going to do whatever it took to bring that cup back. That's what we're focused on from the minute we started walking. And if that meant bringing death itself, then we were going to put our bodies on the line. We did everything we were supposed to do, and everybody knew what they were supposed to do. Tackle, hook, block, discipline. They're the things that you've got to do. And if we did that, then we'd a great chance of bringing back that cup. And if we resolved to do it, then nothing was going to stop us. We were ready. And were going to walk out of Wexford.

'I remember Niamh saying to me, "You make them deep breathe when they're walking up that road." So I said to them, "Breathe long and hard – we're walking out of Wexford. And when we put our feet outside this county, you remember that when we put them back in here, we'll be carrying that Leinster cup."

'I got back into the bus and sat down beside Rory Kinsella. There was silence for a minute, and he said to me, "Where the f**k did that come from? You know now that if we lose this match, you'll be the laughing stock of County Wexford."'

Wexford beat Offaly by 2-23 to 2-15. A conversation with Offaly's Michael Duignan after the match confirmed to Griffin that he was on the right track. Duignan observed to him: 'God, your lads were flying. They went through us as if we weren't there.'

Griffin was purring: 'That was my greatest level of satisfaction because of how well we played that day. And because we were playing such a great hurling team, we were able to express ourselves and still play hurling to that level. We couldn't do that again for the game against Galway in the semi-final – it was a different match-up. And then the All-Ireland final we had to go a different style altogether because we were down to fourteen men. We could express ourselves against Offaly.'

THE SACRED SOD
When Napoli, led by Diego Maradona at the height of his powers, won the League in 1986–87, such was the frenzied nature of the

celebrations that somebody put a sign outside the city cemetery saying, 'You don't know what you missed.' The celebrations when Wexford won the All-Ireland in 1996 weren't quite as intense – but they were pretty close.

Irish soccer legend Kevin Doyle was at the match. He told me: 'I pulled a piece of grass from Croke Park and brought it home because I was so aware of the enormity of the occasion. I still have that piece of grass to remind me of such a cherished memory.'

3

THE MEN BEHIND DWYER

Kerry 1975

They were the team that took me by my small hand and steered me to the cave of treasures.

After leading Kerry to his first All-Ireland title as manager in 1975, how did Mick O'Dwyer celebrate? He went with Mícheál O'Muircheartaigh to the commentator's house in Blanchardstown for a cup of tea.

As a young boy, I was enthralled by O'Dwyer's first Kerry team because they were so young and had such flair. Watching them was like opening a window and letting the sunlight in. In particular I was mesmerised by the nineteen-year-old Kerry forward who, to my eyes, was a symbol of that team: Pat Spillane.

SHOOTING FROM THE LIP

I had no idea at the time how important a figure he would become in my own life and in the nation as a whole. Mindful of the danger of confirmation bias, I sought an outside opinion on Spillane and chose the award-winning sportswriter Brendan Coffey to furnish it.

'Weekends when I was growing up were not complete without

The Sunday Game. Before I understood the concept of controversy, I seemed to know Pat Spillane was controversial. He had achieved notoriety in Kildare for disparaging remarks about the team during the 2000 Leinster final. Things got so bad, he was forced to apologise.

'Beyond the public enemy caricature, I knew little about him. I had no idea that Spillane was one of the most decorated players in the history of the game. His career read like a fairy tale. Imagine, he lifted Sam Maguire at nineteen!

'His recovery from injury – a ruptured cruciate ligament – captured my imagination. The scenes of him slogging around a field wearing ankle weights were unforgettable. As the story of his comeback unfolded, he was recast in my mind as an inspirational character, far removed from the divisive figure I watched on TV.

'By 2005, RTÉ had recast him as presenter of *The Sunday Game* highlights programme. His move from the pundits' couch added another layer of intrigue to the Pat Spillane story. I knew that he'd attended Thomond College, which had since been subsumed by the University of Limerick, where I was then a student.

'On a whim, I decided to approach him about an interview. I thought he would make an ideal subject for *An Focal*, the college newspaper. First, I had to get a contact number. I rang the family pub in Templenoe and explained my mission. The barman called out Pat's mobile: I was away in a hack.

'When I phoned Spillane, he was happy to oblige. Sundays around 11 a.m. were best. By early afternoon, he would be on his way to the television studio in Donnybrook. We met at Jury's in Ballsbridge, where he used to stay the night before the programme. The hotel was lively for a Sunday morning. As we started talking, Spillane overheard a passing conversation. "Keep your voice down," he warned. "There's one fella after calling me a bollocks already." Behind us, another guest had clocked Spillane: "Look, it's yer man off RTÉ."

'I brought an MP3 player to record the interview. The device was relatively new to me but had a microphone that clipped onto your shirt and held the promise of a better audio file. An overriding fear stalks every interview: is the tape working? I was keen to try out this new mic, sure that it would safeguard the conversation.

'We spoke for the best part of an hour and he was exactly as I imagined: lively, engaging, forthright. I travelled back to Maynooth on the train, thrilled. The day had been a triumph.

'That evening, back home, I copied the recording onto my computer. The file played but no voices emerged. All I could hear was the muffled sound of moving fabric. I replayed the file, over and over and over, but the same static rolled without a hint of human interference. A painful reality dawned. No amount of cursing at the computer could alter my situation: I was snared in a technological trap.

'Anger gave way to self-flagellation: I was mortified. My plan for this great article lay in ruin. A few days passed before the feeling subsided. What to do now? I chanced him on the mobile again, explained my predicament. He sounded kind of bemused, as if thinking: "Why is he telling me this?"

'"Perhaps we could meet again," I ventured. He laughed but not in a derisive way.

'"Most lads would have just made it up," he stated. I could only smile. Although it was getting near the end of the season, he could meet again in a couple of weeks: another Sunday appointment at Jury's. Just a basic Dictaphone this time.

'"The glass is always half full with me," he declared when we met for the second time. This creed seemed an appropriate theme for the piece. He had spoken at length about his comeback. "I regretted that suddenly I was out of football and basically nobody gave a shi*e," he recalled. "I just vowed that if I came back, I came back because of me and nothing else. No one came back playing football in Ireland having ruptured their cruciate in the 1980s. I came back a much harder individual. In everything, I was just focused. From that day on, I don't think I ever worried about anything. My motto has always been: 'I do it because I want to do it.' And I don't give a shi*e whether people agree with me or disagree with me. I say it because I want to say it."

'Spillane in full flow was compelling. And he continued in this fashion while assessing his own abilities. "I was never blessed with skill or brains," he admitted. "I was a slogger. If I was into anything I gave it 110 per cent." Spillane's parting words captured something essential about his breed: "Football is a drug. It's my life."

'We walked out together. He had a bunch of newspapers folded under his arm. At his car, he popped the boot and placed a suit inside. Early afternoon and a long day's work was just beginning. Already much of his week had been given over to football: club meetings, training sessions, underage matches. Whatever hour *The Sunday Game* finished airing that night, Spillane could hop into his saloon again. His journey home to Kerry would take him into the small hours of Monday. However handsome his rewards, to sustain such effort surely required searing passion.

'All that time in his company left it hard not to warm to Spillane. I came away from those interviews with a concrete sense of the man behind the popular image. As a journalist, you cannot ask for much more.'

NOT LOOKING BACK IN ANGER

I still feel great nostalgia when I think of the 1975 incarnation of the Kerry team. They showed intimations of greatness. Three years later though they would begin to make the case to be considered the greatest team of all time.

4

SWEET DREAMS ARE MADE OF THIS

Cork 1990

It was like the first and best days of love when everything is new, and nothing ran on empty if you were a Cork fan.

Literally at the centre of everything was a man born of warrior stock.

In September 1990, Teddy McCarthy wrote himself into the annals of the GAA. He starred in midfield in Cork's historic double: defeating Galway in the All-Ireland hurling final, then adding the second leg to a remarkable double a few weeks later when he helped, again in midfield, the Leesiders to beat old rivals Meath in the All-Ireland football final.

Cork's double was possible because of some remarkable men.

PROPHETIC
The coach of the hurling team was Michael 'the Canon' O'Brien. He was ahead of his time. He took over when Cork fortunes were at a low ebb and Tipperary were in the ascendancy. In 1990, at the team's first training session, he arrived in a new car. The registration was: 90-C-27.

The ninety was for the year.

The C was for Cork.

The twenty-seven was to signify that Cork were going to win their twenty-seventh All-Ireland in 1990. They did. It was another motivational masterstroke from the Canon.

He was a very kind man, but in full flight he was an intimidating sight. Once, he was taking part in a press conference, where one of the most challenging questions came from Donal Keenan, the Roscommon-born Gaelic games correspondent with the *Irish Independent* at the time. Donal's father (also Donal) had won two All-Ireland medals with Roscommon in the 1940s and served as president of the GAA in the 1970s. The Canon was irked by his question and responded by asking in turn: 'What the f**k would someone from Roscommon know about hurling?'

Ace defender Johnny Crowley once thought Fr O'Brien was gone safely home and lit up a cigarette while he was getting a massage. To his horror, O'Brien hurried back into the room, and the cigarette was quickly dispatched into the masseur's pocket. The Canon sniffed the air and asked, 'Do I smell smoke?'

'Oh God no,' came the reply. 'That's just the smell of the massage oils.'

By the time O'Brien had left, the masseur was in agony with a burning leg and his trousers had to be discarded into the dump that evening.

Ger Loughnane was a big fan. He was denied the ultimate dream of every young hurler – to win the Harty Cup. In the process he learned an invaluable lesson about the value of an inspired tactical ploy that would remain with him throughout his managerial career. He could not have learned from a more astute teacher.

'We played in a Harty Cup final against St Finbarr's of Farranferris. The opposition were trained by Fr Michael O'Brien. He came up with a masterstroke which cost us the match. He had this midfielder, Dan Dwyer, a wonderful player who never really fulfilled his extraordinary potential, primed to win the game for them. Just before the puckout, Dan would stand at one sideline then take off and just get to the other sideline as the ball landed there. It was a brilliant tactical move. Michael O'Brien was pulling stunts like that all his life!'

I once asked the Canon what the secret to his success as a coach was. The sun had almost sunk below the treetops. Watery beams of light spilled beneath the branches. He was in a mood that was remarkably close to contentment, his face bright and flushed with laughter. Even the fire in the parlour itself seemed to flicker with renewed strength as the words tumbling out of him were liberated, surfing a wave of excitement and anticipation.

'I'm a big believer in giving people opportunities. I'm fascinated by Roy Keane. I know for a fact that he does tremendous work for the people in Cork. Do you ever read about it? No. That's what real giving is about – no publicity, no expectation.

'In July 1993, Alex Ferguson broke the British transfer record of £3.75 million for the 21-year-old Cork man when he signed Keane from Nottingham Forest. As a teenager, he wrote to most top English clubs asking for a trial, but he didn't bother to write to United because he didn't think he was up to their lofty standards.

'He was born and reared in a Corporation housing estate in Mayfield on the north side of Cork City, an area synonymous with Gaelic football. Keane took part in the national game in the corner-forward position. He also showed promise as a pugilist and never lost a fight in the boxing ring.

'He spent ten years with Rockmount AFC, a well-known club in the north side of Cork. He had the good fortune to be part of a very successful side, with a number of his playing colleagues winning schoolboy caps for Ireland and drawing the discerning eyes of scouts from cross-channel clubs. Keane was not at the forefront of the scouts' attention. Following one trial game for the Irish under-15 side, he was informed he was surplus to requirements because he was too small. It is now difficult to match that diminutive, slight figure with the imposing frame which later filled the United jersey.

'When he was seventeen, he got a part-time contract with League of Ireland club, Cobh Ramblers. Part of the package was a football course in Dublin. A year later he was signing for Nottingham Forest for a snip of £25,000. Brian Clough's comments would prove to be well founded: "It's a long time since I've been so excited by a young man ... I'd quite happily have paid £500,000 for him."

'Nobody in the soccer world had ever heard of him, but one evening the late Brian Clough saw him playing twenty minutes in a reserve match for Nottingham Forest. Clough, often lampooned as an arrogant alcoholic, saw enough to pick this unknown youngster to play against mighty Liverpool a few days later at Anfield. Keane grabbed his chance and the rest is history. In his book, Keane thanks Clough for giving him the opportunity. Those who succeed in sport are those who take risks and give opportunities. It won't always pay off, but sometimes it will and sometimes it will pay off big time.'

Canon O'Brien always said a Cork team well prepared is very hard to beat. Galway had a seven-point lead over Cork in the 1990 All-Ireland hurling final and appeared to be cruising to another All-Ireland victory, particularly as Joe Cooney was giving a torrid time to Jim Cashman and calling the shots. However, two goals from Cork's John 'Schillaci' Fitzgibbon turned the match decisively in Cork's favour and they ran out comfortable winners.

IT COULD HAPPEN TO A BISHOP

The sun was dipping low into the horizon, bursting the sky red. The whirling wind was picking up and the temperature was dropping. Sheeting rain was coming in, and it would soon turn wet and miserable. But in that moment, there was a simple beauty that was bone-deep and undeniable as I went to meet the former Bishop of Killaloe and Clare selector Willie Walsh. He always took great pleasure from stories about positional changes.

One of the things that always struck him in hurling was the strange ways positional switches were made in a match, particularly in the 1990 hurling final between Cork and Galway. After about fifteen minutes, he was wondering what the Cork selectors were going to do about Jim Cashman. Joe Cooney was destroying him and he couldn't understand why they left Jim there. They went in at half-time and Bishop Willie said in the stands, 'Well Jim Cashman won't be centre-back in the second half,' but amazingly he was, and he went on to win his battle with Joe Cooney in the second half and Cork won the All-Ireland.

When Bishop Willie went back to Clare, some people said to him, 'Ah, you can't beat those Cork guys. Now if that was Clare, we'd have panicked and taken Jim Cashman off, but the Cork guys were wise and knew what was best.'

Of course that was a bit hurtful to Bishop Willie as a Clare selector, so when he went down to Cork a month later, he headed straight to Dr Con Murphy and asked, 'Up front now, what happened with Jim Cashman and why didn't you change him?'

Dr Con replied, 'Well we all agreed that Jim was being beaten and we'd have to change him. The problem was that none of the selectors could agree on who we would replace him with. So we decided to do the usual thing and give him five minutes in the second half.'

5

TOP CATS

Kilkenny 2006–09

They are a team engraved on the collective consciousness.

In 2008, such was the scale of Kilkenny's trouncing of Waterford, and because each player on that team produced peak performances, the RTÉ panel uniquely made Brian Cody, the manager, Man of the Match. It was the zenith in Cody's long reign – which yielded no less than four All-Irelands in a row.

In an exceptional interview with Anthony Daly in his podcast for the *Examiner*, former Kilkenny goalkeeper David Herity revealed that: 'Cody's phrase to me was that: he's not here to build friendships; he's here to build a legacy, and that to me sums him up.'

If one player symbolised Cody's tactical nous, it was Henry Shefflin's 1-14 against Waterford in the 2009 All-Ireland semi-final. King Henry's versatility and comfort in any of the six attacking positions allowed Cody the luxury of identifying a potential vulnerability in an opposition defence, at which to send his most trusted forward to do the rest. In the '09 semi-final, Shefflin went straight into full-forward and, within minutes, had set up Eddie Brennan for Kilkenny's first goal. Within minutes Tommy

Walsh spotted Shefflin isolated with Aidan Kearney and hit him a sublime 80-metre delivery for Kilkenny's second. The game was effectively won.

NATIONAL TREASURE

Tommy Walsh has become a national treasure since he started reporting on hurling on *Off the Ball*. In recent years, he has given fascinating insights into the Kilkenny philosophy. Bill Hennessy, a fellow Tullaroan clubman, once passed him on some advice he was given by one of the best hurlers to ever come out of Kilkenny, Willie O'Connor.

'Willie told Bill that if it came down to it, he'd much rather be fresh than fit. That stuck in my mind throughout my career. I'd liken the mindset you need for Championship hurling to sitting down to your dinner having not had a scrap to eat all day. No matter what's put in front of you, you'll have it demolished in no time. But if you've eaten an hour before your dinner, then you'll end up picking at it and pushing it around the plate. When it comes to Championship hurling, you better be ready to eat your dinner. And fast.'

Walsh added: 'I remember playing for Leinster in the Railway Cup in 2008 and we had a training session one night in Tinryland down in Carlow. A few of us Kilkenny lads went down together in the car and it was a miserable night for hurling – raining hard and freezing cold. Eddie Coady from the Mount Leinster Rangers club in Carlow marked a couple of the Kilkenny lads in training that night in a game of backs and forwards and tore strips off them. He won the ball high, low, in front, behind; it didn't matter what way it came. Absolutely hurled the ears off them. We were going home in the car that night from Carlow and we knew we weren't at the races. We knew we weren't ready. We had no edge or zest for it the way Eddie Coady had. We had thought we wanted to win the Railway Cup, but we weren't acting like it. Eddie was.

'We were proud Leinster men and we wanted to win it, but we weren't doing what it took. So we promised ourselves on that car journey home that we'd be ready the next day. We ended up beating Connacht in the semi-final and Munster in the final. That's what hunger does. It drives on the whole team and has you ready for game day. That's what belief can do for you. It can drive a Carlow hurler to tear into Kilkenny hurlers and come out with the ball time after time.'

Walsh identifies two key ingredients of the great Kilkenny team: belief and hunger. 'There are many ingredients to win a Championship hurling match, but they are two of the most vital.

'The fundamental law of the game is that matches are won by teams who are better equipped to win their own ball. Many people believe the best ball-winners have to be six-foot-plus and weigh fourteen stone, but they're mistaken. A broad set of shoulders and a big arse can be handy under a dropping ball, but they offer no guarantee you'll win the thing. Speed, skill, timing, technique and self-belief are just as important as strength when it comes to winning your own ball. And to be the best, you need them all. Because you have no chance of succeeding at the highest level of the game unless you can combine skill with a savage will to win that ball. You need that self-belief to persuade yourself mentally and physically that you're going to win it. The only thought running through your mind should be, *I'm going to win that ball and nothing is going to stop me.* That's what self-belief is.

'When I think of that sort of mindset, I think of Noel Hickey in the 2007 All-Ireland final against Limerick. He pulled his hamstring in the first few minutes when the ball came into the danger area and he was chasing Mike Fitzgerald. Another fella would have hit the ground and no one would have said anything, but not Noel. He kept going, ran Mike Fitz out to the corner of the Cusack Stand, danger averted. That was Hickey; that was self-belief and hunger.

'The best county hurlers all have an iron-clad self-belief and steely will to win, so the margins can be very fine when it comes to Championship hurling. And to give yourself the best chance of having an edge over your man, I think it goes back to that freshness that Willie O'Connor prized so much. That doesn't mean to slack off on your gym programme because you're tired. That's laziness. You don't do it because you've tried it already a few times and it hasn't worked for you. You might have been in better physical condition than you ever were before, but you were missing that edge, that zing, that absolute hunger to win every ball that came into your patch. Your focus should be on preparing yourself in the best way possible to have you in that mindset for game day.'

Walsh feels that Cody had a great knowledge of his Kilkenny players.

'He knew we took our hurling as seriously as he did so he'd give us that little bit of latitude. He'd figure out fairly quickly if you were pulling the wool over his eyes, because all would be revealed in a training game or the match at the weekend. Belief, hunger and freshness.

'Nothing got me better prepared for Championship matches than people doubting the team. I don't think you can win all the All-Irelands we did by playing safe. You have to take risks and go for the jugular. That's what Kilkenny always do best.'

6

WE ARE MEATH

Meath 1986–91

To corrupt the famous line from the acclaimed film *Fight Club*, the first rule of talking to Seán Boylan is to expect ferocious energy, passion, humanity and more depth than a 3D printer. In 2020 I got a mighty shock when I rang Seán and that energy field was missing.

'I went for a vaccination for pneumonia and the flu. Some six days later, I wasn't feeling well. It turned out that I had Covid. I ended up in hospital and was discharged from hospital on 31 March. I lost ten kilos in six days. But the terror, the fear – it was uncanny; it was unreal. I was never as afraid of anything in my life and I'm always very happy. It has taken me weeks to recover. Tina [his wife] said to me one day and even the kids were saying that I was still a bit snappy and short. I went out walking in the fields. I remember saying to myself, I got a ferocious fright and I'm probably shaking off my post-traumatic stress. It's been an extraordinary time, but in a strange sort of way, it's brought us very close together as a family. Does the lockdown suit me? No it doesn't, but it's been good for me. It makes you think about things, about your vulnerability, and makes you understand you'd like to have a cut at it for another while.'

Having previously battled cancer, the resilience which is at the heart of his DNA kicked in again and he bounced back as strong as ever. His great Meath team replicated the energy and passion that comes off him in relentless waves. After years in the wilderness, they won five Leinster titles in six years, contested All-Irelands in four years, winning two in 1987 and '88. To their critics they were defined by their performance in the 1988 All-Ireland final replay which did not make the case for Gaelic football to be labelled 'the beautiful game'.

The watershed moment for the team came in 1985 after they bombed against Laois in the Leinster Championship. Harsh words needed to be said afterwards if the Meath ship was to sail to brighter horizons. Padraig Lyons was one of a delegation who came to visit Boylan in his own kitchen. The Lyons brothers are renowned for doing their talking through their actions. Mick appeared in a major RTÉ documentary about Boylan in the summer of 2020 and did not utter a single word. Yet that night thirty-five years earlier, Padraig looked Boylan straight in the eye and said, 'Will you put your shyness in your arse pocket?' The words were heeded and the fortunes of the Meath team would be changed dramatically for the next generation as a consequence.

Bernard Flynn looked back wistfully on the 1991 All-Ireland final for me.

'I still feel we had more All-Irelands in us. I think the savagery we inflicted on each other in training sessions over all those years came back to haunt us. We also were suffering from playing so many games. By the time we got to the final, Colm O'Rourke was suffering from pneumonia, Padraig Lyons had broken his leg, Bob O'Malley had broken his leg. Mick Lyons would wreck his knee in the final. No team can afford to leave four of their best players in the dressing room when they go out to play an All-Ireland. We were slow out of the blocks that day, but we came good at the end and nearly pulled it out of the fire again, and if we'd had a few more minutes, people tell me we would have won.'

Flynn feels that it was a turning point in the perception of the team nationally.

'Two things happened. There was a lot of worry after Italia 1990 that soccer was going to take over and the GAA would lose out, but our four games against Dublin in '91 captured the imagination of the country and in the process we brought the GAA back to the forefront – 240,000 came to those games. We took our defeats in the All-Irelands against Cork in '90 and '91 with good grace. It's strange but people have said to me that we won more friends for the two All-Irelands we lost than for the two we won.'

7

WATERFORD WIZARDS

Waterford 1998–2010

Rapper Yung Shakur captures the passion Waterford fans have for their hurling team: 'Should be in Croydon with the fam. But I loves me county like John Mullane.'

It was in the 1998 Munster final and replay that the Waterford hurling team really announced itself on the national stage. The intensity of those games were on a scale few had ever seen before. To get an insight as to how this situation arose, I turned to the Clare captain on both days, Anthony Daly.

'At the end of 1997, the Clare squad were at another All-Ireland function when I approached a few of the boys. "Hi, your man [Ger Loughnane] is kinda delaying his commitment to staying on," I said. I was anxious for an answer so I only saw one way of getting it. "We'll go down and ask him straight out."

'A few days later, [Brian] Lohan, Jamesie [O'Connor], Seánie [McMahon] and myself arrived down to Loughnane's house in Shannon. As soon as we arrived, Loughnane began testing us as much as we were testing him. Did we have the same hunger and commitment? Loughnane put it straight up to me: "Where are you at, Dalo? You're after lifting the Liam MacCarthy twice. Do you want to lift it again?"

'I answered, "I'm still only twenty-eight, Ger. I think I've at least another couple of good years left in me. We'll never have it as good as we have it now. We'll never have as good a management."

'We all desperately wanted Loughnane back, even though we knew that if he did [come back], we were going to be tortured later that winter; we were going to be abused high up and low down. I could already hear his comments in my own head: "Milk would turn faster than you. Some lad from Tipp will make an ape out of you again. The whole country will be laughing at you." I still wanted Loughnane so badly because I believed so much in him, and in his way of getting the job done.

'We won just three games that spring – against Antrim, Dublin and Offaly – but we somehow ended up in a semi-final against Cork. We were flat on the day, and Cork gave us a right hiding. When we went back to a pub that night, a handful of customers gave it to us between the eyes. "Hi, Dalo, ye might let us know the next time ye're not going to bother yer arses, so we might save a few quid going to Thurles."

'Loughnane was equally as disgusted with us. We were struggling for form, but when he rang me the following day, the May Bank Holiday Monday, I said, "Ger, get me a few quid and a bus because we're going drinking up the coast."

'"What the . . .?"

'"Ger, just get me a few pounds and a minibus and I promise you we'll be right for the next seven weeks."

'Loughnane agreed. I remember asking Jamesie [O'Connor] and Colin Lynch, who didn't drink, to drive up and meet us there at 9 p.m. We went into a side room and I addressed the group. "Lads, I'm as fond of a pint as any man in this room but I won't be touching one drop again after tonight until we bate that shower." I didn't care what anyone else thought and neither did Loughnane. That was the beauty of our manager–captain relationship – he trusted me. If I said I was going to go down a certain route, Ger would back my plan if he agreed with it.

'We trained very hard in the lead-up to that Cork game. At one stage, we did twenty nights out of twenty-two. As I was leading the lads out the tunnel, I nearly knocked down Jimmy Barry-Murphy and Dr Con Murphy. "Get out of my fu**ing way," I roared at them. They did. So did Cork.

'At one stage of the game, the TV cameras caught me hissing in the face of Fergal McCormack. In his *Sunday Independent* column the following week, Kevin Cashman was critical of me. I got a great kick out of reading that piece. This was where I always wanted to be. I grew up looking at Cork and Tipp walking all over teams. I wanted to be like those guys.

'One of the lines in that piece more or less said "if that's the price of success for Clare, it isn't worth it". What? If he was writing about hurling back in the 1960s, I'd love to see what he'd have said about Tipp's "Hell's Kitchen". Or Christy Ring after some of those Cork–Tipp battles. Ring was well able to look after himself. I laughed reading that Cashman article. The wheel had really turned full circle. Before 1995, we were labelled as the greatest chokers that ever took to a hurling field. Three years later, we were depicted as a ruthless bunch.

'Even Loughnane was as high as a kite the same day. Towards the end of the match, he marched down towards the Killinan End terrace. When he pumped his fist up to the terrace, Semple Stadium exploded.

'It's not in our nature for Clare people to get carried away, but it was inevitable that some people would. I remember my brother Martin telling me some of the stuff Clare supporters were saying to Cork people as they left the ground early that afternoon. "Lads, make sure ye don't send up the minor team again next year."

'We all felt a little untouchable. There was definitely a sense that evening around the county of, "Ah, we'll have no problem taking care of Waterford in the final." I won't say we felt invincible, but we had an aura about us at the time.

'Gerald McCarthy and Waterford knew that we'd probably lost the run of ourselves. They had some brilliant players, but Waterford were also fully aware that if they could match us for aggression, they would take away some of our power – they would strip away some of that mystique around us. They certainly did. We felt they were the aggressors, both on the pitch and on the sideline. We were only hanging on for a finish. Paul Flynn had a late free to win the game.

'Dan Shanahan took me for three points. I was kinda embarrassed with my performance. I asked Loughnane if I could speak to the lads before he did. I took them out to the conservatory, which was baking hot, and told them of a nasty personal comment that had been said to me.

'Loughnane never asked me what I said to the players but I told him anyway the following night at training. He didn't need it. All it did was reaffirm how we, both the players and management, had been bullied all day by Waterford. We all knew what was coming before we even arrived into training. Our heads were down. We knew Loughnane was going to savage us, but we knew we deserved it too. On the Wednesday, we played a forty-minute match in training that was absolutely filthy. There were fights breaking out all over the field, lads leathering one another with hurleys and fists. "Now," Loughnane roared, "we're ready."

'On the Friday night, he brought us in to the goal at the bottom of Cusack Park and had us in the palm of his hand as he laid down the law. We were never going to be bullied again. We were never going to dishonour Clare again.

'On the Sunday, we would have nearly belted each other in the dressing room if Loughnane didn't let us out when he did. I didn't say too much, but I remember going into the shower area with Davy Fitzgerald and the defenders beforehand. "I can guarantee ye all, what happened to me the last day won't happen today. A lot of talking has been done all week but by Jaysus the talking is over now. We'll do whatever we have to do out on that field." Both sides went at it, but we were like men possessed.'

Waterford lost the battle in the replay, but they would be back. Later that year came an early indication that they were about to take their place at hurling's top table when Tony Browne was chosen as Hurler of the Year. But in the noughties they really came of age. What cemented their status in the popular imagination was their games against Cork.

It is telling that in their eleven Championship games between 2002 and 2010, Cork's five-points win in the '05 All-Ireland final was the highest winning margin. Who will ever forget the '04 Munster final? Thunderbolt City, when despite having John Mullane sent off, the Déise won 3-16 to 1-21.

Before they played in '02, the counties had met fifty times in the Championship. Cork had won thirty-nine, Waterford just eight. When Waterford won their first Munster title in 1938, they defeated Cork on the way, their first win against them in nineteen contests.

In the noughties, games between both counties were inextricably bound to drama. Think of Ken McGrath's coming off the bench to hit the winning point in '02; John Mullane's three goals in '03; Paul Flynn's stunning goal in '04; Dónal Óg Cusack stopping Ken McGrath's late free going over the bar in '06; Eoin McGrath going man for man with Dónal Óg Cusack in '07; and perhaps the end of an era in 2010 with Tony Browne scoring the equalising goal in the seventy-fourth minute of the drawn Munster final, and Dan

Shanahan scored the winning goal late in extra time of the replay in characteristic high-octane contests.

There was even an interesting subplot. Cork royalty Gerald McCarthy and Justin McCarthy coached Waterford teams against Cork. When Gerald returned to manage Cork against Justin in three games in '07, the rivalry increased even more.

LEGACY

Anthony Daly looks back on that Waterford team with great affection.

'They never won an All-Ireland, but they were a swashbuckling, flamboyant group who brought so much more to the game than just their skill and quality. The brilliance of their hurling was only one element – the shaved heads; the tattoos; kissing the crest on their jerseys; how they wore their collars up; how they stuck their chests out.

'That breakthrough win in 2002 was a landmark victory for hurling in the province because it also announced Waterford as a serious force on the national stage for the rest of the decade.

'Fergie Tuohy and I travelled down together for that Munster final. As we strolled back to the car afterwards, fully intending to head home, we decided to go into the city for one pint. We wound up in this bar celebrating all evening with Waterford fellas. The craic was so good we stayed on overnight. It had been just four years since the fallout from the 1998 Munster final but there was no animosity or ill-feeling that evening. Tuts and I could relate to the beauty of that moment when you finally make the breakthrough.'

8

PLAYERS OF THE FAITHFUL

Offaly 1980–82

Sometimes we are at our most stupid when we are at our most certain.

Eugene McGee brought Offaly back to the top table after Kevin Heffernan's Dublin had reigned supreme in Leinster for years.

Like Ger Loughnane in Clare, getting the Offaly job in the first place was one of his biggest challenges. There were four hurdles to be jumped. He was not from Offaly. He had no pedigree as a player. Even worse, he was a journalist! Some of the Offaly legends from the All-Ireland winning teams of 1971 and '72 fancied their chances of succeeding their teammate – 'The Iron Man from Rhode' Paddy McCormack.

Enter a man of vision, foresight and bold moral courage. In 1976, the new county chairman Fr Seán Heaney knew intuitively that radical surgery rather than a band-aid solution was necessary if Offaly football was going to scale the summit again. They had just been relegated to Division Two and had lost emphatically to Meath by nine points in the Leinster Championship. Their glory days looked like they were consigned to the dustbin of history. Fr Seán persuaded McGee to take over the reins.

The appointment was far from universally welcomed. By 1980, McGee led Offaly to a Leinster final, in which they were beaten by Dublin. But the county board delegates hadn't taken to McGee. They attacked him covertly by insisting that he appoint four more selectors. During one match in Cork, the team manager stood on the line while the selectors sat in the stands. When he sought to make a change, McGee had to run up the steps for consultation and a vote. It was obvious to all and sundry that he was being publicly undermined. In response, for a big tournament game, McGee selected the team himself and didn't tell the selectors anything. He informed them, 'That's the team we're playing.' Fortunately for him they won. That night, the four selectors wrote to Fr Heaney telling him they could not work with McGee. For the second time Fr Seán had the courage of his convictions and swam against the prevailing tide. The following morning, each selector found a brief note through their postboxes thanking them for their services. History would vindicate the man who today continues to minister to his flock in Tullamore but away from the sometimes shark-infested waters of GAA politics.

IT'S FIVE IN A ROW

McGee would reward the faith placed in him and mastermind perhaps the most famous All-Ireland win in history in 1982. The team had been building nicely. After defeating Dublin in the 1980 Leinster final, they contested a thrilling All-Ireland semi-final. In a match played at ferocious pace that generated a feast of scores, Kerry came out on top by 4-15 to 4-10. An astounding statistic from the game is that all of Offaly's scores came from just two players – Gerry Carroll who got 2-1 and the extraordinary genius of Matt Connor who scored 2-9.

The second instalment came in 1981 in a tight All-Ireland final. The Kingdom won their four-in-a-row because of the goal of the year which saw six Kerry players handling the ball in a sweeping move which culminated in Jack O'Shea unleashing a rocket of a shot. An indication of the confidence in Kerry of winning the All-Ireland in 1982 came a few weeks before the match in the team's victory song, 'It's Five in a Row'.

Páidí Ó Sé recalled his memories of the game for me.

'It was a massive disappointment to lose in '82 and a memory that has never left me because we were minutes away from immortality. We had plenty of chances to win the game but we became too defensive when we went four points up and this allowed Offaly back into the game. People say if Jimmy Deenihan was in there, the famous Séamus Darby goal wouldn't have got in, and they were right. Jimmy knew how to "put manners" on anyone. I think it was a bigger deal for our supporters than for us. I think we were the better team, but the result said otherwise. Fair play to them, and if ever a footballer deserved to win an All-Ireland it was Matt Connor.

'The first half was open and it was a very good game of football. During the second half it started raining fairly heavily and the game deteriorated a good bit. Kerry dominated for a long time and Offaly were lucky enough to stay with us. Martin Furlong's penalty save from the normally lethal Mike Sheehy was very important. If we had scored that, I don't think they would have come back. The rest is history. They were four points down and got two frees to put them two points behind. Then a long ball came to Séamus Darby and he banged it into the net. All Croke Park went wild, but there was still a minute and a half left in the game and they had to hold on with all their might.'

The closest I ever saw Eugene McGee come to glowing was when I asked him to describe Séamus Darby's goal. We sat as the night closed in around us. 'I'm sure it's probably a false memory but when I think of it now, over twenty years later, I remember everything slowing down and the ball smashing into the net, and because it was a wet day there was a shower of raindrops. I was never so happy to see raindrops.'

9

SHANNON WATERS TEARS
OF JOY THAT FLOW

Limerick 2018–21

The secret thoughts that swirl undetected in the mind became suddenly real. Limerick reigned supreme.

One of the stars of the 1990s Clare team compared his side with the Limerick team of 2018–20. Jamesie O'Connor likened Limerick's All-Ireland triumph in 2018, their first since 1973, with Clare's triumph in 1995. Then, just as Clare had lost their crown to Limerick in 1996, after Ciarán Carey's never-to-be-forgotten point, Limerick had stumbled against Kilkenny in 2019, despite playing some thrilling hurling that year. As I turned my collar to the cold and rain, Jamesie highlighted how all through 1997 Loughnane had drilled into his players that they needed to win a second All-Ireland to be considered a great team, and Clare duly accounted for Tipperary in the All-Ireland final that year. Likewise, Limerick secured their place in the pantheon by beating Waterford in the 2020 All-Ireland final.

Limerick did so under the inspired leadership of John Kiely. I want to single him out for special attention because his actions were so countercultural. The year 2019 was a disappointing one for Limerick when they lost the All-Ireland semi-final to Kilkenny in controversial circumstances. Referee Alan Kelly got the biggest call of the game wrong in failing to give what TV replays show was a clear sixty-five to Limerick and denying them the opportunity of a last-minute equaliser. John Kiely was my man of the year for the grace he showed in defeat and his refusal to enter into any recriminations, even though the match officials gave him an obvious scapegoat. For those who admire sportsmanship, it showcased the GAA at its very best.

Of course, he could not have done so without some extraordinary players. Witness Gearóid Hegarty's man-of-the-match performance in the 2020 All-Ireland final, but the displays of the likes of Tom Morrissey, Kyle Hayes and Cian Lynch were also top notch. Then there was Dan Morrissey's move from number seven to number three after Limerick lost Richie English and Mike Casey to injury, which became a masterstroke. Of course, it helped greatly that Barry Nash was also having a brilliant year at corner-back.

FROM BOOM TO ZOOM

After the win, John Kiely said: 'We had Zoom calls out to them in their garages and their gardens; they're running around the place and lifting weights, then breaking out into outbreak rooms and chatting to each other, then getting back into it again. I think that was the telling moment of the year for us – how hard they worked through March, April and May. They were relentless.

'And the break for the club over the summer was brilliant. They came back so fresh. I remember the first evening back, I said to myself: "Oh my God, look at these fellas, they are literally like cattle coming out of a shed after the winter – raring for the road." And they kept that freshness right through the autumn. It was constantly there. Friday night they were just busting to get out onto the field. We had to hold them back.'

Wexford's Diarmuid Lyng claimed Tommy Walsh was an 'artist in the moment'. Walsh's view of Kiely is worth considering. 'You often hear the term hunger, the will to win, the want to win. The great teams bring themselves up to a level that they can do it every day. It's a consistent performance whether it's in the early pre-season competitions in January or an All-Ireland final. John Kiely brought that standard which reminds you of the Alex Fergusons, the Brian Codys, the Mickey Hartes of this world.'

After Limerick's second All-Ireland, Anthony Daly captured their place in the new hurling order: 'Limerick are the supreme governing tribe now. They don't rule the hurling landscape the same way that Kilkenny once did, but they're threatening to. And every other clan out there has to devise a way to put a stop to that.' With the benefit of a sensational individual goal by Kyle Hayes, Limerick clinched a third successive Munster crown in 2021 after trailing Tipperary by ten points at half-time. It was the first time Limerick achieved this feat since the 1930s.

Just five weeks later, Adare's Declan Hannon became the first player since Christy Ring to captain their team to three All-Ireland victories. Limerick trounced Cork in the All-Ireland final. In an exceptional performance the Shannonsiders were piloted superbly by 'the Messi of hurling' or 'Harry Potter' – Cian Lynch. This Limerick team have not played brilliantly because they are excellent. They achieved excellence by consistently playing brilliantly.

10

LILYWHITE LEGENDS

Kildare 1997–2000

When Alexander the Great was just thirty-three he cried salt tears because he had no more worlds to conquer. After he finished as Kerry manager, Mick O'Dwyer might have been forgiven for thinking the same, but instead he went wandering in search of a new Holy Grail. Kildare were the beneficiaries.

First, he came, he saw and didn't fully conquer. He was replaced by Dermot Earley in 1994, but after two bleak years in the Leinster Championship, the Kildare back-room people persuaded Micko to return and break the Kildare curse. A priest in Clane, who was left behind after being promised a lift to a match, made a foreboding promise that Kildare would never win another All-Ireland. The curse is usually ascribed to the senior footballers, given that their last title was in 1928.

Another 'nearly year' came in 1997 – with a defeat to Meath after three tremendous, thrilling games. Kildare drew, then drew again after extra time (3-17 to 2-20), then finally lost in the first week of August by two points.

But the phoenix rose from the ashes in 1998. It was a slow start.

Another draw, with Dublin, but the replay, two weeks later, saw Kildare through by a point. A month later they decimated Laois and then climatically extracted revenge on Meath when Brian Murphy's shot hit the net. Hill 16 was alive to the sound of music – at last it was the Kildare fans' turn to sing with gusto. Famously Glenn Ryan sang 'The Curragh of Kildare' and the county went into rapture.

Then Micko put one over his native Kerry in the All-Ireland semi-final. Kildare were in an All-Ireland senior football final. Happy days had finally arrived. The hype in the county was unreal but John O'Mahony's Galway denied them the fairy-tale finish they craved, though another memorable Leinster title would come in 2000. Written off by Pat Spillane at half-time, they blew Dublin away in the second half.

THE LIFE OF RYAN

One man typified that Kildare team more than any other. I shopped local to get some insight into perhaps the most iconic player in Kildare football in the form of sportswriter Brendan Coffey.

'Glenn Ryan announced his retirement on a boring Wednesday in October 2006. His final year playing with Kildare had seen the Lilies bow out of the Championship in meek fashion away to Derry. Ryan didn't feature during that dispiriting defeat (1-17 to 0-11), so Kildare's controversial loss against Offaly in that year's Leinster Championship proved his final appearance.

'Ryan's last game on home turf at St Conleth's Park also resulted in defeat to Offaly. For many Kildare fans, that display remains one of his bravest hours. His performance was heroic; only for him, the Lilies might have been wiped out. I think every fan watched in awe that day as Ryan almost single-handedly drove his team to victory. Even at the time, that skirmish felt like the last stand of a great general.

'On the morning that he retired, Ryan was interviewed at length on local radio. In the KFM studios, he heard messages of gratitude from far and wide. The depth of feeling expressed that morning reduced him to tears.

'Ryan's reaction touched a chord with every listener. To hear a man of his stature overcome with emotion was strangely uplifting because you could sense just how much Kildare meant to him. No words could express his feelings quite as forcefully. Anyone with a passion for GAA could relate to him because all of us feel that way to a greater or lesser degree.

'On the pitch, Ryan embodied the very best of what it means to represent your county. Fearless, resolute, inspired: he seemed to grow bigger and stronger every time he wore the white jersey. With him at centre-back, you always felt Kildare were in safe hands.

'John Roddy, a beloved GAA reporter in Kildare and a great mentor to me, once wrote of Ryan: "He might not be the fastest from A to B, but then he doesn't always start at A."

'Ryan had that gift of timing that is perhaps unique to all great players. Invariably, he was in the right place at the right time. He played according to an instinct few possess. Doubts about his fitness engulfed Kildare during the build-up to the 1998 All-Ireland final. Nobody knew if he would make it.

'"Glenn Ryan is supposed to be injured," Pat Spillane noted at half-time on *The Sunday Game*. "Boy, if he's injured, it's the new recipe for success. He's playing absolutely superb at centre-back."

'Kildare led 1-5 to 0-5 and looked on course for their first All-Ireland since 1928. Even with Ryan at his best, they couldn't curtail Galway in the second half. Two years later, Galway dashed Kildare's hopes again, this time in the semi-finals. Two Leinster titles in three years was an incredible haul for a county that hadn't won their province since 1956, but Ryan retired with one overbearing regret.

'"You could say it's an exaggeration, but probably it might just breeze by you at some stage in every day," he told me in December 2006, when we met ahead of his testimonial match. "For some reason, the thought enters your head."

'The pain of 1998 had still not left him. "It might look foolish from the outside, for fellas that weren't in the position that I was in, captaining your county, an All-Ireland winning team. I don't know what way the rest of the lads feel about it. I missed out on what could have been a huge part in history, something huge in my own life and something huge in the lives of thousands of people in Kildare."

'For the captain, the planets seemed to be aligning that season. "The last man to win an All-Ireland in 1928 was from the town here," he said, referring to Bill "Squires" Gannon, the first man to lift Sam Maguire. "It looked like it was fairy-tale stuff. I honestly don't remember much of the day, anything about the dressing room afterwards, because I haven't tried to think about it or I've tried not to."

'One thing Ryan said that day has stayed with me since. "What I'll miss most of the county set-up is the whole effort that goes in," he insisted. "That the sole goal of fellas is wanting to go out and do a real hard training session. That you're really just flat out, and you come off the field on a bit of a high because you see everyone else doing it. You won't get that buzz out of anything else you do in life."

'Perhaps his answer lodged in my mind because it was so unexpected. I assumed that all players live for the big days in Croke Park. Everyone dreams of kicking a score into Hill 16, but it is harder to appreciate the satisfaction that comes from being part of a team. No wonder Ryan was such an effective captain and leader. He relished every bit of it and learned to love the labour of football as much as the glory and the games.'

11

THE FAMINE DAYS ARE OVER

Tipperary 1987–91

You could cut the atmosphere with a knife.

Nicky English won six All-Stars in seven years and was Hurler of the Year in 1989. He is ideally placed to give an insider's guide to the 1987 Munster final.

'When I came on the scene, Tipperary changed managers almost every year because we weren't winning Munster Championships. It's a bit like what happened in Galway in the noughties – in a county where you have a lot of hurlers, there is a massive turnover of players with each new manager, and that means there is little or no continuity and a lot of good players are thrown out in the wash before they have the chance to develop. We came close in a high-scoring Munster final that we should have won in 1984 when Seánie O'Leary scored a late goal to win for Cork.

'Winning the 1987 Munster final was my greatest day in hurling. The fact that we beat Cork after extra time in a replay added to it. Tipperary hadn't won a Munster final since 1971 so that's why Richie Stakelum's comment that the "famine days are over" struck such a chord. The emotion our victory unleashed was unreal. Nothing has ever matched that feeling.'

Nothing captures the unique magic and tribalism of the GAA more vividly than that Munster final.

TIPP TOP

In 1989, Tipperary beat Antrim in the All-Ireland final. Nicky English scored 2-12 in the game. His genius was best encapsulated in his own second goal right at the death. A long ball from the right wing sent in by Aidan Ryan dropped into the path of his run. Off his left-hand side, the strike just after the bounce of the sliotar was nothing less than perfect. He also set up Pat Fox for his goal, a slick half-volleyed finish.

English felt a second title was essential to secure the team's reputation.

'We won the All-Ireland again in 1991 and it was important to us that we beat Kilkenny in the final because there were those who devalued our win in '89 because it was Antrim we beat and not one of the powers of the hurling.'

FAMILY TIES

My own father died when I was five. A lot of the memories I have of him are sad because of illness and his premature death. However, one cherished memory that I will carry with me until I take my last breath is of the day he brought me to see Roscommon play for the first time.

The GAA is about so much more than games. Above all it's about memories. So many are about the link between parents and children bonding attending games, and I could think of nobody better to speak about this than Ireland's greatest writer Donal Ryan, a man whose life's work is built on the beauty and power of words.

For those of us who believe John McGahern was Ireland's greatest writer of the last century, Donal Ryan is his successor. The Tipperary-born writer shot to fame with the publication of *The Spinning Heart*, a portrait of recession-hit rural Ireland in twenty-one voices, which won the Guardian First Book Award in 2013 and was longlisted for the Booker Prize. This was quickly followed by other publications, set around the same area, a composite of various places in Limerick and Tipperary. Ranging from the boom years of the Celtic Tiger to the experience of Irish Travellers, they dig deep into the psyche of Irish communities, with marginal voices summoning the intensity of small-town loves and hates to uncover a complicated history and uncertain present.

It's as if John McGahern has leaned over the bannisters in heaven and stretched out to pass on his torch to Ryan. Donal follows in McGahern's wake and pushes and pushes towards the truth of things. His writings serve a noble purpose, to oust secrecy, to obliterate shame, to stand as mirror to the soul of humankind, to delineate the terrible propensity for violence and abuse and to use narrative as a blessed valve to relieve the awful pressure of the ignored, pent-up, unspoken pain of existence. His words are written from scraps of memory and then written on his heart. Donal has vivid memories of that Tipperary team.

'I was eleven years old in 1987 when Galway beat Tipperary 3-20 to 2-17 in the All-Ireland hurling semi-final. It was the first time I'd felt the full power of the spirit of rivalry. Until that day I'd been a semi-interested observer of hurling, never playing it properly, only getting excited or upset when my home club of Burgess, and later Nenagh Éire Óg, were playing against their neighbours Portroe or Toomevara, because proximity breeds sporting rivalry like no other element. Neighbouring clubs go at it with all the pent-up frustration and resentment and desire for superiority of siblings close in age, and of course, like most siblings, return to being friends when the fire of battle goes out.

'But that day in Croke Park, watching Galway score 1-4 in the opening minutes, something ignited inside me that has never been quenched, a kind of madness, a burning away of reason. We were within four points of them at half-time. "We'll do it all right, lads", my father said. "We have them on the run." I could hardly speak; the excitement was almost too much to bear.

'The sides went to war in the second half. Pat Fox burst through from midfield with fifteen minutes to go and scored a goal that put us a point ahead. I remember seeing flashes of red and bursting stars before my eyes as I screamed for joy, hoisted into the air by my six-foot two-inch cousin. Nicky English followed Pat's goal with a beautiful point and it seemed like we would pull away, put these Tribesmen to the sword.

'But it slipped away from us. Noel Lane sealed it with a goal for Galway, and our Tipperary hearts were broken. I'll never forget the desperate sadness I felt as the whistle went, the look of disappointment on my father's face, the ferocity of my feelings towards the Galway supporters as they celebrated.

'There was a sway in the crowd as we exited the Hill that threatened to become a crush, and my father lost his grip on my hand as I was knocked from my feet. A giant bear of a Galway man lifted me up and carried me through the melee to the steps and to my father's arms, and he and my father laughed and shook hands and we all walked together towards Jones's Road.

'The next year Galway beat us in the final, and the year after that we met in a bloody, bad-tempered semi-final, Tipp winning by three. In 1991, Tipp won well against Galway in the final, and the mad intensity between the counties eased, for a few years at least. Rivalries like that can smoulder for years, for generations even, without ever really conflagrating, until circumstances and personalities and events line themselves up to be fed to exponential, uncontrollable growth. Simultaneous comings-of-age of promising players, serendipitous fixture draws, repeatedly convergent paths to semi-finals and finals; all sorts of factors lead to certain teams at certain times seeming to be the absolute embodiment of the "against each other spirit" that makes sport so exciting, that makes victory so beautiful and defeat so utterly devastating.'

12

LAOIS LEGENDS

Laois 1988–2001

They have an uncanny ability to tug on the heartstrings.

Sometimes a player defines a team. Think of Maurice Fitzgerald with Kerry in 1997; Matt Connor in Offaly in the early 1980s; Peter Canavan with Tyrone in the 1995 All-Ireland final.

The first ladies' football team to take a major hold of my affections was the great Laois team. The sheer brilliance of Sue Ramsbottom grabbed my attention initially, but I would discover that one player was the heart of the team that would reach the holy grail of an All-Ireland win: the one and only Lulu Carroll. With this in mind, I sought the help of the person who knew her best as a player, her teammate and great friend Sue Ramsbottom.

'It was her persistence and nagging of our teacher, Mr Sayers, that led the way for girls to play on a boys national schools team. Lulu got a great kick out of saving penalties on the boys and would taunt them with: "Ah you couldn't score a goal on a girl." Lulu dreamed of playing in Croke Park on All-Ireland final day – which she did first in 1988 against Kerry.

'Lulu played in the forwards, midfields, backs and goals. Many people have done this before, and many will do this in the future, but the difference is, Lulu was brilliant in all these positions, with All-Stars and replacement All-Stars to prove it. We had a wonderful time together on that journey to get an All-Ireland medal. Girls came and went, but Lulu's steely determination, focus and energy made sure her dream was realised.

'The year 1996 was a great one for Lulu as the sports commentators commented that she was "the Liam McHale of ladies football with her long, tanned legs". It was also on the day of the final that Lulu got that marvellous equalising goal for Laois in the last seconds, so we could have another bite at the cherry.

'It was in 2001 that the Laois ladies won that famous All-Ireland. Not many people remember that Lulu got Player of the Match in the 2001 Leinster final. This was the hardest game Laois faced and played en route to the All-Ireland in 2001. While all her teammates lay down, Lulu rose above everybody else that day and ensured the dream was kept alive. Lulu was a real hero and only for her there would be no All-Ireland medal in Laois.

'Lulu was a proud Timahoe and Laois woman and wore her jerseys with pride. When she finished playing for Timahoe, she enjoyed coaching and passing on her skills and knowledge to the new kids on the block. She had eight county medals to her credit. I know the last county medal she won the year she died meant so much to her. The Timahoe club owes a great deal of gratitude to Lulu as a player and a manager, helping it to the dizzy heights of reaching a club All-Ireland in 2000.

'Lulu was the epicentre and the heart and soul of every team she played on. We will all play again someday with Lulu in the great pitch called heaven. The best of things come in ones – one great friend, one Croke Park, one All-Ireland medal and one Lulu.'

GONE BUT NOT FORGOTTEN

Lulu won an All-Ireland title with Laois in 2001 and eight Leinster titles. After her retirement from playing, she was still actively involved in Laois ladies football, and she was a selector with the Laois team.

Although I never had the good fortune to meet her, I was shocked to the core to hear of her premature death in 2007 after a typically brave battle with a long illness. The shock was accentuated by the fact that she was just thirty-five. It seemed that a light was quenched when she left us. Words fell like silent raindrops. Few gave so much so often. If we want to see the true essence of the GAA, her career and spirit captured its power, magic and heroism. That was her legacy on this earth when she left this world: how many hearts she touched.

As her husband Ozzie told me, 'Lulu was one of a kind.'

Life is not forever. Love is.

We don't own our memories. They own us.

13

PEOPLE OF GALWAY, WE LOVE YOU

Galway 1980–88

He was exactly what I expected.

He was the total opposite of what I expected.

There are two people I have met in the GAA who can most change a room just by walking into it because of their energy and the sheer force of their personality: Joe Connolly and Anthony Daly. It is no coincidence that they both have made the most iconic speeches in the history of the GAA.

Yet what shocked me most about Joe Connolly was that for all the passion he brings to everything he does, he generally goes to great lengths to avoid the limelight. Opportunities for self-promotion tend to be firmly rejected, including ones that have the possibility to bring significant financial gain.

In the noughties, Connolly returned to Galway as a selector with the senior team. He brought the same intensity to the task as he had to playing. One morning he was lying awake at 5 a.m. mulling over a decision of which was the most effective position for Iarla Tannian. His wife turned over and didn't ask him what he was thinking of. Instead, her question was more specific: 'Backs or forwards?'

He is a fascinating combination of extrovert and introvert and seems happier talking about his life off the pitch than his glories on it. He grew up in a very different Ireland which was brilliantly chronicled by the peerless Con Houlihan: 'Thomas Wolfe, the brilliant half-forgotten novelist, used to say that the most evocative of all American sounds was the whistle of a distant train. For my generation in rural Ireland, the most evocative of all sounds was the lowing of cattle being driven to the fair in what Thomas Hardy called the non-human hours. Rounding up those same cattle was not quite as romantic as in the novels and the films about the Old West. The cowboys had horses and lassoes; we had our voices and wattles. Some cattle can spot a gap in a fence as quickly as Paddy McEntee can see a flaw in the case for the prosecution. And if you think that we enjoyed a full Irish breakfast, it wasn't so. I don't remember all that honey and soda farls, whatever they are. I remember mugs of tea and slices of bread and butter.'

One of Joe Connolly's neighbours killed pigs at the weekend for the princely sum of a pound: doing the first half of the job on Saturday afternoon, actually killing the pig, and finishing it on the Sunday and curing the bacon. Some of the bacon was hung up the chimney and was smoked in the process. Half the homes cured bacon; the pork steaks and the pudding went around the countryside. Everyone got some of it, and by the time it was distributed, there was little left for the pig's owner, but still no one went hungry and that was what real community was about, giving and sharing.

Pleasures were generally simple – one exception was 'castration day' on 1 June – when on one day a local man was invited to castrate the dogs in the area. In lieu of payment, he was called into each house after the job was done and given a glass of poteen. This meant that his hands were nice and steady in the morning but by the end of the day the dogs who were last suffered greatly because the poor man's eyes were glazed over as the drinking took its toll.

To listen to Joe Connolly speak is to get a masterclass into social history. He grew up in a house when one room was shared between seven brothers. His father, Pat, was struck down by TB in 1948. It would take ten years for the miracle cure to arrive – which led the family to move from Connemara to a cottage in Castlegar, to be close to the TB sanitorium. Pat would go on to live until he was ninety-four.

The family was devastated by emigration. In 1990, Mary Robinson popularised the phrase 'the diaspora', but ten years earlier Joe Connolly had pointed to the importance of our immigrant community in his famous All-Ireland winning speech.

Connolly chipped in four points in Galway's 2-15 to 3-9 win over Limerick in the 1980 All-Ireland for only the county's second All-Ireland, their first in forty-seven years. He describes himself as 'a Junior B Catholic' but nonetheless ended his famous speech by paraphrasing the pope: 'People of Galway, we love you.'

A mhuintir na Gaillimhe tar éis seacht bliain agus caoga tá craobh na hÉireann ar ais in Gaillimh.

('People of Galway, after fifty-seven years, the All-Ireland title is back in Galway.')

Over forty years on, Joe Connolly's speech still has the power to make the heart skip a beat.

What made those words all the more remarkable was that they came from a 23-year-old.

The team were a great unit on and off the field. After League matches, they would congregate in Salthill. After sufficient liquid refreshment, Niall McInerney would intone one word: 'McDonagh.' The late Joe McDonagh was an acclaimed singer, with a sideline career in musical theatre, and had a unique ability to bring out the wildness of the team. He would lead the other great singers like Conor Hayes and Cyril Farrell in song, and the whole squad would follow suit with gusto.

Sylvie Linnane retains great memories of his first All-Ireland win.

'I remember the incredible reception we got when we won the All-Ireland in 1980. It was clear how much it meant to people. The great thing was they were all there again when we lost the next year.'

BACK IN THE FAST LANE

For star forward Noel Lane, winning the 1980 All-Ireland was a proud day: 'We won that day because our leaders, especially Joe Connolly, stood up and were counted. We were a powerful team and that side should have won more than one All-Ireland. It suited us that day that we were playing Limerick rather than Cork or Kilkenny, and that gave us confidence. It felt like it was for us that day, though Limerick could have considered themselves unlucky. What was even better though was going to beat Tipperary in two finals to win back-to-back All-Irelands in 1987 and '88.'

14

KING SIZE

Cavan 1997

In 2020, Tipp people got in touch with their emotions, the dam burst by a sobbing Sam Bennett after his first Tour de France stage win. Nicky English wrapped things up after the footballers' triumph in the Munster final on the centenary of Bloody Sunday: 'The first time I've cried after a match.' The uniqueness of the occasion meant that Cavan's win in the Ulster final on the same day was eclipsed. It had been twenty-three years since the Breffni men had previously won an Ulster title.

Stephen King's exploits for Cavan have elevated him to the status of local hero, but his innate self-possession has saved him from being overwhelmed by the celebrity that has engulfed him. His lengthy inter-county career has left him a treasure chest of memories from which he can quietly plunder its pleasures for himself.

Growing up in Killashandra, the biggest influence on his career was Sgt Peter Maguire who nurtured his talents with his club Killashandra Leaguers, with whom he won a minor league and a Junior Championship and three Intermediate Championships. As a youngster he was always a precocious talent.

'When I was fourteen, I played under-16 for the county. When I was sixteen, I played for the county minors; when I was minor, I played under-21 for the county; and when I was eighteen, I played my first match for Cavan seniors against Meath in a challenge match in Kells, and I never really looked back after that.'

Despite the disappointments with Cavan, his zest for the dramas of the game was undiminished.

'It probably wasn't as difficult as people might think to keep going. I got great enjoyment from playing, and it was a great way of meeting people. Having said that, it was hard to lose Ulster Championships year after year. You would ask yourself: "Why am I doing this to myself?" Then a few months later the League started, and after you won a couple of matches the hunger came back as strong as ever.'

The longevity of his career saw him playing under a number of different managers. He admired them all, but one stood out for him.

'I would have to say they were all very good, people like Gabriel Kelly and P. J. Carroll were very committed. Eugene McGee came with a big reputation, having won an All-Ireland with Offaly, and he certainly was a very deep thinker about the game. Martin McHugh was definitely the best of them all. He was the first to really adapt our style of football to the modern era and really move us up with the times in terms of taking us away from a catch-and-kick style of play and to a faster style.'

Apart from the change of style and Martin McHugh's influence, why did Cavan make the breakthrough and win the Ulster title in 1997?

'Ulster is such a minefield that it's very hard to win the title. In Martin's first year in charge of us we got to the Ulster final. We could have won it but we were too naïve on the day. In 1997 we were a mature outfit, and for a few players like me it was the end of the line so it was do or die. We got out of jail to snatch a draw with Fermanagh and I think we knew then that it was going to be our year.'

Cavan's victory in the Ulster final prompted celebrations the likes of which had not been seen in the county since the glory days of John Joe O'Reilly. The local media and local radio station, Shannonside/Northern Sound, celebrated the win as the major news story of the year.

'Everyone in Cavan went haywire. I'll never forget the scene in Clones after we won. You couldn't see a blade of grass on the pitch because of the sea of blue and white.'

If 1997 provided King with the highlight of his career, it also provided him with his greatest disappointment because no one is more happily stirred by the special magic of an All-Ireland final, more alive to its electricity.

'Definitely the low point of my career was losing the All-Ireland semi-final to Kerry. As a team we didn't perform to the best of our abilities on the day. We missed the boat. It was all the more galling because I still believe we would have won the All-Ireland that year had we beaten Kerry.'

Having climbed the mountain in 1997, Cavan football went into something of a decline afterwards. King saw it more as a transition than a crisis.

'The change of management probably had something to do with it. Then there were players like myself who stepped down so that a new panel had to be developed, and it takes time for things to settle.'

Major controversy erupted when Martin McHugh's successor Liam Austin was forced to resign as Cavan manager because of so-called 'player power'. King was the punters' favourite to take the job, but he declined to run for the post.

'I had just started up my own pub in Killashandra at the time so there was no way I could even consider taking the position.'

How does King feel about 'player power'?

'In general I think it's a bad thing. The one thing I would say though is that players should be properly looked after by the GAA because it's the players that generate the big crowds and the revenue for the Association. Once that happens, I think players should concentrate on playing and not get involved in politics if that's what you want to call it.'

15

THE REBEL YELL

Cork 2002–18

It was the end of an era.

In February 2021, one of the GAA immortals retired from inter-county camogie.

No camogie player won more All-Stars than her. A remarkable total of eleven.

Gemma O'Connor was a great player on a great team. The nine All-Irelands provide confirmation of this: 2002, '05, '06, '08, '09, '14, '15, '17 and '18.

There were some setbacks on the way, notably a heavy beating to Wexford in the 2012 All-Ireland final. The fact that a great Wexford side won four All-Irelands in this period is indication that Cork's dominance was not easily won.

A snapshot to illustrate her career: having started centre-forward, she and wing-back Briege Corkery moved to midfield at half-time in the 2005 All-Ireland final when Tipperary had been on top. From being behind by five points at the interval, Cork rallied to win by four.

OLD RIVALS

In the latter part of her career, it was Kilkenny who threatened the Leesiders' supremacy. It began in 2016 when rank outsiders Kilkenny, managed by Ann Downey, prevented a Cork three in-a-row with a seven-point victory that gave the county its first title in twenty-two years. The game was overshadowed somewhat by a media frenzy that followed a bit of pushing between two players before the game. This generated sensational headlines such as: 'Handshakes turn to handbags' and 'Heated scenes at camogie final'. Would such a minor incident in hurling have provoked such major headlines?

The following year it looked as though Kilkenny were about to confirm their status as the new queens of camogie. But, in dramatic fashion, two magnificent injury-time points from Gemma O'Connor and Julia White saw Cork through by 0-10 to 0-9.

In 2018, in another thrilling crescendo, a late free from sixty metres out on the left wing from Orla Cotter gave Cork a one-point victory over their great rivals and Kilkenny hearts were broken again. Cork won a fourth title in five years with survivors from the team which played in eight successive finals in the noughties.

LEADERS

That team produced a number of stars who have used their profile on the pitch to raise important social issues off it. Midfielder Ashling Thompson has courageously opened up about her mental-health problems with a view to bringing greater focus on this issue at national level.

Julia White's credentials as a natural leader on the pitch were forcefully illustrated by her dramatic winning point in the 2017 All-Ireland Senior Camogie final against Kilkenny. She subsequently used those leadership skills on the GAA/PDST Future Leaders Transition Year Programme. The cross-curricular programme – comprising of eight modules in subjects as diverse as coaching, sports journalism and event management – is designed to provide a learning experience based on the practical application of the skills from each module, by empowering every student to play an active role in the organisation of a Gaelic games opportunity in their school or community.

NOTHING COMPARES TO YOU

Most of us do not inhabit what Leonard Cohen memorably described as 'the prison of the gifted'. One player did more than any other.

Driving that team like a mighty engine at full-back was one of Ireland's most distinguished and decorated sports personalities of all time, Rena Buckley. She holds eighteen senior All-Ireland medals in football and camogie. Despite the claims of Sonia O'Sullivan and Katie Taylor, is Rena Ireland's greatest sportswoman? In fact, should she not be considered one of Ireland's greatest sportspeople?

Rena took the Gucci view about hard work on the practice field – long after you have forgotten the price, the quality remains. Rena's commitment was total. The team followed her lead. Not since Joan of Arc has one woman accrued so many victories on the battlefields.

Nulli secundus. Second to none.

16

NO FANCY DANS

Galway 1998–2001

'There's only one f**king answer to that.'

It was a classic old-school move but it worked.

In the run-up to the 1998 All-Ireland final, Kildare were hot favourites, having impressively deposed of reigning All-Ireland champions Kerry in the semi-final. A Connacht team had not won an All-Ireland in thirty-two years. Eugene McGee had dismissed the Galway team as 'fancy dans'. A gentleman to his fingertips, O'Mahony held up the newspaper in the dressing room and, in uncharacteristic unparliamentary language, told the players that an emphatic response was demanded. 'Lads, I am not a Galwayman,' he began and went on to make a Churchillian speech that was nothing less than a call to arms. A surge of resolution crossed the room like a Mexican wave.

In the first half, it wasn't obvious that it was working as Kildare were in the ascendancy. Michael Donnellan though produced a surging run, a little shimmy and scored a stunning point. In 2005 this run and score was voted 'the greatest GAA moment of all time' by a poll carried out for RTÉ television.

At half-time it looked as if it was to be another defeat for the Westerners as Kildare led 1-5 to 0-5. In the second half though, Ja Fallon dazzled. He began by kicking a marvellous point from under the Cusack Stand and later scored with a sensational line ball under the Hogan Stand. Pádraic Joyce announced his arrival on the national stage with the decisive goal in their 1-14 to 1-10 victory.

JOHNO

Our obsession had become an oppression.

We didn't know at the time, but he could reverse the weight of history for an entire province. The appointment of John O'Mahony as Galway manager in October 1997 would change everything. O'Mahony had been great at making teams good, but would he be good enough to make this Galway team great?

Within twelve months he'd taken his side to an All-Ireland final. Galway captain Ray Silke said in the dressing room before he led his team out: 'Right, lads. I'm going out to win an All-Ireland. Who's coming with me?' One of John O'Mahony's favourite maxims was now to come into play: 'A winner never quits. A quitter never wins.'

Prisoners of hope, at first the fans from the west were both beguiled and sceptical, talking to each other to persuade themselves, listening to be persuaded that what lay before them was exhilarating – the combined intricate talents of the team fitting together in the second half like an expertly designed puzzle.

The win restored the hope that sport can still be the simple, challenging life enhancement it was first meant to be. Galway lost the final to Kerry in a replay two years later but in 2001 confirmed their status as a great team with a crushing victory over a hotly fancied Meath team.

The Galway team gave football fans from the west of Ireland back our dream.

17

KEEPING THE FAITHFUL

Offaly 1994–98

Destitutus ventis, remos adhibe.
If the wind does not serve, take to the oars.

Offaly entered 2021 in hurling's third tier after a shock penalty shoot-out loss to Down in Newry in the Christy Ring Cup. It was a spectacular fall from grace in the county's fortunes, especially as their celebrated team won All-Irelands in 1994 and '98, as well as five Leinster titles in eleven seasons from '88 onwards.

In the memorable 1994 All-Ireland final between the counties, Offaly staged an incredible recovery to score 2-5 in the final five minutes in a 3-16 to 2-13 win. Five points clear in the 1994 All-Ireland Senior Hurling Championship final with as many minutes to go, Limerick looked certain to end a twenty-one-year drought and return home with the Liam MacCarthy Cup. But less than ten minutes later, they could collapse in despair after an extraordinary turnaround.

For sixty-five minutes of the seventy, Offaly had been uncharacteristically listless, with even a 'spirited' half-time bollocking from

71

their manager Éamonn Cregan, himself a Limerick icon, doing little to stir them from their slumber. 'He really ripped into me,' said Johnny Pilkington, one of several players whose fondness for 'a few scoops' had long been the subject of folklore.

HERE'S JOHNNY

Enter Johnny. He was one of three Dooley brothers on the pitch. Socks around his ankles, he stood over a 21-yard free with a battalion of Limerick defenders across the goal line, then glanced to the sideline where management signalled him to pop the ball over the bar for a point that would reduce the lead to four. With the insouciance that only an Offaly player of that time could muster, Dooley blasted low towards the corner and Offaly were a mere two points behind. As RTÉ viewers watched replays of Dooley's goal, Johnny Pilkington dispatched the puckout back goalwards, with Pat O'Connor catching it on the bounce with a swing of his hurley. Another green flag in less than a minute and suddenly Offaly were leading. Then for an encore they hit five unanswered points with Billy Dooley chipping in three of them from almost identical angles.

One night in Gleeson's in Roscommon, Eugene McGee gave me a unique insight into what makes Offaly tick: 'They rarely just win All-Ireland finals. Instead, they steamroll their way to victory in dramatic fashion, usually with late goals, most famously in Séamus Darby's goal in 1982. In 1998, their hurlers did what no county has ever done before. They played eight games to win the All-Ireland Championship and at the end of all that they looked the fittest, freshest and most convincing hurling team we have seen.

'Once again they broke away from the shackles of GAA history and tradition. After losing two games out of the eight, Offaly had to put on a super show to silence the knockers who were saying that they should never even have been in that final. Offaly pulverised Kilkenny in the second half of that fabulous All-Ireland final.'

Heroics and Offaly hurling and football teams seem to go hand in hand in the modern history of the GAA. One of the truest tests of a great player is his ability to recover from adversity during the course of a high-profile game. Most players are not able to do that. Brian Whelahan got off to a disastrous start in the half-back line as Eugene McGee recalled: 'Then the Offaly mentors made the first of a few brilliant moves when they switched Brian to wing half-forward and put Michael Duignan to the half-backs to mark Brian McEvoy. In the second half, Brian was moved to full-forward. This switch was the winning of the game. Whelahan scored one goal and two points from play and showed how a great player can overcome disaster and still triumph. Offaly simply had too many heroes on the day for Kilkenny to cope with like Whelahan, Duignan, Kevin Kinahan, Pilkington, Joe Errity and the Dooleys. It was a parable of Offaly's talent and their capacity not just to win but to do so with polish and plenty of drama.'

Myths abound about that Offaly side. Johnny Pilkington suggests that perception and reality were somewhat, if not completely, different.

'It's just something that we seemed to be kind of easy-going, but when Kilkenny were on top, their A versus B games and this, that and the other, their indoor [in-house] matches were better than any Championship matches. Kilkenny didn't invent that. That was going on with every All-Ireland team. I remember there would be odd arguments there in matches inside our training games. I know I was on [Daithí] Regan at one stage, and even though he's a foot taller than me, he still managed to pull across my ear and we had words, so you had that intensity there. I suppose what was a bit unique about it, we had a laid-back kind of an attitude in a way. If you take a look at the 1994 All-Ireland and you see Offaly running out onto the field, it seems as if the first lad comes out fast and the others just jog out one after another and Limerick are sprinting out into it. We had some kind of laid-back characters.'

18

THE EARLEY YEARS

Roscommon 1977–80

The savage loves his native shore.

The four happiest years of my life were 1977 to 1980. It was a time when Roscommon won four consecutive Connacht titles, an under-21 All-Ireland and their only National League title. The best eleven minutes of my life came at the start of the 1980 All-Ireland final when Roscommon had the great Kerry team reeling. Sadly, the next sixty minutes were considerably less enjoyable. Mick O'Dwyer said that was an All-Ireland his Kerry team could have lost and should have lost.

Roscommon's star player Dermot Earley reflected on that game for me.

'It was just incredible to reach the All-Ireland final in 1980. Our manager Tom Heneghan had us really well prepared. He arranged for us to get two weeks off work, and for those two weeks we trained twice a day, at noon and in the early evening. By night-time you couldn't wait to get to bed. We had Kerry reeling early on, but I feel we lost because we weren't attacking enough. We had great attacking half-backs, and on the day, they did a good defensive job, but we didn't use them to attack Kerry. Offaly beat Kerry in 1982 by attacking them. We had the class to do the same, but we didn't.

'We were gutted afterwards, especially for the supporters. They gave us a massive reception when we got home. What stays with me is that there was no real celebration from the Kerry players, nor the fans. That's what hurt me the most. Winning had become so routine it didn't seem to matter to them. When they won in 1997, you could see it did matter to the Kerry lads because they hadn't won an All-Ireland for eleven years at that stage.'

That evening a convoy of cars and buses made their way home. The normal buzz of chat and banter was noticeably absent. One of the songs that came on the radio was the big smash from ABBA at the time 'The Winner Takes It All'. Those five words said it all for Dermot Earley.

'It was not a great All-Ireland final. Both sets of defenders were well on top, and scoring chances were at a premium. Marking was extremely close, and this resulted in too many frees from each team, but it wasn't a dirty game. However, many of the decisions left the players bewildered, not to mention the crowd. Roscommon suffered more than Kerry in this area. We became frustrated, and our game suffered as a result. Kerry deserved to win because they took their chances well. We had the winning of the game from placed balls alone, but the concentration slipped and so did the opportunity for victory.

'I was disappointed that Eoin Liston didn't play as it was a shame for any footballer to miss the All-Ireland final for any reason, but particularly for ill health. We felt all along we could have beaten Kerry with him because in Pat Lindsay we had a full-back who could have held him.

'The start was magic – a goal from John O'Connor followed by sustained pressure from Roscommon and a further point from

Seamus Hayden. Then Kerry took over and threw the ball around, but our defence was good. Gerry Connellan and Mike Sheehy appeared to be booked by the referee, and then Tommy Doyle and I got our names taken. This happened as Kerry came forward. I turned hard to the left to follow the attack and bumped hard into the back of a Kerry player. He turned and let me have one in the face. The ref called us together as I got off the ground. The Kerry man was my former army colleague, Tommy Doyle. The referee booked me. I asked him: "Why are you booking me, ref?" He said nothing. He booked Doyle then moved away. Tommy and I looked at one another. We shook hands. There were no hard feelings, but I was disappointed to be booked in my first All-Ireland final.

'Michael O'Hehir in his commentary said: "Tommy was a lucky man – he wasn't sent to the sideline," but then the referee decided to hop the ball and O'Hehir wondered who hit who. Now I got frustrated as I felt doubly punished, booked and had lost a free to a hop ball.

'We had the wind and we didn't want to waste time. Tom Heneghan was told to stay in the dugout. Mick O'Dwyer was up on the line for much of the first half and nothing was said to him. Time was being wasted and selective justice was administered – more frustration.

'The final score was 1-9 to 1-6. Kerry won and deservedly so, before a crowd of 63,854. As I pondered the result, it stood out that the difference between the teams was Mike Sheehy's accurate free taking. He scored six frees and a goal from play. Although Roscommon scored 1-4 from play to Kerry's 1-3, we missed frees we should have scored. After a marvellous start, Roscommon seemed to change their style of play as the openings which were there in the first few minutes were quickly closed off by the Kerry defensive unit. I have explained this change of play many times as a self-conscious feeling that Kerry would whittle down our early lead. What happened was that the fear of losing overcame the will to win.'

It is noteworthy that three of that Roscommon team were selected on the GAA's 'Football Stars of the 1980s' team which was honoured on the 2013 All-Ireland SFC final day. After back-to-back winners Meath (1987 and '88) were honoured at the previous year's final, the Association availed of the opportunity to acknowledge a specially chosen team deemed to be the best fifteen footballers from the 1980s who did not win All-Ireland senior medals. All of those included in the final fifteen were deemed to have made special contributions to the GAA through outstanding performances over prolonged periods. The three Roscommon players were Harry Keegan, Dermot Earley and Tony McManus.

EARLEY RISER

Dermot Earley had a reflective streak. In my last proper conversation with him before the fatal illness had too strong a hold on him, I asked him if he had any regrets. He asked me to wait for a moment. Then he went to his desk and removed a piece of paper. He read for me.

'If I had to live my life all over again, I would finger-paint more and point the finger less. I would do less correcting and more connecting. I would take my eyes off my watch and watch with my eyes. I would care to know less and know to care more. I would take more hikes and fly more kites. I would stop playing serious and seriously play. I would run through more fields and gaze at more stars. I would do more hugging and less tugging. I would be firm less often and affirm much more. I would build self-esteem first and the house later and I would teach less about the love of power and more about the power of love.'

19

DALO'S DUBS

Dublin 2008–14

Anthony Daly does not so much walk into a room as bounce into it. It came as no surprise that this explosion of energy, enthusiasm and charisma would achieve the GAA's equivalent of the story of the ugly duckling that was turned into a swan.

In 2008, he gave a massive lift to Dublin hurling when he agreed to manage the county team and in his first year brought them to an All-Ireland quarter-final – which seemed to confirm the view that he was the messiah of Dublin hurling.

When he became manager, Dublin were not at the top table but firmly in the second tier. His job was to put them on the map. At the time all the Dublin footballers were household names but hardly anybody in Dublin would have been able to name a single Dublin hurler, though he would change that.

There followed the great highs: winning the Leinster title in 2013 (first in forty-two years), the League title in 2011 (first in sixty-two years) and beating the mighty Kilkenny in the Leinster Championship – all of which would have been unthinkable for Dublin fans before Daly took the job.

Dalo also felt the bitter disappointment when the path to progress was not smooth and the team suffered what seemed like crushing disappointments on the way – notably in 2012 when they underperformed and lost tamely in the Leinster Championship and then suffered a crushing defeat to Daly's native county Clare. He looks back on his time in the role with searing honesty.

'In 2013 after narrowly losing the All-Ireland semi-final to Cork, management spent twelve hours in a hotel in Mullingar with a facilitator that September. I never felt so drained that night in my life. The facilitator, who had experience from the labour courts, absolutely grilled us, before putting this substantial document together. Looking back now, the whole process could have been done over an hour and a half, followed by a round of golf. All we needed was a couple of basic themes to work on, not the thirteen we were presented with in the document.

'We thought we had it all sorted for 2014 but we forgot the most basic one of all – to fight the fight against Kilkenny and Tipperary in the Leinster final and All-Ireland quarter-final.

'Maybe we clapped ourselves on the back too much. It happens with the likes of Dublin very easy. Clare too. The highs are almost too high; the lows get too low. Kilkenny get the balance right.'

Dalo could be the subject into a study of 'Catholic guilt'. He seems more affected by the lows than the highs. He talks about being able to live with the pain but not the shame, honourable defeat like the 2013 semi-final to Cork rather than a limp display like the 2014 Leinster final. Kilkenny cast a long shadow over Dalo's Dubs.

'In 2011 we won the League final, beat Offaly in a dogfight in the first round, then beat Galway in Tullamore being fourteen men down, looking like we'd a real team. But then it came. We never mentioned the words, but it got into everyone's heads – the backlash. What everyone else was thinking: "Oh, Kilkenny, the backlash, you'll get it for the League final now." It got into the psyche, even though we tried everything for it not to.'

Daly offers a revealing insight into the mentality of the team: 'Dotsy O'Callaghan said to me once, "It's just them, Dalo. Whatever it is in our heads about Kilkenny, we can't get it out of our heads."'

Daly uses that Kilkenny team as the benchmark not just to measure his Dublin team but all teams with aspirations to greatness.

'Jackie Tyrrell told a great story that encapsulated the difference between Kilkenny and the rest. The Wednesday after the 2011 All-Ireland final, Jackie and a raft of the Kilkenny lads found themselves drinking in Quinn's pub on the Drumcondra Road. A recording of the match was playing on the TV. Jackie was happy and merry but already found himself thinking about the 2012 Championship. While everyone else would wait until January to refocus on the following season, Kilkenny give themselves three days.

'Cody has driven that culture, but it doesn't just exist within the squad. When I was Dublin manager, my brother Michael travelled around the country following us. He was always taken aback by the ferocity of the Kilkenny supporters any time Dublin played them.

'"They were always one of my favourite teams until I started going to their matches," Michael said to me once. "Never mind them slating you coming up from Clare, or giving it to the Dublin Jackeens, they're vicious to their own players."'

PICTURE THIS

With the benefit of insight, Dalo looks back on one incident from his time with the Dubs that encapsulated the distance between his team and Kilkenny.

'In my first year as Dublin manager in 2009, we had a press day ahead of the Leinster final. One of the tabloid papers sent this model to the event, who arrived in this sky-blue minidress, for a photo shoot with the players. I don't want to appear sexist but it was probably natural that a group of young players, in their athletic prime, would find the girl attractive, and that her appearance at the event would seem novel and distracting.

'I sent a couple of the subs over to the girl for the photo. She was draped across them as they were holding her up like you'd unload a coffin out of a hearse. I've always believed in treating players as responsible adults but, in my own mind, I was still thinking, *How did I allow this to happen? Cody or Loughnane certainly wouldn't.* But when you're not used to success, this kind of stuff is harder to control.

'One very noticeable trait of Kilkenny and the Dublin footballers' modern success is how much they have controlled that environment. We all saw Jim Gavin at multiple All-Ireland winning banquets when it seems more like he's won the Walsh Cup than the Sam Maguire. I certainly wouldn't want to be Brian or Jim, although I have huge admiration for them. But maybe that's the reason they won all those All-Irelands as a manager, and why I don't have any.'

20

THY KINGDOM GO

Cork 1987–90

In July 1990, Cork football fans savoured one of their sweetest moments: old rivals Kerry were hammered 2-23 to 1-11 in the Munster football final.

THE BOSS

Between 1987 and '90, Cork and Meath dominated the football landscape, winning all four All-Irelands and three leagues between them. It is remarkable that the great managers notice the little things and store every perceived slight as fuel for battles ahead. In 2020, after Liverpool won the Premier League after thirty years of waiting, Manchester City gave them a guard of honour in their next match. City then thumped them 4-0. Yet Pep Guardiola made a point of mentioning in his post-match interview that Liverpool had not thanked them for the guard of honour.

Billy Morgan is a man of deep conviction. He is a serious Liverpool fan. In 2007, a journalist from *The Irish Sun* rung him seeking an interview. Morgan turned him down because of the English *Sun*'s treatment of Liverpool in the wake of the Hillsborough disaster in 1989.

Nemo Rangers' Billy Morgan led Cork to four consecutive All-Ireland football finals – initially losing to Meath in '87 and '88 before beating Mayo in '89 and old rivals Meath in 1990.

Billy Morgan 'hated' Kerry so defeating them was huge for him. After Cork beat Kerry by 0-13 to 1-05 in the Munster final replay in 1987 in Killarney, Morgan was in seventh heaven because Killarney had been a torture chamber for Cork for so long. In the dressing room afterwards, an official told him that the team bus was ready to take the squad to the hotel for the meal. Morgan emphatically told him: 'We're not taking the team bus; we are going to walk to the hotel. I don't care how far away it is. We have lost here so often and driven away hiding but today I want everyone to see us.'

It was equally sweet to hammer Kerry in the Munster final. Colm O'Neill was not originally part of the twenty-one-man squad. Cork had six injuries. Billy Morgan rang Larry Tompkins and asked him who did he think should be selected at corner-forward. Larry suggested O'Neill. Tyrone's Frank McGuigan is rightly immortalised in the GAA because he scored eleven points in the 1984 Ulster final – seven with one foot and four with the other. Colm O'Neill scored eleven points in the 1990 Munster final but for some reason that incredible achievement has largely been ignored.

None of the Cork players sat down in the dressing room in the 1990 All-Ireland final at half-time, they were so keen to get back on the pitch. They barely noticed that Colm O'Neill had been sent off. Larry Tompkins did his cruciate in the 1990 All-Ireland final but played through the pain barrier.

The homecoming for the footballers was a dual celebration for the double winning teams. The two captains, Larry Tompkins and Tomás Mulcahy, exchanged the trophies.

Bishop Buckley said: 'There are two types of people: those from Cork and those who want to be from Cork.' The cheer of the night though came for Billy Morgan. He was a bit emotional and very pumped up. Think Mel Gibson rallying the troops in *Braveheart*. In the run-up to the All-Ireland final, there was a lot of talk that Cork didn't have the bottle to beat Meath. That had driven Morgan crazy. He said on the night: 'There was a lot of talk about us not having the bottle. Well, we showed that you can take the Cork off the bottle, but you will never take the bottle out of Cork.'

21

FIVE-IN-A-ROW

Kerry 2014–18

It will come as a surprise to some people to read that Kerry really did win the five-in-a-row.

It did come though at minor level. In 2018, Kerry beat Galway 0-21 to 1-14 to make history as five-in-a-row All-Ireland minor winners. It was a landmark victory for their manager Peter Keane, who was leading Kerry to his third consecutive minor title. That victory was more gruelling than the previous year as Kerry fell seven points behind initially. They conceded 1-7 without reply between the eleventh and twenty-sixth minutes before achieving greatness. It should be noted that this was the first year of the new under-17 age grade, having previously been under-18.

The five-in-a-row is noteworthy in its own right, but they also brought two names onto the national stage. In the 2017 Munster final, Kerry beat Clare 2-21 to 0-3. David Clifford notched six points. He had scored 2-8 against Cork in the previous round. The Kerry manager was asked why he didn't haul the Fossa man ashore with the match in the bag. Peter Keane replied, 'If you've a Merc, do you put it in the garage?'

The hype surrounding Clifford was on the level only generated by that of the teenage Joe Canning. In the All-Ireland final against Derry, Clifford's impact was immediate. Within ten seconds of the throw-in, he soared above the Derry full-back, stepped off his right and smashed the ball into the back of the net. He concluded his minor career as an All-Ireland winning captain and with a tally of 10-68 in twelve Championship matches. Such were his performances winning two All-Ireland medals and being named the 2017 Young Player of the Year, there was concern that the big teams from Australia would come knocking at his door waving their chequebooks.

Pat Spillane was happy he wasn't lost to the game. 'The most skilful Kerry player I ever played with was Maurice Fitzgerald. I would say David has the potential to be one of the best we have ever seen.'

THE HOT SEAT

Winning three minor All-Irelands was the stepping stone for Peter Keane to become the manager of the Kerry senior team. Pat Spillane has a nuanced assessment of Keane.

'There are loads of similarities between Manchester United and the Kerry football team. However, the main one is that both are so successful that they are considered aristocrats of their sport. Their fans are loyal, passionate, and hugely demanding. And they treat every result as a defining moment. So after a win they are certain this is going to be "their" season, whereas every loss is treated as a crisis.

'The two teams have been underachieving of late. United last won the Premier League title in 2013. Kerry's last All-Ireland win was in 2014 – and they have won just one in the last eleven years. Believe me, that's a famine down here.

'Just as the Kingdom was emerging from the official "period of

87

mourning" after the Cork loss in 2020, somebody got up to a little mischief. My phone lit up with calls and text messages. Numerous radio stations wanted to talk to me about an alleged mutiny by the players against team boss Peter Keane. Frankly, I hadn't a clue what they were on about. Let me explain a few facts about the inner workings of the Kerry team. I'd have a better chance of discovering what North Korean leader Kim Jong-un had for his dinner than finding out what's happening inside the Kerry senior football squad.

'In terms of expertise and experience, the Kerry management team is lightweight compared to other counties. Jim Gavin's crew included Jason Sherlock, Declan Darcy, Paul Clarke and Bryan Cullen, who oversaw their strength and conditioning programme.

'Late 2020, Kerry had a post-mortem on the season. Down here, we'd all hope it went like Dublin's after the loss to Donegal in the 2014 All-Ireland semi-final. I'm told Jim Gavin stood up at the start of that meeting and said he was taking full responsibility for the defeat – that he got the tactics wrong. He promised he would learn from it. And, boy, how Gavin learned.

'I'm not too sure whether Keane took responsibility for what happened against Cork. But I think he must put his hand up and accept the blame. He got the dreaded vote of confidence from the county board who wanted him to bolster his management team. It was not a ringing endorsement as Keane must eat a portion of humble pie.'

22

NO ORDINARY JOE

Galway 2008–21

Although he has now retired, his creation is proof that God loves hurling.

It is a truth not yet universally acknowledged but a truth nonetheless.

It was like the hours before a birth or death – with no knowing when it will happen, only that it must happen. Time itself behaves differently in that interlude. It has a kind of weight that slows it down and elongates it. It was always a question of when not if Joe Canning would reach the hurling summit.

Careers are defined by moments as well as medals. There is surely a case for a TV special like a film montage complete with melodramatic score to showcase the many extraordinary moments produced by Joe Canning. However, if there was one moment above all others that encapsulated his genius it was in 2017 when Galway ended a long drought, stretching back to 1988, and won the Liam MacCarthy Cup. It was Joe who produced the most outlandish on-field moment. The Tribesmen were level with reigning champs Tipp in the All-Ireland semi-final – and it was going to take something magical to separate the sides. Cometh the hour, cometh the man. Joe Canning rose to the occasion, firing over a stunning point from under the Cusack Stand with seventy-four minutes on the clock to send his team into the final.

Canning is unusual in that he had already gained a place in the hurling immortals when he was a teenager, given his exploits with his club Portumna and with Galway's underage teams, winning two minor All-Irelands and captaining the team as they sought a three-in-a-row, only to lose to Tipperary. Canning is a sports-writer's dream: boy-next-door manner, quick-witted, intelligent and, above all, immensely talented.

Although still a minor in 2006, Canning was given the opportunity to join the senior squad. He declined then, though he did win an All-Ireland under-21 medal that year. In 2008, he made his senior debut for Galway. Canning showed what he was made of when he starred in Galway's narrow loss to Tipperary in the League final. However, he really announced his arrival on hurling's centre stage in bold print with a stunning performance against Cork in the Championship. Although Galway lost, Canning scored two goals and twelve points of Galway's total of 2-15. He was rewarded with an All-Star and the Young Hurler of the Year award.

In 2009, he once more lit up the Championship, notably in his first-half performance against Kilkenny when he strode through the defence like a colossus. Again, disappointment came when Galway were surprisingly defeated by Waterford in the All-Ireland quarter-final, but still Canning finished the top scorer in the Championship with 3-45. He scored 4-7 in the All-Ireland under-21 semi-final defeat to Clare. Consolation came for him in the form of his third All-Ireland club medal with Portumna and his second All-Star award.

His Galway team haven't always been great, but whenever he played, he consistently produced moments of greatness. He made that team box office. But it comes with a price. Canning has had to deal with complete strangers chastising him while he's out minding his own business. He gives an amusing if slightly frightening anecdote of when he was at a concert and a random man gave out to him for holding pints before a big game. The drinks were for others. He was only drinking coffee! The game was two weeks away.

THE PROMISED LAND

Canning is aware of how important the All-Ireland title was for the county.

'Winning the 2017 All-Ireland was a big thing for the Galway team. You're always going to feel pressure when you're going into an All-Ireland, but the big thing for this group of players was that a lot of the guys were on the team in 2012 and '15. We didn't want to lose three on the bounce. We didn't want to be on another losing team. It had been twenty-nine years since Galway last won it – in our own minds enough was enough.

'It was also a big deal for my family. My brother Ollie played for Galway almost fifteen years and never won it – he was unlucky not to win it. It was a sense for him that we have it in the family now. I could've got taken off ten times in that game and my dad wouldn't have minded. He was more overjoyed than anything.

'It's great for the next generation, for the kids. For twenty-nine years they've never witnessed the All-Ireland Hurling Championship in Galway. If we can inspire the next generation of Galway hurlers, then that's the main thing.

'It's brilliant because Galway isn't a traditional county for winning All-Irelands – it's only our fifth-ever All-Ireland compared to the likes of Kilkenny, Cork and Tipperary. For us to win just our fifth All-Ireland is pretty special – we have to embrace and celebrate it as well, and they don't come round very often.'

23

CONNACHT GOLD

Mayo 1987–89

Some players have their careers defined in moments. Willie Joe Padden is such a player. In the All-Ireland semi-final in 1989 against Tyrone, he was forced to the sideline with a dangerous cut to his head. In one of the most iconic images in the history of the GAA, he later returned to the fray, his head wrapped in a bandage, his shirt splattered in blood.

'Everybody had written us off before the match. I got an injury. I'm not too sure which Tyrone player it was. He was going for a ball and he hit his knee off my head and I got a few stiches in it. You don't mind getting a few things like that as long as you win the game. It was our first experience of getting to a final after all our endeavours from the previous years. From our point of view, and from a spectator's point of view, it was a great period because we were basking in the build-up to the final, especially being in our first All-Ireland for so long.

'That year was one of the more open All-Irelands. Unfortunately, Jimmy Burke, our full-forward, got injured and he had to go off. That really took the wind out of our sails because he was in there as a target man and did that job very well. We were forced to rejig the team. Having said that, when we took the lead in the second half, we looked as if we were in the driving seat, but we got another injury and had to rejig the team again. I think it was that which cost us the game rather than a lack of concentration. We were just as well prepared as Cork so it certainly wasn't a lack of fitness. We didn't press home our initiative, so we didn't get the extra couple of points up to have the cushion there for the end of the game. Cork rallied and pipped us in the end.'

BIG TIME

Martin Carney had been through big games for Mayo but had never experienced anything like this.

'This time things were a bit different. Up to then Mayo had always been a rollercoaster, from one extreme to the other. We were either fully up or completely down, but our manager John O'Mahony kept things grounded. We won our third consecutive Connacht title in 1989, when Liam McHale literally owned the ball and gave one of the great individual displays against Roscommon. We also had Seán Maher in the side, who was a very underrated player, and he gave us that enforcer rather than a creator presence we badly needed. Anthony Finnerty famously described Jimmy Burke's goal that year as "the push-over goal". It kind of bounced off him.

'For a county that hadn't won an All-Ireland final for so long, there was such an outpouring of goodwill and an incredible longing to win. Johno tried to control it as best he could, but a lot of local interests were looking for a slice of the action. When we scored the goal, I can recall looking down the Cork bench and seeing the sense of shock. They were as brittle as us in a different way, but John Cleary and Michael McCarthy took over and they deservedly won. Although we lost, the team was fêted and there was plenty of back-slapping that created its own problems – the team was distracted the next year, and the opportunity to build on the advances of 1989 was lost.'

SO NEAR AND YET SO FAR

T. J. Kilgallon believes the '89 All-Ireland is yet another case of what might have been for Mayo.

'After Anthony Finnerty got the goal, we were in the driving seat, because having lost the previous two years, they were starting to doubt themselves, but in the last ten minutes we went into disarray and let them off the hook. They finished strongly and got the final three points.

'There were 10,000 people waiting for us when we flew back to Knock. It was awfully moving. There was a real party atmosphere, and we went on the beer for three or four days to kill the pain. There was none of the back-stabbing you normally have after a defeat. It was almost a mini-celebration, and Mayo people were proud of us for getting there and playing well. There was a feeling that we needed to do a tour of the county as a political move as much as anything else. I went back to work on the Wednesday though because for me it was over and done with – but not achieved.'

PART II

The Gamechangers

'The whole problem with the world is that fools and fanatics are always so certain of themselves, and wiser people so full of doubts.'

BERTRAND RUSSELL

There is hardly an individual on the face of the earth who has not been affected in some way by the Covid-19 crisis, and that is surely unprecedented in our lifetime at least. The tiny, silent, obnoxious killer crept into all our lives and will colour our existence for the foreseeable future. Suddenly Disney was out of magic and New York was asleep. Hugs had suddenly become weapons, and not visiting grandparents became an act of love. Yet against all the odds, the GAA managed to run off its Championships. Two teams caught the popular imagination: Tipperary by winning the Munster football title and Cavan by winning the Ulster title.

Unlike Bruce Springsteen, I was not born to run so I limped through the Covid crisis. My mother assured me that wearing a mask was a big improvement on my face.

Nonetheless I decided that a good crisis should not go to waste, which led me to a study of great teams. One set of teams which held particular interest for me were those who set the bar for others to follow – trailblazers. In their unique ways, they helped change the culture of Gaelic games from Mick O'Dwyer's swashbuckling Kerry team to Mick Mackey's Limerick, who brought the solo run into fashion, to Éamonn Ryan's Cork ladies' team who bestrode the world of Gaelic games like a colossus.

This section celebrates some of them.

24

WHERE WE SPORTED AND PLAYED

Cork 1939–47

He had the key to unlock the door of perception.

After I finished college and entered the workplace, I rented a flat in Rathgar. To my surprise, I found myself a near neighbour of the then only player to win All-Ireland medals in six consecutive years, Jack Lynch. He had retired from the political stage after his time as Taoiseach came to an abrupt end in 1979. A mutual friend arranged for us to meet.

I sat in silence and stillness, and like the soloist in an orchestra moving towards the centre of the podium, he took control. There is no easy way to describe the next few hours other than to say 'something happened'. The experience felt like a sacred time when the perpetual restlessness of the human heart was stilled and transformed in the face of this heartfelt, rhythmic and charismatic character. Time shimmered and paused, slowing its relentless pace as I sat enthralled. He shared the story of his great Cork team with me at a leisurely pace.

'We won the Munster Championship in 1939, but were beaten by Kilkenny by a single point, scored in the last minute of the

All-Ireland final. That game was played in atrocious weather conditions and, incidentally, the date was 3 September, the day World War II began. Although we were beaten by Limerick the following year in the Munster final, we knew we had an All-Ireland winning combination. That defeat by Limerick in the 1940 Munster final was the only defeat suffered for two seasons by the team and therefore, when we came to face Dublin in the All-Ireland final of 1941, we were firm favourites.

'I played practically all my games for Cork at midfield, although I started at left half-back and played a few times at right half-forward. Towards the end of my career, when I was slowing down, I was moved to full-forward. I was at midfield for all the All-Ireland finals, including our first victorious one, in 1941. We played only one Championship match before reaching the final that year. That was again against Limerick, and this time we won easily by 8-10 to 3-2. I was playing well in that 1941 final, before first being injured and then being forced to leave the field. Cork won by a huge margin, 5-11 to 0-6.

'Dublin were our opponents in the 1942 final again. We had beaten Limerick by 2-14 to 3-4 in the Munster final, and this time we beat Dublin by the less convincing margin of 2-14 to 3-4. In those days there were enormous transport difficulties because of the war. As in previous years, in 1942, several cycling parties set out from Cork on the Saturday before the final, stayed in Portlaoise that night and cycled on to Dublin the following day. We met Antrim in the 1943 final, and of the 48,000 people in Croke Park that day, at least 30,000 were hoping for an Antrim victory because of the fillip this would give the game in the north. It was a disappointing match, largely because Antrim were suffering from stage fright and we ran out easy winners by 5-16 to 0-4.

'In 1944, we were going for our fourth title in a row, which would have established a unique record in itself. We beat Tipperary 1-9 to

1-3, Limerick by 4-6 to 3-6 and Galway 1-10 to 3-3, in what were all very tough games, on the way to the final. Nine of that Cork side had, by then, won three All-Ireland medals, myself being among them, so we were a very experienced side. The final was perhaps the easiest match of the Championship that year for us – we won over Dublin by 3-13 to 1-2.

'We failed to get out of Munster in 1945, being beaten by Tipperary, who went on to beat Kilkenny in the final. In 1946, we beat Kilkenny in the final by 7-5 to 3-8. I blame myself for us not retaining the title again in 1947, this time to lose to Kilkenny by a single point in the final. I had the equalising of the game twice in the closing minutes but hit wide on both occasions. It was the end of an era.'

Having had the opportunity to interview a former Taoiseach about that team, I thought it might make for a nice symmetry to interview the current Taoiseach about its two greatest stars: Jack Lynch and Christy Ring.

RINGY AND THE CHAMP

From ancient times, Irish men and women carried the gift and treasure of Gaelic games. To the Americas, Australia, England and beyond, they brought stories that reminded them of their homeland that sustained them in crisis and hardship, legends to respond to all life situations, and the ability to create new legends to answer new needs. In these crucibles of separation and suffering, Gaelic games were a fixed beam they could hold on to so that they retained their sense of Irishness.

Today GAA fans at home and abroad are attuned to the rhythms, tones and harmonies that communicate their deepest feelings of identity across barriers of region and language. They share stories that speak to our hearts, that touch and move us, none more so than An Taoiseach, Micheál Martin. He has the benefit of being able to underpin his interest in the nation's past with an academic training, having obtained a master's degree in history.

'My thesis was on the formation of the Irish party political system from 1918 to 1932: including the War of Independence, Civil War and the elections: local and national. I didn't focus to any degree on the GAA, but there was one significant political figure in Cork (who once shared digs with Jack Lynch's father) – J. J. Walsh. He was in the GPO in the 1916 Rising and that didn't do him any harm in Cork! He got over 20,000 votes and was first elected in the 1918 general election. He was Minister for Post and Telegraphs in the first Free State government but was also chairman of the Cork County Board and heavily involved in the promotion of Gaelic games. The divisions caused by the Civil War manifested themselves less forcefully in the city than in the county in Cork, and there was a desire to heal the hostilities as quickly as possible.'

THE BOXER

On a deeper emotional level, the Taoiseach's love for Gaelic games was nurtured by his late father, Paddy, who shot to fame as a boxer. He was said to have never been floored in a fight.

'My father fought with the Glen Boxing Club. He had joined the Irish army during "the Emergency", which was when he was introduced to boxing. He was an Irish international, Munster champion, All-Ireland finalist and a regular at the tournaments on a Friday night at Cork City Hall. Boxing in the 1940s and '50s was a very popular sport, and he explained to us that the workers from Ford and Dunlop would come up to the environs of City Hall with their sandwiches, into the local hostelries, a few pints and then into City Hall. It would be packed to the brim. By popular acclaim, his greatest night in City Hall was his victory over the then British champion Joe Bygraves.'

Paddy Martin earned the nickname 'the Champ' in beating Bygraves, 'the boxing master of the British Empire', who, in turn, went twelve rounds with World Heavyweight Champion Ingemar Johansson.

HIT THE ROAD, JACK

Paddy Martin was a northsider. He was born on the Old Youghal Road, and as a massive Gaelic football fan, geography determined that he joined St Nicholas, the sister club of Glen Rovers.

'My father would have boxed for Ireland or competed in the national trials on the Saturday night and then come down to play for St Nicks on the Sunday.'

The star of that St Nicks team was the future Taoiseach Jack Lynch. Although best known as a hurler, Lynch was also an accomplished footballer, winning an All-Ireland football medal in 1945.

Jack entered folklore in the 1938 county final in Bandon. The match was played on the old Bandon field which had a river running parallel to it. Back in the day, footballs were scarce and the clubs had only two on the day of the final. The first ball was punctured early in the game, and later, with St Nicks ahead and looking in control, the second ball was kicked into the middle of the river. Knowing that the match would be abandoned if the ball wasn't reclaimed, Lynch leaped into the river and retrieved it and St Nicks subsequently went on to win the title. This story was told to future generations as an example of the dedication that was required to be successful in the club.

'My father got involved in politics because of his friendship with Jack Lynch in the sense that he used to canvass for Jack. Glen Rovers came out very heavily for Jack and that caused some bad feeling initially with the other Fianna Fáil candidates. (The tension died down when Tom Crofts, the director of elections, personally intervened and suggested that when canvassing, the Glen Rovers members should ask for support for the other Fianna Fáil candidates and this they agreed to do.) We were all brought into the sitting room to watch Jack's big speeches on television.'

FROM A JACK TO A RING

Paddy Martin's career with St Nicholas led him to an even deeper friendship with Christy Ring. In 1948, St Nicholas played UCC at Douglas. St Nicks only had fifteen players and trailed by 4-1 to 2-1 at half-time. Early in the second half, a Nicks player received a bad injury and had to retire from the game. Ring was among the spectators and offered to step into the breach. Playing gear was found, and Ring scored two goals and created two more as Nicks won 6-2 to 5-1. From 1949 until 1956, he played in most of the St Nicks Senior Football Championship games.

Ring was sent off once when St Nicks played Macroom in the 1949 county football semi-final. The referee in his report said Ring had obstructed him in the course of his duty by making a remark. The club vigorously pleaded Ring's innocence, and Jack Lynch, who also played in the match, left the Dáil to travel to Cork to attend the board meeting as a witness on Ring's behalf. The referee's report, however, stood, and Ring received a one-month suspension.

'Ring always played corner-forward, and my father played either full-back or full-forward. As a light heavyweight, my father was a big, strong man and had a great physical presence on the football pitch. He needed it because those games were very tough. Diarmuid O'Donovan of *The Echo* sent me on the referee's reports from some of those games. One read: "Once the ball was thrown in, neither side showed any interest in it. They were only interested in the battles they were having with opposing players."

'St Nicks were very competitive during those years, reaching the county finals of 1950, '51 and '54, and winning the 1954 final.

It always annoyed my father that he never won a county medal. When they won in '54, he was disqualified from playing because he'd lined out for CIE in an inter-firm match.

'That time in Cork the club Championship was fiercely competitive because back then both the Gardaí and the army had teams competing in the Cork Championship and both were like inter-county teams because of the pools of talent they could draw from. So St Nicks were doing really well to hold their own. My father had great friendships with some of the Garda team like Con McGrath, whose son Paul went on to win two All-Irelands with Cork.

'It was very fluid in Cork in the club scene. Jas Murphy captained Kerry to the All-Ireland in 1953. He played for the guards against St Nicks, then played for Nicks against the guards and later on became president of Nemo Rangers! There was also a lot of movement between clubs in families. Those games were a huge deal back then, and you would have up to 25,000 people attending the county finals.

'Another star of that St Nicks team was the late Donie O'Donovan, who coached the Cork footballers to the All-Ireland in 1973, the first one they won since 1945. He sent a ticket for that final to our house for my father because he "heard that Paddy Martin didn't have a ticket for the game".

'Ring was very competitive, and in 1956, when playing against Millstreet, his jaw was broken. He was very unhappy afterwards, not so much with the guy who did it but with my father! He said to him: "It was your man who did this to me. You should've been keeping him busy." The sending off of a Millstreet player in the second half led to a pitch invasion by the crowd, which escalated into a mini riot!'

Ring was also a big believer in the truth and could brutally deliver it.

'He strove for perfection and demanded it off everybody else.

103

My father would tell me of times when he would go for the ball and be beaten by an opponent and Christy would turn to him and say: "You should have got it." There was no room for letting your standards drop.'

The Champ's friendship with Ring did have an unexpected outcome.

'Ring and my father were great personal friends and, in many respects, he had an influence on my father's career. Ring was leaving his job in CIE and he told my father: "There's going to be a job for you here." My father duly got a job there: first as a truck driver and then as a bus driver.'

Having gained a fan base first in the boxing ring, then a new one on the GAA fields, a third set awaited Martin in his new role. He was a handsome man so legend has it that there was a faithful group of ladies who would hang around the No. 3 bus route to wait for him to come along.

More recently, the Taoiseach has come to a keen appreciation of Ring's involvement as a mentor to the Cork hurling team in the 1970s.

'Ray Cummins tells a great story of how Cork played Wexford in the League. Tony Doran lost his hurley and ran the best part of a dozen steps before passing the ball into the net. Everybody expected the goal to be disallowed, but it wasn't. Later that season, the two sides met again in the 1976 All-Ireland final. The same referee was in charge. Ring told the Cork players the week before the game that they could take as many steps as they wanted because the referee wouldn't penalise them. During the game, Ray Cummins got the ball and took a dozen steps before kicking the ball to the net after hearing Ring's advice. It just was a wonderful illustration of how brilliant a hurling mind Ring had.'

The passing of the years has done nothing to diminish the Taoiseach's memories of his father and Christy Ring.

'My father adored Ring. We were brought up on the mantra that there never had been as good a hurler as him and there never will be as good a hurler as Christy Ring. It was wrapped into our brains because my father ensured it would be so.

'The word I would use to describe the feeling for Ring in my family was reverence. The image I had of him from my father was of a very humble man, quiet and unassuming and very kind. We were reared on stories of this exceptional man who did exceptional things and who brought thousands to watch him. My father always said that the Railway Cup would never have taken off the way it did without Christy Ring. People literally came from every corner in Ireland just to see him play. He had that kind of impact. We were brought up to think of him as a god really.

'I regret that I missed Ring's funeral. I was tied up with college commitments. My father went with my brother, and when I asked my brother about it afterwards, he said it was the first time he ever saw my father crying.'

FINDING NEMO

The Taoiseach had his own football career.

'I grew up in Nemo Rangers, a club situated in Turners Cross, the birthplace of my mother. Our cousin Colm Murphy, who won many honours for the club, asked my twin brother Paudie and I when we were eight to the Nemo Street Leagues on the Tramore Road where Nemo had a leased field from the city council. The field we played on was on a hill, so if you were lucky you played up the hill in the first half and down the hill in the second! Our clubhouse was a tiny unit on Patrick's Road, the dressing room a galvanised shed which always looked the worse for wear.

'When my brothers and I were playing for Nemo Rangers, Christy Ring was at one of our games, and he turned to my father and said: "'Tis a great shame to see your sons play for Nemo Rangers!"

'At underage level in the club, the emphasis was not on winning but on developing the young players. I wasn't a great footballer. My major contribution was to entertain the lads on the team bus by mimicking Ian Paisley. Once we got to minor level though it became very serious.

'One highlight came in 1979 in an under-21 County Championship final against Beara. I was a sub on a very talented panel! My brother Seán was captain and in goal. We have a long history of goalkeepers in my family. Maybe it's because we don't have enough pace to play outfield! My twin brother Paudie was full-back. We won well thankfully because one year we lost a minor final we were expected to win and there was a major inquiry in the club as to how we lost. It was worse than the Spanish Inquisition!

'It was a golden age for Nemo Rangers, and they had so many great players, like Dinny Allen – who was, by the way, a very tasty hurler.'

In recent years, the Taoiseach has savoured watching his son Cillian play for Nemo and his older son Micheál Aodh play in goal for Nemo and Cork.

'Cork had a good year last year, though my son would disagree with me because they lost to Tipperary in the Munster final. My father taught me that any year you beat Kerry is a good year!

'It was a very proud day for me to see my son play for Cork for the first time. It was away to Tyrone, and I drove up with a friend to watch it. I thought of my father because he loved Cork football so much. I thought of all the Cork games he brought us to as children and how fortunate I was to have him. It was magical.'

SPEECHES FOR ALL SEASONS
Given his role in politics, the Taoiseach has attended many GAA functions and has had a lot of exposure to that unique literary creation 'the GAA speech'.

'One of the best speeches I ever heard was by Frank Murphy, the former Cork secretary. He was invited to Nemo Rangers to speak about the history of the club. There were times when Nemo were in a spot of bother with the county board, having been embroiled in a bitter row over an expulsion from the Senior Hurling Championship after a brawl in Ballinspittle against Bandon. Some in the club believed the county board had it in for us, and Frank had been associated with that era. However, he came with this incredibly well-researched speech and had a lot of detail that many club members had never heard before. He showed the club great respect by the care he took in preparing that speech.

'My favourite speaker to listen to though for entertainment is Kevin Hennessy. He has a great fund of stories going back to his playing days. In the 1990 All-Ireland final, Cork were trailing Galway badly at half-time. The team manager Canon O'Brien read the riot act and gave a tirade of a speech with one knee on the ground, a jersey in one hand and a hurley in the other, and tears in his eyes. The Cork team were ready to take the hinges off the door on their way out.

'There was one light moment though. During the Canon's tirade, he said there were only two of the team who had played well in the first half. Just before they left the dressing room, Kevin, as only he could, shouted out to great hilarity, "Canon, who was the other fella who played well in the first half?"'

25

THE HEATHER BLAZING

Wexford 1955–56

The philosopher Gabriel Marcel (1889–1973) distinguishes between a problem and a mystery. A problem is generic. You see a broken window or a computer glitch and it needs fixing. It is a straightforward solution. A mystery is unique. It is one of a kind that you have never managed before. It has multiple origins and you cannot understand it from outside. You need to bring your whole life experience to enter it. Often it is the flip side of something good and wonderful.

The mind is a physical thing – but it is not like a leg, arm or ribcage. Its trials are seldom ones that medicine alone can fix. William Shakespeare fused mind and heart together with this relevant question:

> Canst thou not minister to a mind diseased;
> Pluck from the memory a rooted sorrow.
> Raze out the written troubles of the brain.
> And with some oblivious antidote

> Cleanse the stuffed bosom of that perilous stuff
> Which weighs upon the heart?
> *Macbeth*, ACT V, SCENE III

When you're a county like Wexford that didn't have a tradition of winning hurling All-Irelands, you need someone who can unlock the mystery of how to win big games and how to give confidence to those around you that they could do the same.

THE RIGHTEOUS BROTHERS

Nicky Rackard was such a man. Witness his performance against Antrim in the 1954 All-Ireland semi-final. According to folklore, Rackard had been held by Paddy Donnelly in a National League game between the counties the previous year. To compensate, he scored 7-7 of Wexford's 12-17 in a forty-four-point victory, after which Antrim withdrew from the Championship for seventeen years. It was the highest individual Championship tally for any hurler. Rackard had scored no less than 5-3 in Wexford's previous game, the Leinster final win over Dublin – remarkably, a tally he also scored against Galway in the '56 All-Ireland semi-final. He contributed 12-19 in the '54 Championship alone.

If any man was responsible for the Slaneysiders' emergence as a major force, it was him, as Wexford's 1996 All-Ireland winning manager Liam Griffin argues: 'Nicky Rackard was one of the most colourful characters I ever met. He changed the whole sporting and social structure of Wexford. He went to St Kieran's College in Kilkenny and developed a love for hurling which he brought home to his brothers and to his club, Rathnure. Wexford had traditionally been a football power going back to their famous four-in-a-row side. But Nicky Rackard turned Wexford almost overnight into a recognised hurling bastion. He was crucial to Wexford's two All-Irelands in 1955 and '56. It was a tragedy that he died so young.'

Griffin has no doubt about the high point of his county's rivalry with Cork.

In the 1956 final between Cork and Wexford, the crucial contest was that between Christy Ring, playing at left corner-forward and Bobby Rackard. Ring went into the match in search of a record nine All-Ireland senior medals, having won his first in 1941. Outside of Munster, Cork's greatest rivals were Wexford at the time. It was the Wexford man who would win out in every sense.

Wexford had the advantage of a whirlwind start with a goal from Padge Keogh after only three minutes. Two minutes later, Ring registered Cork's first score with a point from a 21-yard free. Wexford went on to win by 2-14 to 2-8.

Wexford had a special place in Ring's affections: 'We in Cork treated Tipperary as our greatest rivals, but I always loved our clashes with Wexford in Croke Park. It's a different climate in Croke Park because you didn't have the pressure of the Munster Championship on your back. It was the same for Wexford – they didn't have the pressure of beating Kilkenny on them. Both of us could relax a bit.'

Liam Griffin sees the rivalry between the two counties as a parable of all that is good in the GAA.

'After the 1956 All-Ireland final – which was the great Christy Ring's last match for Cork – the Wexford players carried him off the pitch. It was a stunning act of sportsmanship. If you ever wanted to know what made that Wexford team so special, that incident tells you all you need to know.'

Mícheál O'Muircheartaigh is another big evangelist for that Wexford team.

'The first hurling team to make a lasting impression on me was the great Wexford team of the 1950s. I had seen John Doyle's great Tipperary three-in-a-row side of '49 to '51, but because of Tipperary's tradition you somehow didn't wonder at that. It was different with Wexford because they came from nowhere. Remember, this was a county that had only won one All-Ireland in 1910, and by the 1950s, they had only added a solitary Leinster title back in 1918. They showed they had promise when they reached the National League final in 1951, only to lose to Galway. They took another step forward by reaching the All-Ireland that same year, even though they lost heavily to Tipperary. By the next year, they were able to run Tipp to a point in the League final and then they swept all before them in 1955 and '56, winning two All-Irelands. The '56 All-Ireland final against Cork was an epic, with a late surge ensuring perhaps their greatest-ever triumph.

'In the 1990s, there was a famous racehorse called Danoli, a Cheltenham winner, who was known as "The People's Champion". It may not have been fully on the scale of the reaction to Clare's triumph in 1995, but when Wexford won in '55 they became the People's Champions.

'The star of that side was Nicky Rackard, but sometimes the invaluable contribution of his brother Bobby is neglected. Bobby was probably the best right full-back I have ever seen. He started off as an elegant centre half-back, but because of an injury to their great full-back Nick O'Donnell, he had to move back to plug the back there. When Nick recovered, Bobby was slotted into the corner and he produced a string of astounding performances there. He had a marvellous ability to catch the sliotar – high or low – and sending it far out field in sweeping clearances. He was key to Wexford's supremacy at that time.'

BACK FROM THE DEAD

That Wexford team also created one of the greatest comebacks in the rich history of the GAA. In 1956, Wexford and Tipperary drew a then record crowd for a hurling league final of 45,902 to Croke Park. It was the second successive year that they had contested the League final. The previous year, Tipperary had won by 3-5 to 1-5, but the match had been overshadowed by the death of Bob Rackard, father of the legendary brothers Nicky, Bobby and Billy, who had all withdrawn from the match.

During the 1956 League final, an exceptionally strong breeze blew into the railway goal at Croke Park, and by half-time Tipperary led by fifteen points, 2-10 to 0-1, through goals from Paddy Kenny, who lined out at right corner-forward beside Billy Quinn, father of soccer international Niall. Tipperary had produced some of the greatest hurling seen in Croke Park in the process. Within five minutes of the restart, Nicky Rackard and Tom Ryan had scored goals. A third Wexford goal, by Tom Dixon, cut the arrears to just 3-7 to 2-13, and with three minutes left, Nicky Rackard pointed to reduce the lead to two. In injury time, Rackard and Dixon scored a goal each, and Wexford won by 5-9 to 2-14 to complete one of the greatest resurrections since Lazarus.

26

MICKO'S MAESTROS

Kerry 1978–86

It was a time when the most exotic thing on Irish television was an ad for a drink, which featured an Irishman overseas reminiscing on everything he missed about home. Chief among the things he missed was Sally O'Brien 'and the way she might look at you'. Her knowing smile sent pulses racing. At a time when we hadn't yet heard the term 'va-va-voom', we knew we craved it. A football team gave us a taste of it.

In American basketball they use the phrase 'Ride the ref'. Most people like to be liked. So if you scream at the referee every time, even when they've blown you up legitimately, they're more likely to give a marginal call in your favour. While it's difficult to imagine Mick O'Dwyer using the phrase 'riding the ref', he was familiar with the concept. Pat Spillane contends that nobody was more adept at getting into the heads of referees than him before Kerry played in big matches, particularly in the era when the handpass reigned supreme.

It was one of his many talents. Dermot Earley would help the Kildare team managed by O'Dwyer to beat Kerry in the

All-Ireland semi-final in 1998. He saw O'Dwyer's genius up close and personal in his half-time talk in the 2000 Leinster final replay against Dublin, which saw Kildare overturn a six-point deficit at the interval to win by five. 'I think one of the things Micko was very good at was calming the situation. Micko would have said, "We're not playing well. These are the things we're not doing good. This is what I want you to do, and now just go out and do it."'

O'Dwyer is without question the greatest football manager of all time, and his team were long considered to be the greatest side of all time. Dublin's six-in-a-row has led to a revisionism in this area. The mid-1970s witnessed the thrilling rivalry between Dublin and Kerry. While the Dubs won in 1974, '76 and '77, Kerry in contrast only won in 1975. By 1978 and '79, Kerry reigned supreme. They thrashed Dublin in both finals, winning by seventeen and eleven-point margins respectively. In the 1980 All-Ireland semi-final, they would play out a high-scoring classic, with Kerry beating Offaly 4-15 to 4-10. Roscommon awaited them in the final, with the Kingdom winning a bruising encounter by three points. The Roscommon side were both puzzled and bewildered by many of the decisions of the referee, and after thirty-three minutes the Roscommon fans started chanting: 'We want a ref; we want a ref.' This might seem like sour grapes, but it is worth noting Michael O'Hehir's words at half-time to the television audience: 'It can only be described as unsatisfactory, and I must say contributing to the unsatisfactory nature was the referee who appeared to lose control of the game and whose decisions were more than mysterious.'

The following year, Kerry and Offaly clashed once again, this time in the final, and a brilliant Jack O'Shea goal would ensure that Sam Maguire would again return to Kerry. In 1982, Kerry were confident of achieving something that had never been managed before in either code: win five All-Irelands in a row. Séamus Darby's sensational late goal denied Kerry by a solitary point. Offaly completed the greatest upset in football history.

PUTTING A CORK ON IT

Kerry dramatically lost the 1983 Munster final to Cork by just a point. It is often forgotten that Cork were frequently the biggest threats to Kerry's supremacy at the time.

By 1984, Kerry found their groove again and began another extraordinary run, winning three consecutive All-Ireland titles. Five players won a record eight All-Ireland medals during the period: 'Ogie' Moran, Páidí Ó Sé, Ger Power, Mikey Sheehy and Pat Spillane. As a famed pundit Spillane has no doubts about O'Dwyer's contribution.

'Mick O'Dwyer is the greatest manager of all time. It wasn't that he was great on tactics. He wasn't, but he was a great man-manager. O'Dwyer always told you that you were the best. Before big games we never concentrated on the opposition. We just focused on our own game. The great leader is the one who enthuses others to rally to the cause. O'Dwyer had that gift.'

27

RAISING THE BANNER

Clare 1995–97

Napoleon famously said that the only generals he wanted were lucky ones. In his later years, Ger Loughnane's luck appeared to desert him, but in the early years, he was blessed with it when his team needed it the most.

'People often say to me, "Ye were very unlucky not to win three All-Irelands." I always say in return, "Do you realise how lucky we were to win two All-Irelands?" You have to have luck to come from where Clare did to win two All-Irelands.

'I think back to the match against Cork in the Munster Championship in 1995. We should have been beaten out of the gate, but we weren't, and we went on to win the All-Ireland. It could be said we picked the wrong team against Cork. We didn't start with Ollie Baker. We picked Stephen Sheedy, who had been a brilliant underage player, but he had a lot of problems with injuries. He didn't play well on the day. If we had lost that day, the Clare officials would have had the perfect excuse to bury me. It's a very fickle thing.'

With the benefit of hindsight, Loughnane can now see that some of the apparent setbacks were actually huge strokes of luck.

'In '95 Tony Considine and I were coming out of the dressing room after losing the League final to Kilkenny. We saw their captain, Bill Hennessy, going out with the cup in his hand. He just dumped it into the boot of his car. I said to Tony, "Imagine if we won the cup – it would still be floating around." It would have been a massive victory but the worst thing that could have happened to us because everybody's ambition would have been satisfied. In '95, we just had a magical year. What was wrong was right. In '98 on the other hand, what was right was wrong! We were lucky to have lost the League final in '95.'

Hurlers could learn to block out external criticism by ignoring a sometimes-hostile media and filtering the feedback they received from others. However, the most difficult voice to silence is internal.

'The toughest voice to block out is the one inside your head. That was always the biggest problem in Clare – to blot out the voice which said, "Ye can't win. Ye won't win." You can only get rid of that voice when players are convinced that you absolutely believe that you will win. If you do, gradually that voice melts in the players' minds. The old Clare wanted to win, prepared to win, but they couldn't block the voice of self-doubt. In the '97 All-Ireland final, we were four points down at half-time, but we could get each other to believe we would win. I had drilled into the players that we had to win that second All-Ireland to be considered a great team. It's something I'll never be able to do again, to hold a group of men in such a vice-like mental grip.'

THE CLARE SHOUT

A new ritual emerged at Clare matches with the appearance of 'the Clare shout'. This was said to have dated back to the time de Valera came electioneering in Clare. Loughnane had tasted the bitter pill of disappointment too often to get carried away, yet he found it impossible to conceal the swelling of hope his team engendered. The jury of experts was still out before the '95 All-Ireland final, but even after beating Galway in the All-Ireland semi-final, the team had as yet to prove themselves in Croke Park. The real test would come in the All-Ireland.

'On the day of the match, everything was very relaxed and I believe we made the right decision in flying up from Shannon that morning. If we had travelled up the day before and stayed in Dublin, we were bound to meet all the Clare crowds and run the risk of getting caught up in the "occasion". We had a workout around noon, doing a bit of stretching and pucking a few balls, before we sat down and talked with the players.

'I was the first into the dressing room, and Jimmy Barry-Murphy and Dr Con Murphy came in to wish us luck. They had been there with the Cork minors that day. There was no discernible air of tension. We had been through the semi-final against Galway, which in a way is a more difficult occasion to cope with. There were very few words spoken. We just told them that Clare people were there in their thousands and that people had come from all over the globe to be here so a massive effort was needed. Above all, we stressed that all the plans we had for Offaly were to be implemented, and stressed the importance of work rate, discipline and taking any opportunities that came our way because they would be scarce. We also emphasised that if they suffered any disappointment or setback, they were to put it behind them. When they left the room, they nearly took the doors off the hinges they were so charged up.'

Across the nation, enthralled radio listeners were listening to the peerless Mícheál O'Muircheartaigh with breathless enthusiasm saying the magic words, 'We're gone forty-five seconds into injury time. It's all over and the men of Clare of '95 are All-Ireland champions.' Almost before the roars that greeted the final whistle, Loughnane was eulogising the talents of his young team.

'I wanted to be back in the dugout with the other three mentors when the final whistle went. When it did, I thanked them for all they'd done. Then the crowds descended on us. Every inch of Croke Park was covered with Clare people.'

Croke Park takes you like no other place, but add in Anthony Daly's famous speech to the emotional mix and it's a recipe for emotional release. 'There's been a missing person in Clare for eighty-one long years. Well today that person has been found alive and that person's name is Liam MacCarthy.'

Loughnane was buzzing.

'When the cup was presented, I didn't go up the steps. It was just a thrill to stand there and soak it all in. It was surreal. Those players will be heroes forever, and that is more lasting than cups or medals. The best way I can think of summing up the day is from the lyrics of a Paul Simon song when he sings of "days of innocence and wonder".'

THE LIFE OF BRIAN

Jamesie O'Connor is keen to pay tribute to the men on and off the pitch.

'We had great players like Brian Lohan. I made my Championship debut with Brian in 1993. He was such an important figure in our dressing room, and his iconic red helmet will never be forgotten. Nobody seemed to galvanise the Clare crowd like him. I will always remember playing Tipp in a League match in 1997 – he blew a Tipperary player away with a shoulder, won a ball he had no right to win, opened his shoulders and cleared the ball way up the field, and such was the roar of the crowd that the roof almost came off the Cusack Stand.

'Loughnane was exceptional. He changed the mindset and made

us believe we could win. When we won the Munster title in '95, he wasn't content to leave it there as others would after waiting for sixty-three years, but he drove us on to win an All-Ireland. I don't think anyone else would have got out of us all he did.'

ON THE OUTSIDE LOOKING IN

Meanwhile in Tipperary, attitudes to that Clare team would change quickly as Ireland's greatest living writer Donal Ryan acknowledges.

'When the great Clare hurling team of the mid-1990s ended an eighty-one-year search for All-Ireland glory against Offaly in 1995, we were largely congratulatory in Tipperary. Four years later, we lined out against Clare in the Munster final and I walked up the steps of the Blackrock end into a Páirc Uí Chaoimh packed to bursting, the air humming and crackling with tension. Insults were flying across the grass from terrace to terrace and stand to stand: nothing mattered in the world in that moment to any man, woman or child in that place but victory. This nascent enmity between the counties had become superheated over the previous few years, had spun and spiralled outwards, gaining density and mass until it collapsed back under its own weight into a black hole of ambition and passion and wounded pride that sucked in and destroyed all reason, all logic, all reserve. Davy Fitzgerald ran from his goalmouth to take a penalty in the game's dying moments and the Tipperary fans were concomitant in censure. As Davy ran back after scoring the equalising goal that would lead to a replay and an easy win for Clare, we coalesced into a single screaming pulsating body of rage and despair and thwarted hope.'

28

GALWAY BOYS HURRAH

Galway 1964–66

Their culture was to put principles before personalities.

Before Mick O'Dwyer's Kerry swashbuckling team of the 1970s, Galway's three-in-a-row-winning team of the 1960s were widely considered to be the greatest football team of all time. They produced a history maker. Having previously won an All-Ireland in 1956, Mattie McDonagh became the only footballer with a Connacht team to win four senior All-Ireland medals. His daughter Joanne recalled not just her father but the man who was also her teacher for five years for me.

'As a family, we were probably more Simpsons than Waltons! Daddy invented the first remote control and called it Shane – well Shane was the youngest at the time and he needed the exercise. Daddy couldn't watch just one programme. We got a video recorder as soon as they came on the market and Mammy duly became an expert at taping one sports event while we watched another.

'In winter we played cards. We started off playing spot, moved on to twenty-five and later graduated to poker. Daddy was no softie and believed in the "tough love" route. He never let us win – ever!

He told us losing would give us the fire in our bellies that would teach us to win.

'Daddy had a great interest in poetry. One day when he was training with Galway, one of his teammates wasn't passing the ball and Dad changed Patrick Pearse's line to describe him from the "the beauty that will pass" to "the beauty that will not pass"!

'Daddy loved the simple pleasures of life – watching a match, playing a game of cards in town with the usual suspects, having a cuppa and a lump – his word not mine – of apple tart or kicking a football around the back garden with the grandchildren. His friends, neighbours and family gathered around his bed the weekend he slipped away and he'd have wished for no more than that.'

Grace is but glory begun and glory is grace perfected. Mattie made each game he played in Croke Park a day of grace and glory. He scored the only goal against Meath in the 1966 final. He also had the distinction of playing minor hurling for Roscommon and minor football for Galway in the same year. The big Ballygar man exploded on to the national stage when, as a nineteen-year-old, he formed a potent midfield partnership with Frank Evers as Galway beat Cork in the 1956 All-Ireland final. In 1966, he won the ultimate personal award when he was chosen as Texaco Footballer of the Year. Mattie managed Galway to a National League title in 1981 and took them to an All-Ireland semi-final in 1982 and an All-Ireland final in 1983.

Mattie died on 10 April 2005, the same day as Enda Colleran's first anniversary Mass. Enda had furnished me some revealing insights into Mattie's character.

'He fired our imagination when Galway won the All-Ireland in 1956, and because Mattie was only nineteen but playing at midfield, I think young fellas like me had a special identification with him.

'When we played Kerry in the All-Ireland final in 1965, they had a very physical side and hit us with everything. Mattie was concussed during the game but played on. That's the sort of man he was. He was going to put the team before his own health. He was a real father figure to that team. When I became captain, I felt at first he really should have been captain because he had won an All-Ireland medal eight years before the rest of us. Thinking he should have been captain raised my performance because I knew if I didn't, I would feel terrible about it because I would have been letting Mattie down. Then I grew into the captain's role and became confident in it.'

29

MIGHTY MACKEY

Limerick 1934–40

The founder of the GAA, Michael Cusack, said of hurling: 'When I reflect on the sublime simplicity of the game, the strength, the swiftness of the players, their apparently angelic impetuosity, the apparent recklessness of life and limb, their magic skill, their marvellous escapes and the overwhelming pleasure they give their friends, I have no hesitation in saying that the game of hurling is in the front rank of the fine arts.'

Hurling is the ultimate virtual reality because it can take you anywhere you want to go. The heart of all sport is the quality of experience it provides. Contrary to real life, sport offers us a state of being that is so rewarding one does it for no other reason than to be a part of it. Such feelings are among the most intense, most memorable experiences one can get in this life.

Hurling is a parable of life at its innocent best, the world as it ought to be, the ideal for a moment realised. Our national sport is an expression of optimism: enshrouding sports lovers with a redemptive feeling, melting away depression, pain and bitter disappointment, hinting at a bygone age of innocence and values that no longer obtain.

Hurling is drama's first cousin. It is theatre without the script. It has the capacity to stop your heart and leave the indelible memory of a magic moment. A great hurling match is something thrilling to watch, a miracle of speed, balance and intense athleticism, a thoroughbred leaving a trail of mesmerised opponents in his slipstream, who have been as transfixed in wonder as the crowd by his silken skills.

Hurling is like a gift wrapped up in deliciously pretty paper, to be given, with discretion, to the faithful. It transcends mere sport. It is about identity and how we feel about ourselves, individually and collectively. Hurling produces a defining moment, an experience that redirects, the revealed truth by whose light all previous conclusions must be rethought.

In the words of Justin McCarthy: 'Hurling identifies my Irishness. I'm not an Irish speaker, so the game portrays my national spirit – it's so Irish, so unique.'

Despite its vast history and our radically different cultural, social and economic context, hurling has in many ways changed very little – the changeless is what it's been about since the beginning. Hurling takes us, at heart, into a mythic place, an ageless space alight with Celtic warriors – not men but giants – who know who they were, are and will be. It's not just part of who we are – it could be argued it *is* who we are. The great hurling teams and the great hurlers make that possible. Sometimes the two seem synonymous, notably Mick Mackey's Limerick. The team won three All-Irelands in 1934, '36 and '40. When I spoke to Jack Lynch, I was keen to get his opinion of Mick Mackey.

'Christy Ring was the greatest hurler that I knew. I know there are some who will contend that others were better – Mick Mackey, for example. Mackey was great, but in my opinion, Ring's hurling repertoire was greater. He was totally committed to hurling, perhaps more so than any player I have ever met. He analysed games in prospect and in retrospect. In essence, he thought and lived hurling.

'I think Mick Mackey was the most effective hurler that I played against. If there was one game which proved that, it was when he scored no less than five goals and three points in the 1936 Munster final against Tipperary. His fifth goal in particular was a thing of beauty. It came on the end of a solo run. He mightn't have pioneered the solo run, but he turned it into an art form, and his presence brought a golden age for Limerick hurling.'

30

SMALL HEADS AND SMALL ARSES

Cork 2004–16

He was the GAA's answer to Robin Williams in *Dead Poets Society*.

Few men knew how to motivate players better than the manager of the most successful GAA team of all time, Éamonn Ryan. He put the emphasis on humility and fitness. Hence his instruction to his team to be like nuns and have 'small heads and small arses'. In January 2021, the GAA community mourned his passing.

The Glenville/Watergrasshill man led the Rebels to their first All-Ireland title in 2005, and they went on an incredible run which brought them nine more titles over the next ten seasons. He was a towering figure of his time with a unique capacity to redirect the traffic of sporting destiny from the back alley of failure towards the grand concourse of triumph and glory.

We stand in awe.

He could relate to the type of dedication that caused a top jockey like Tony McCoy to live solely on a diet of chicken and Jaffa Cakes. He could understand why Herb Elliott, the 1500 metre Olympic champion from Australia, retired at the incredibly tender age of twenty-one. He hung up his spikes because he had never been beaten over his Olympic distance and was unsure how he would handle the trauma when it inevitably came. To outsiders, these competitors are not of this world, but for those like Ryan who have competed at the highest level in their chosen sport, or as Macbeth would have put it, acquired 'the sickness', they all think they are madly normal. They live and breathe the game.

Ryan knew why second best was just not good enough. He knew that it was the small things that make the big differences. He understood that a lot of the time winning is not about being one hundred per cent better than your opponents but about doing a hundred things one per cent better than the other team. He knew that in the lead-up to a big game what players want – no, what they need – is an atmosphere as reassuringly familiar as the odours of home cooking; he understood how the hours peeled away like layers of insulation before a match, and he could decipher the throb of misgiving that can be detected in strident predictions of success. He went through what Clive Woodward calls the T-Cup, i.e. 'thinking correctly under pressure'.

AMONGST WOMEN

In the rich history of the GAA, the Cork ladies' team of the noughties and beyond are the greatest team of all time. From never having won a senior title to winning ten All-Irelands in eleven years (2005–09 and 2011–15), nine League titles and ten Munster titles, their record is simply breathtaking. They made household names of players like Valerie Mulcahy, and were led magnificently by the peerless Juliet Murphy, who ranks with greats like Mary Jo Curran and Cora Staunton as one of the GAA immortals. Famously in 2013, Murphy came out of retirement to lead Cork to another All-Ireland.

Éamonn Ryan was not prepared to accept the old ways. His message was: 'As a team we were feared by everyone out there, but we don't believe in ourselves. The dream can become a reality if they want it bad enough, but they need to believe.'

He told the players to realise the sacrifices needed to get to the top. They had to be more committed, loyal to their teammates and play with pride in the jersey. There was to be no cliques, no gossip and what was said in the dressing room stayed in the dressing room. Three times they beat Dublin in All-Ireland finals, including the never-to-be-forgotten 2014 final when Dublin led by ten points with just sixteen minutes to go.

The players responded to his motivation. Before the 2011 All-Ireland quarter-final against Dublin, he told them how he'd listened to a woman on the radio whose husband had died. Asked how she was able to keep going and see light at the end of the tunnel, 'She said she was able to keep going because she walked down that tunnel and turned on the feckin' light herself ... Now go out there and do the same.'

31

THE BLACK AND AMBER

Kilkenny 1969–75

Mícheál O'Muircheartaigh ranks with the likes of Peter O'Sullevan, Dan Maskell, Bill MacLaren and Michael O'Hehir as one of the all-time giants of sports broadcasting. Who better to canvas for an opinion on the great GAA teams?

'When you talk about the great teams, it's not near as clear-cut in hurling as it is in football. Despite their achievements under the guidance of Brian Cody, for a certain generation of Kilkenny supporters, the Kilkenny side of 1969–75 has a claim to be considered their finest ever, and with good reason. That team featured in the side reads like a who's who of the hurling world – greats such as Eddie Keher, Frank Cummins, Noel Skehan, Liam "Chunky" O'Brien and Pat Henderson but to name a few.

'If I were pushed to it, I would say that the best hurling team of the last century – with the emphasis on team – that I ever saw was that Kilkenny side. They won the All-Ireland in 1972, '74 and '75 and played the final in '73 against Limerick. When I think of their great games of the time, especially against Wexford, who had a great team at the time but couldn't get the better of Kilkenny, usually in Leinster finals, I think that Kilkenny team were good in all sectors. Take Eddie Keher in the full-forward line, Pat Delaney at centre-forward, Frank Cummins in midfield, Pat Henderson at centre half-back. They had super men in all parts of the field and played like a team.

'I suppose though I'd have to single out Eddie Keher from that team as one of the all-time greats. I always say to score, we'll say, a point in an All-Ireland final is something special for a player. I could be wrong now, but I think it's seven goals and seventy-seven points that he scored in All-Ireland finals alone. What memories must that man have? That tally is a measure of the man's greatness.

'D. J. Carey became the next great modern star. There is no doubt about it. The crowd got very excited when the ball came towards him. He had speed and tremendous skill. On his day he was unbeatable. You'll often be asked on the day of a match when a guy shines if he is the greatest player you ever saw. I always say that you have to wait a few years after a guy retires to judge him properly. Eddie Keher played senior for Kilkenny for the first time in 1959, having starred in the minor All-Ireland final that year. The senior final ended in a draw and he was drafted on as a sub for the replay. He was still playing for the seniors in 1977, so apart from his superb skill, that he remained at the top for so long was also a factor.'

John 'The Legend' Doyle was part of the formidable Tipperary full-back line of the 1950s and 1960s known as 'Hell's Kitchen' with Mick Maher and Kieran Carey. It was a time when, in the classic GAA euphemism, players 'had to be able to look after themselves'. Few people in hurling were ever better equipped to talk about toughness than Doyle. He described Keher as the toughest man he ever played against.

GLORY DAYS

One of the highlights in the showreel of that great Kilkenny team came in 1969 when they regained their Leinster crown from Wexford and beat Cork in that year's All-Ireland final by six points. Although Wexford wrestled supremacy back the following year in the province, between 1971 and '75, the Leinster title never left Kilkenny. They also reached the All-Ireland final every year during that period; a record which stood until Brian Cody's Kilkenny side broke it in 2011.

In 1971, Kilkenny faced old rivals Tipperary, and despite a heroic effort from Eddie Keher, who scored 2-11, Liam MacCarthy made its way to the Premier County after an absolute thriller of a game – Tipp emerging victorious, 5-17 to 5-14. Kilkenny regained the All-Ireland in 1972, beating Cork. Eight points down at one point, Kilkenny staged a remarkable comeback, winning by seven.

32

THE KINGS OF ULSTER

Cavan 1947–52

For the first half of the last century, Cavan were the kings of Ulster. Before Down's breakthrough in 1960, Cavan were also the province's sole All-Ireland winners.

Although they won their first two All-Irelands in 1933 and '35, it would be the Cavan side of the 1940s that would carve their name on football immortality. In winning the All-Ireland Championship of 1947, Cavan earned a unique place in GAA history. That final was played for the first and only time outside of Ireland. In the Big Apple at the Polo Grounds, Cavan beat Kerry to lift Sam Maguire for a third time. They were captained by 'the Gallant' John Joe O'Reilly. The following year they beat Mayo by a point to retain their title. In 1949, they were back in the final looking to complete a three-in-a-row only to lose by four points to a Meath side winning its first-ever title.

YES, MINISTER

Right half-back on that team was the late John Wilson, who went on to become Tánaiste in the Irish government. He recalled his memories of the highlight of his career for me.

'The 1947 final was held in New York as a gesture of goodwill to the Irish people in America by the GAA. Once it was announced, it aroused great interest in every county. To get there was a great prize in itself. The teams left Cobh together for a six-day trip on the SS *Mauritania* to New York, after getting our vaccinations against smallpox, which were compulsory at the time. The fact that we were playing the aristocrats of football Kerry added to the occasion for us, but the fact that it was the first final played abroad gave it a much more exotic quality, so it really grabbed the public imagination.

'The pitch was used for baseball and was much smaller than the usual Gaelic pitch. The grass was scorched and even bald in a few places, and there was a mound in the playing area. Kerry got off to a great start, but Peter Donohoe was on fire for us that day. The American press described him as "the Babe Ruth" of Gaelic football after the greatest star in baseball of the era. We had a great leader and one of the all-time greats in Gaelic football in John Joe O'Reilly – the young army officer who died so tragically at the Curragh Camp's military hospital after a short illness in 1952 at the tender age of thirty-four. By coincidence, one of the biggest stars of our team, Mick Higgins, who scored a goal and two points in that match, was born in New York.'

I had the great good fortune to know 'the voice of Kerry football', the famed presenter of *Terrace Talk* Weeshie Fogarty. It was cold outside, with a raw wind howling from the north, with the promise of more rain that had dogged the country for the past week. In fact, the first drops of rain were falling as I reached the front door. I quickly found myself chattering about all matters of Cavan's fairy tale of New York: 'In blistering hot conditions and played on a bone-hard pitch, John Joe O'Reilly led Cavan to a controversial 2-11 to 2-7 win. The loss of Eddie Dowling through injury from the Kerry midfield on top of some debatable refereeing by Martin O'Neill was a big turning point in the game.'

33

STRIKING IT BIG

Cork 2003–06

They were like surging waves in the sea.

One of the unfortunate consequences of the high-profile strikes involving the Cork hurlers in the noughties is that they overshadowed the greatness of the Cork team who contested four consecutive All-Irelands losing to Kilkenny in 2003 and '06 and winning back-to-back All-Irelands in '04 and '05, defeating Kilkenny and Galway respectively.

STAR-STRUCK

That Cork team were a team of stars. Dónal Óg Cusack in goal; full-back Diarmuid 'The Rock' O'Sullivan; a half-back line for the ages: John Gardiner, Ronan Curran, Seán Óg Ó hAilpín; the energy, dynamism and creativity of Jerry O'Connor and Tom Kenny in midfield; Joe Deane, Ben O'Connor and the peerless Brian Corcoran in the forward line. Wayne Sherlock was as hard as nails.

Then for a brief period there was Setanta Ó hAilpín. Pat Spillane feels that the GAA missed a trick in not adequately drawing on his superstardom, particularly as he claimed that Setanta was 'the first sex symbol in the GAA since Marty Morrisey'.

Moreover, this was a team of innovation as they apparently reinvented the face of hurling with a brilliant running game that was described as 'a new game'.

The biggest compliment to the greatness of the Cork team was how Kilkenny dealt with them in the 2006 final. The Cats hadn't won an All-Ireland for two years and knew they would have to perform at a very high level and try to stop Cork's running game. Kilkenny were in a good place until J. J. Delaney, their star defender, suffered a training-ground injury ten days out from the final. Noel Hickey though would step into the breach.

In 2003, Tyrone had harassed and hustled Kerry into submission in the All-Ireland football semi-final. Kilkenny did the exact same to Cork in '06. Henry Shefflin has spoken about the importance of beating Cork that year.

'Intensity was the big word. We were so fired up and so hungry. There was so much spoken about the way Cork were playing and the Cork tactics over the previous couple of years, especially in their drive for three-in-a-row, there was a lot more media attention on it. When you watch the video back when one of the Cork lads had the ball, it went from one, two, three Kilkenny players surrounding him. The game flowed from there; we just outworked them and brought that intensity. Because Cork obviously liked possession, we needed to turn them over a lot with that manic aggression of tackling.

'While Kilkenny and Cork didn't like each other during that period, what I will say, behind it all, I went on trips with a lot of those lads and we had great craic together, and we had the height of respect for each other.'

34

KINGS OF THE KINGDOM

Kerry 1903–14

It was a slow burner.

Limerick won the first All-Ireland played in Beech Hill, Donnybrook on 29 April 1888. The first edition of the All-Ireland Championship featured club teams who represented their respective counties after their county Championship. The first final was contested between Commercials of Limerick and Young Irelands of Louth, with Commercials winning by 1-4 to 0-3.

Gaelic football really came of age in 1903 when Kerry won their first All-Ireland. They beat Kildare in a three-game saga, which grabbed the public imagination. Kerry won the first game, but the match was replayed because Kerry had been awarded a controversial goal. So intense was the second game, which finished in a draw, that the referee collapsed at the end. On the third occasion, Kerry were comprehensive winners by 0-8 to 0-2.

The background music to this Kerry team was a growing cultural nationalism. The historian W. E. H. Lecky wrote in 1861 of the 'ceaseless ridicule, the unwavering contempt, the studied depreciation of the Irish character and intellect habitual in the

English newspapers'. The Catholic Church was also swept up in the changing mood of the national pulse. In the late nineteenth century – thanks in no small part to the work of Cardinal Paul Cullen – the Catholic Church exerted a massive cultural influence in Irish society. To have its blessing – and, above all, to be *seen* to have its blessing – was important for the GAA. Archbishop Croke was a shrewd choice as a patron of the GAA. He was one of Parnell's most outspoken supporters among the hierarchy. In fact, he was summoned to Rome by Pope Leo XIII to explain his support for nationalist politicians. Croke's biases and prejudices were very clear in his letter of acceptance as patron:

> We are daily importing from England not only her manufac-tured goods [. . .] but together with her fashions, her accent, her vicious literature, her music, her dances and her manifold mannerisms, her games and also her pastimes, to the utter discredit of our own grand national sports, and to the sore humiliation, as I believe, of every genuine son and daughter of the old land.
>
> Ball-playing, hurling, football, kicking, according to Irish rules, 'casting', leaping in various ways, wrestling, handy-grips, top-pegging, leap-frog, rounders, tip-in-the-heat, and all such favourite exercises and amusements among men and boys may be said not only to be dead and buried, but in several localities to be entirely forgotten and unknown. And what have we got in their stead? We have got such foreign and fantastic field sports as lawn-tennis, croquet, cricket and the like – very excellent, I believe, and health-giving exercises in their way, still not racy of the soil, but rather alien, on the contrary, to it, as are indeed, for the most part, the men and women who first imported and still continue to patronise them [. . .]
>
> Indeed if we continue traveling for the next score of years in

the same direction that we have been going in for some time past [. . .] we had better at once and publicly retain our nationality, clap hands for joy at the sight of the Union Jack, and place 'England's bloody red' exultingly above 'the green'.

KING CON

As a young student I shared a cheap flat in Rathmines which was less than salubrious. The only thing in its favour was that it was very close to a hostelry favoured by Con Houlihan. One evening I almost literally bumped into him. I was in awe, but in the following months we had a few chats, and he tried to explain the spiritual importance of Gaelic football in the Kingdom.

'As you come from Limerick into Kerry, the road starts to rise at Headley's Bridge. After about three miles, you reach the summit of the road in the townland of Gleannsharoon. Now you are looking down at a great valley ringed all around with hills and mountains. Geographers call it the Castle Island Gap; sensible people call it the Heart of the Kingdom. In the middle of the valley, you can see an old town sloping from east to west. In the days when the Gaelic language prevailed, it was known as *Oileán Chiarraí*, the Island of Kerry. The island was a great outcropping of rock surrounded by marsh. Eventually the marshland was drained for grazing and tillage. The Normans came and built a castle in the western end of the outcropping of rock. Trade followed the flag. Houses were created from the rock – and on both sides of it a town began to grow. If you were farming in an area like that, it was tough to eke out a living, and as Ireland marched to its independence, people looked to football as an escape from the harshness of their lives.'

STAR POWER

The year 1904 saw the first taster of what would become one of the great rivalries in the GAA when Kerry beat Dublin to claim their second All-Ireland. By now, the first true star of Gaelic football, Dick Fitzgerald, had emerged. He won five All-Ireland medals, captaining the team to All-Irelands in 1913 and '14. Like many men of the time, Fitzgerald was active in the IRA, as the movement for Irish independence gathered momentum.

35

THE TIPPERARY TRAILBLAZERS

Tipperary 1949–52

The sharpest blades are sheathed in the softest pouches.

As Jack Lynch happily puffed on his pipe when I spoke with him, inevitably the focus was on all things Cork hurling. However, the surprise for me was that I left with a huge interest in the Tipperary team of the early 1950s. He explained that alongside Cork, Kilkenny and Tipperary are one of 'the big three' in hurling. From the earliest days of the GAA they were making their mark on it, but it wasn't until the late 1940s that the first true great Tipperary team and its stars – like Mickey 'Rattler' Byrne, Tommy Doyle and Jimmy Finn – emerged. In particular he had me spellbound as he spoke about the goalkeeper on that team, Tony Reddin.

I was surprised to learn that Reddin began his hurling career in his native Mullagh, in County Galway. He made one appearance for the Tribesmen, but because of the form of Seánie Duggan, Reddin couldn't get his place on the team. When the offer of employment across the Shannon came up in 1947, he took it.

His display for Lorrha in the 1948 North Tipperary final caught the eye of the Tipperary management, and at the age of twenty-eight, he became the Premier County's number one, winning his first National League title the following year in 1949. Later that year, Reddin was between the posts when Tipperary beat Laois by 3-11 to 0-3 in the All-Ireland final.

ANARCHY

The Cork–Tipperary rivalry was intense during this era, and in the 1950 Munster final, it came to a head during one of the most famous matches to ever take place and one in which Tony Reddin confirmed his legendary status in the minds of Tipperary hurling fans. The official attendance in Fitzgerald Stadium was about 40,000, but it's believed that more than an additional 10,000 people poured into the stadium, breaking down gates on their way.

Tipperary enjoyed a pleasing seven-point lead at half-time, but Reddin emerged from the dressing rooms after the break to see that supporters had broken down the fence and were now placed directly behind his goal. Christy Ring scored a goal; however, both he and Jack Lynch were denied further goals by stupendous saves from Reddin. Lynch was already a TD at the time, and he made a beeline for Reddin as he went up to catch a high ball. But the Tipperary goalkeeper was too quick for him, gathering the ball and dodging Lynch, who went crashing into the goalpost. Reddin turned to him and in a tone that left no room for ambiguity said, 'Try that again and there'll be a f**king by-election.'

There was a twinkle in Lynch's eye as he told me about some of the folklore about the game. Legend has it that Reddin was pelted with various stones and bottles and even an orange, which he controlled on his hurley and partially ate before hitting it back. The tone in his voice suggested that Lynch might have felt some of the tales might have been a tad exaggerated.

The match became known as the 'Anarchy in Killarney'. Despite a premature pitch invasion by Cork fans, Tipperary held on to retain their Munster title on a scoreline of 2-17 to 3-1. There was further drama after the final whistle when Reddin ran to the middle of the pitch with a posse of furious Cork supporters on his tail. He was met by a priest who dressed him in a clerical hat and coat to disguise him. He stayed on the pitch until the crowd had dispersed, and it wasn't until the Tipperary convoy were well outside of Killarney that the disguise was abandoned.

After beating Galway in the semis, a more formidable threat awaited them when they accounted for Kilkenny in that year's final. In 1951, Tipperary emulated the side of 1898–1900 by winning a third successive All-Ireland crown when they beat Wexford 7-7 to 3-9.

36

MAYO'S MAGNIFICENCE

Mayo 1950–51

It was the classic confrontation between Gaelic football's beauty and the beast. The late Mayo full-forward Tom Langan went shoulder to shoulder with the celebrated Paddy Bawn Brosnan in the All-Ireland semi-final replay in 1951. In conversation with this writer, the great John B. Keane explained the legend of Paddy Bawn with a hushed awe in his voice.

'Once, Paddy Bawn suffered a nose injury in a club Championship match. To stop the blood that was flowing with the ferocity of Niagara Falls, a piece from *The Kerryman* was stopped up the nose, but true to form, Paddy played on. A week later he felt a stinging pain and went to the doctor. The poor medic had much more difficulty in extracting the paper than healing the fractured nose.

'The Bawn loved to play up his image of a hard man. Stories abounded about his ability to stand up to a hard tackle. "How hard was he hit?"

'"Hit hard is it? If he was a stone wall, he'd be in rubble."

'"And he still played on?"

'"He played better than ever. Sure, the blows only straightened him."

'The Bawn is one of the giants of Kerry football. The only player I ever saw make him look like a dwarf was Tom Langan in Croke Park in 1951. If he wasn't before, that was the day Langan became one of the all-time immortals of Gaelic football.'

Mayo's full-back on that team was Paddy Prendergast. His conversation drew you to him like a warm fire in a blizzard. He recalled Tom Langan with undisguised affection.

'Tom was one of the best footballers I've ever seen. Above all, he was one of the original thinking footballers. He won many games for us, but he was very badly done by the Mayo selectors in the early years. Our whole history is peppered with stories like that. I could think of a litany of them. Our centre half-back Henry Dixon was the same. He was nearly over the hill when he was brought onto the team.

'Tom was all knees and bones and was very shy at times. He was from Ballycastle and there we are not allowed to be too forward! As a Garda, he was more inclined to give people a warning than apply the full rigour of the law. He was very special. One of my clearest memories of him was when we played Kerry in the drawn game in the 1951 All-Ireland semi-final. We were four points down but Éamonn Mongey gave Tom the ball and he flashed it into the net.

'My abiding memory of him though was the night before the 1951 All-Ireland final. He was in the lobby of the hotel and he had one of the lads pretending to be the Meath full-back Paddy O'Brien, who of course was chosen as full-back on the Team of the Century, who was as tough a marker as you could get. Tom would do a sidestep to the left and a sidestep to the right with the ball, and I remember at one stage he went crashing into a chair. When the game began, the first ball that came into him, he sidestepped Paddy O'Brien and stuck the ball into the net.'

THE FLYING DOCTOR

Mícheál O'Muircheartaigh believes that one of the reasons why that Mayo team were so successful is that they had very strong characters.

'Characters are good for sport. There were a lot of characters in the old days in Gaelic games when there was no managers and players were individuals. Nowadays, with managers controlling players and not allowing them to talk to the media, characters are not as plentiful as they once were.

'In the olden days, there were great characters like Gunner Brady of the Cavan team that won the Polo Grounds All-Ireland in 1947. I think even his name was one of the reasons that he had this aura that surrounded him, and also from that side, Bill Doonan was as interesting a character as I ever met.

'Another character was Paddy Prendergast from the great Mayo side of 1950 and '51. 'The Flying Doctor' Paddy Carney, also from that side, was a wonderful character. Sometimes he would even hold up the ball to show to the crowd and usually it went over the bar. He had a little bit of arrogance, but he also had the skill to match. His Mayo team won back-to-back All-Irelands, and there's no doubt they rank as one of the great teams.'

37

THE STRIFE OF BRIAN

Kilkenny 2000–03

Alexander the Great was marching with his army. They had gone a few days without water. One evening, one of his soldiers came running into camp having discovered water. He proudly handed over his helmet, which was full of lovely water. He was expecting thanks. Instead, Alexander threw the water on the ground and said: 'I only drink after all my army has drank.' It was a brilliant example of leadership and one that Brian Cody would have endorsed.

Cody follows the great tradition of Kilkenny coaches, notably the legendary Fr Tommy Maher. Cody's first three All-Irelands came in 2000, '02 and '03. The team was noteworthy for the end of one era and the birth of another.

D. J. Carey's status amongst the hurling cognoscenti was literally reflected in the box office. The standard attendance in a Kilkenny county final would be 10,000 – when D. J.'s Young Irelands played in the county final, the crowd swelled by fifty per cent with 'fierce hurling people' from as far away as the Glens of Antrim attending just to catch a glimpse of his genius.

There was massive controversy when he wasn't chosen on the hurling Team of the Millennium. The whisperings were that he hadn't really delivered on the big day. He put that to bed with his star performance against Offaly in the 2000 All-Ireland final.

In 2002, Carey had come back from retirement. When the game was in the melting pot in the All-Ireland semi-final against Tipperary, he produced a dazzling solo run with Tom Costello in dogged pursuit and set up a crucial goal for Jimmy Coogan. In the All-Ireland final against Clare, from out under the Hogan Stand, D. J. evaded the formidable Ollie Baker and produced what no less an authority than Mícheál O'Muircheartaigh described as probably the greatest point he had never seen.

Carey had a national profile that no Kilkenny hurler had ever known. He did a promotional event for Flora with Jack Charlton in the new Croke Park. Jack had been in his share of great stadia but was blown away by Croke Park and said he'd never seen anything like it.

Eddie Brennan was another great forward on that team and his pace ensured that he got the nickname 'Fast Eddie', but D. J. was even quicker. Was Carey better than Henry Shefflin? That depends on who you ask. However, in full flight, there was no more exciting player in the modern era.

Cody's first great team had the benefit of not one but two of the handful of men who are part of the conversation as to the greatest players of all time in Carey and Shefflin. Although he is known in the hurling fraternity as 'The King', David Herity rechristened him 'Tenry' after he won his tenth All-Ireland. Having already won two All-Irelands as a coach, the Shefflin story is far from over.

However, Cody's team was also powered by some of the greatest defenders in the history of the game: Tommy Walsh, Jackie Tyrell, Noel Hickey, Brian Hogan and J. J. Delaney. Brian Cody said Delaney was the greatest defender he has ever seen. That is some endorsement. Think of the 2014 All-Ireland final: Séamus Callanan on the ball before Delaney dived, hooked and flicked the ball away. On such moments, big games are won and lost. Hard work beats talent if talent doesn't work. All those defenders had the talent and the hard work. Some, like Brian Hogan and Noel Hickey, were surprisingly fast. To be hit by Brian Hogan was like being hit by a JCB.

Nonetheless, Nicky English believes Cody's contribution was crucial.

'Begrudgers suggest Cody's triumphs can be attributed to the fact that he had so many exceptional players. Perhaps other managers would have won a number of All-Irelands with those players, but could any of them have won so many senior All-Irelands?'

38

HOW THE WEST WAS WON

Corofin 2018–2020

Is iomaí cor sa tsaol.
There is many a twist in life.

In January 2010, I had perhaps my most memorable conversation with Dermot Earley. It was the first time I really became aware of the toll that the illness that would claim his life just six months later was taking on him. Both of us were anxious to deflect the conversation away from health topics so we immersed ourselves into a discussion about the future of the club. Dermot was uncharacteristically downbeat.

'In rural places especially I've seen big changes insofar as the traditional loyalty to the club is weakening. There's a lot more young fellas going to third-level education now, and they're emigrating for the summer and playing hurling in America or somewhere and not in their local club. There's a lot more mobility now in the workplace, and guys are moving around from place to place but are generally not willing to travel back to their parish for training every evening, so they're switching to clubs in Dublin or wherever. In the club versus county stakes, the county is winning. Each of these changes on their own are not that significant, but when you add them all together, they become very significant, and they are decimating some of the clubs, especially in the rural areas. I have to say I'm very worried the old-style club may be in danger.'

STYLE AND SUBSTANCE

I thought about that conversation again in January 2020 when Corofin became the first side to win a third consecutive All-Ireland club football title. In fact, they became the first-ever team in either code to complete the three-in-a-row. In 2020, they eked out a gritty victory earned against a steely Kilcoo outfit after extra time. For the third time in his distinguished managerial career, Mickey Moran found himself on the losing side on All-Ireland club final day following two previous defeats with Sleacht Néill.

In their previous two All-Ireland triumphs, their respective rivals Nemo Rangers and Dr Cokes allowed Corofin the space to play expansive football, but Kilcoo rolled out a blanket defence that suffocated their attack for most of the afternoon. This was a clash of styles that had echoes of Donegal v Dublin in 2011.

The fact that Corofin won those three titles is admirable in itself. But what is so commendable is that they did so almost exclusively playing with style and flair. In 2019, Ciarán Whelan said Gaelic football was coming out of recession. Corofin blazed the trail in that respect. In the process, they proved that Gaelic football can, like hurling, be the beautiful game.

Within two months, the coronavirus struck the world with the ferocity of a tsunami. Apart from the global trail of illness, economic devastation and death, it also sparked a tidal wave of fear. It struck at something deep inside us and shattered many of our cherished certainties. We thought we were in control, but nature reminded us of our fragility, vulnerability and mortality not with a gentle whisper but with a primeval scream. It had echoes of a medieval plague. Corofin left us with wonderful memories to keep the flame of hope flickering of happier days to return.

Dermot Earley would have saluted a terrific team playing the beautiful game – a team who showed the world that the west's awake.

39

THE PREMIER TEAM

Tipperary 1960–71

In January 2021, the death of Theo English was announced. He had turned ninety the previous July and was the midfield general of the great Tipperary team of the 1960s. He was chosen on the best Premier XV of the twentieth century and was part of the great Tipp team of the 1960s.

English played on the 1958 All-Ireland winning side that still included names from their three-in-a-row-winning side (1949–51) such as Jimmy Finn and John Haugh, but by 1960 a new team was emerging that would become widely regarded as the Premier County's greatest ever.

In 1960, they beat Cork for the first time in a Munster final for nine years. They lost to Wexford in that year's All-Ireland final. The following year they began a new era of great success. They defeated Cork once again in Munster, in what was a forty-year-old Christy Ring's last Munster final. They went on to beat Dublin by a solitary point to claim the All-Ireland.

In 1962, they nearly suffered at the hands of an error that befell Clare in 1998 when Jimmy Cooney famously blew up too early in the All-Ireland semi-final replay against Offaly; the referee ended the game prematurely. Thanks to some quick thinking from the officials, the game was restarted and Limerick forced a replay in the Munster semi-final. Tipp emerged victorious, winning Munster and extracting revenge on Wexford for 1960 by beating them in the All-Ireland final by two points.

An uncharacteristic below-par performance in the 1963 Munster final at the hands of Waterford ended any chances of completing the three-in-a-row and subsequently an unprecedented five-in-a-row.

In 1964, Kilkenny were firm favourites to win the All-Ireland, but Tipp crushed their illustrious neighbours, with a fourteen-point win. The next year would see them face their rivals Wexford, but another comprehensive defeat gave Tipp their fourth title in five seasons.

The win saw one of the great icons of the GAA, John Doyle, equalling Christy Ring's record of eight senior winner's medals on the field of play. The Holycross star was one of the corner-stones of that side and had a powerful human-interest story. He had a tough childhood – his mother died weeks after his birth. He did have other great stars playing with him like Liam Devaney, Jimmy Doyle, Donie Nealon and Mick Roche.

Jimmy Doyle too was an exceptional talent. He was selected for the Tipperary minors as a fourteen-year-old, playing four years at the grade and competing in an All-Ireland final in each of those. He won six All-Irelands – captaining Tipp to Liam MacCarthy twice – nine Munster medals and seven National Leagues. Slim and smaller in stature, 'Babs' Keating once revealed a conversation he had with Christy Ring, in which Ring said: 'Do ya know, Babs, if Jimmy Doyle was as strong as you and I . . . no one would ever ask who was the greatest hurler.'

By 1967, Tipp were no longer the dominant force they had been for the past five or six years. Successive All-Ireland defeats in 1967 and '68 furnished evidence of this. One final taste of glory for Jimmy Doyle came in 1971 when Tipperary beat Kilkenny in the All-Ireland final. The side were captained by Tadhg O'Connor. The Roscrea man was just twenty-two at the time, but he was surrounded by great experience in the side, such as Mick Roche, Len Gaynor, and Michael 'Babs' Keating. In front of 61,393 in Croke Park, the game yielded an astonishing ten goals and thirty-one points. When the referee – famous Cork official Frank Murphy – blew the full-time whistle, Tipperary had beaten Kilkenny by 5-17 to 5-14.

The past is a foreign country. The week before, one of the Tipp players, John Flanagan, got married in Gortnahoe. Love was all around him, and he could feel it in his fingers and in his toes, but nonetheless he still managed to score 1-2 against Kilkenny. It is unlikely that Liam Sheedy would allow one of his star players to get married days before an All-Ireland final today.

STEADY EDDIE

Eddie Keher scored a record 2-11 in that game. When I spoke to him, he looked back at the match with surprising affection.

'There was a really big rivalry with ourselves and Tipp in the 1960s. We played in a couple of League finals and they were fairly tempestuous matches, to be honest. It was hot and heavy. Tipperary always had this belief that they could beat Kilkenny, because they were tougher and stronger, whereas we were "fancy" hurlers. Tipp had a spell over us, or at least that was how it seemed. Fr Tommy Maher took the view then that we needed a strong team to beat Tipp. We won two All-Irelands with St Kieran's under Fr Tommy as well. He was the most innovative of coaches. He came in as Kilkenny coach in '57 and revolutionised coaching. Before Fr Tommy there was no real coaching drills or analysis of the opposition. He was very forward-thinking, devising systems to curb certain players on the opposition. Fr Tommy was adamant, though, that we needed to be stronger. This led to two teams that refused to back off each other. Hardy men and tempestuous matches, which was fuelled by the fact we're bordering counties.

'Where I was living in Inistioge, it was bordering Wexford, so the rivalry was with Wexford. For those living in the areas like Callan, and all of that area, the Kilkenny–Tipp rivalry was intense. Personally, I probably didn't realise what the rivalry was really like until I started working with AIB in Callan. The other thing was though, and this is so dissimilar to today, in that era you never met players of opposing counties until you played them. Nowadays, players meet in third level regularly, for instance. So I would never have spoken to those Tipp lads back then.

'We had met in 1964, which Tipp won, and again in '67, which we won. This was probably a great Tipp team coming near the end in '71.

'It was a strange game in many respects, because Tipp had the wind in the first half and made use of it. They were leading by six points at half-time, but we started to haul them in and got level with them. I vividly recall saying to myself at that stage: "We have this now." We seemed to be on top of the Tipp defence at the time. Next thing, against the run of play, Tipp got a key goal. Their backs tightened up and I sensed it was slipping away from us. The game see-sawed after that, but Tipp got their goals at the right times, and we were playing catch-up all the time. They did deserve to win that day.

'After 1971, they didn't win another All-Ireland until '89 when they beat Antrim. Nicky English beat my record for the highest score in an All-Ireland final when he got 2-12. I rang him afterwards to congratulate him. He was a fantastic player, one of so many Tipperary produced.'

40

THE TERRIBLE TWINS

Galway 1956–59

Nothing remains unscathed by the passage of time.

Jack Mangan made history by becoming the first goalkeeper to lift the Sam Maguire Cup when he captained Galway in 1956. When I asked him about the greatest player he ever saw, his answer came instantly.

'Seán Purcell was the best. We were from the same street in Tuam. I took the captaincy off him after a vote. Although I felt bad for him, he didn't hold it against me and we remained the best of friends. He was a natural, with a wonderful temperament. If we were behind, we would always rely on him to do something special.

'The next best I would have seen was another Tuam man, Frank Stockwell. The two of them didn't even have to look for each other on the field of play, they knew each other so well.'

The 1956 All-Ireland final was the apex of the team's achievement when they beat Cork by 2-13 to 3-7 as Seán Purcell recalled for me.

'We had a great lead at half-time and Cork came back to us in a big way. They really put it up to us, and they got back within a point or so. We were lucky enough to get back one or two points at the end.

'We got a wonderful reception at home. I remember that quite well, coming from Dublin into Tuam. By present-day standards, the crowd wasn't huge but it was a great night. The match was broadcast around the town that day, and there would have been a great spirit of victory around the place. When we arrived in Tuam, I think the crowd met us and we were carried shoulder-high or on the lorry down to the town.

'Another national honour came the following year when Galway beat Kerry by 1-8 to 0-7 in the League final. Kerry, captained by Mick O'Connell, got their revenge in the All-Ireland final in 1959 when they beat the Westerners by 3-7 to 1-4.

'I made a stupid mistake early on. I was playing full-forward. My opponent Niall Sheehy was a big strong man and the ball was going wide. I could have let it go, but I saw Niall coming towards me. I said I'd get my retaliation in first and I did. I hit him an almighty crack with my forearm across the head, and he got in under me and put me up in the air. I really thought I'd killed him, but when I looked up, all he did was shake his head a few times and trot away. It was a bad start, a foolish mistake, and after that we were well beaten. We didn't really make much of a show. The lads did their best all right, but we just weren't good enough that day.'

DUNNE DEAL

That 1956 final turned Frank Stockwell into one of the GAA immortals. The late RTÉ Gaelic games correspondent Mick Dunne coined the phrase 'the terrible twins' to describe Seán Purcell's unique partnership with Frank Stockwell. He explained the origin of the phrase to me.

'Galway's Seán Purcell was the best player I ever saw. It could be said that there were better players in different positions, but as far as I'm concerned, he was the best all-round footballer. I remember him at full-back in the Connacht semi-final in 1954 against Mayo. It was one of the finest individual displays I've ever seen. He played on the great Tom Langan, then Dan O'Neill and then John Nallen, but it was all the same – Purcell was superb. He was also a magnificent midfielder, and he was the brains of the great Galway team that won the All-Ireland in 1956 at centre-forward. He had such a wonderful combination with the other Galway maestro, Frankie Stockwell, and they performed such a lethal duo that I described them as the terrible twins, and to my pleasant surprise. the phrase entered the GAA vernacular about them.'

In conversation with this scribe, Seán Purcell reserved a special place for Stockwell.

'We were known as the terrible twins because we had such a great understanding and because we did a lot of damage to opposing defences. Frank was a fabulous footballer. The fact that he scored 2-5 in the 1956 All-Ireland final speaks for itself. They were all off his foot, no frees. He destroyed the Cork defence on his own. It was just a matter of getting the ball in to him the best way we could. We tried the old tricks we'd worked on over the years. Things were much less scientific, I suppose, than they are now. We all contributed to each other, but we all knew Frank was the man to give the ball to and he'd do the rest. You have to remember that was a sixty-minute final. I'm great friends with Jimmy Keaveney, but when he broke Frank's record by scoring 2-6 in the 1977 All-Ireland final, he had a seventy-minute game to do it in.'

41

DUBLIN'S CAMOGIE QUEENS

Dublin 1941–67

In 2013, Dublin City Council invited suggestions from the public to name a new bridge over the Liffey crossing which would carry the Luas Cross City line between Marlborough Street and Hawkins Street. Eighty-five names were proposed and these were whittled down to five. These included the founder of the Alone charity Willie Birmingham, the Dracula creator Bram Stoker and Frank Duff, the Legion of Mary founder. Eventually, following a vote by Dublin City Council, the decision was made to name it the Rosie Hackett Bridge. It was the first time that any bridge over the river has been named after a woman – in this case a trade unionist best known for her involvement in the 1913 Lockout.

A close second in the vote was Dublin camogie player Kathleen 'Kay' Mills, star of one of the greatest GAA teams of all time. For a camogie player to receive such consideration is a powerful testimony to her unique place in the annals of Gaelic games.

Born in Inchicore in 1923, her mother died when she was eighteen months old and she was raised by her grandmother. She was only five when she first held a hurley in her hand, but she was a Renaissance woman and competed in athletics, table tennis and gymnastics with the CIÉ sports club. Throughout her entire inter-county career, she played in the one position – midfield.

Her first attempt to win an All-Ireland medal ended in crushing defeat 7-5 to 1-2 at the hands of Cork in 1941. The match report provides a fascinating social history in terms of the prevailing attitudes at the time: 'Referee Peg Morris had difficulty controlling a game which also produced the unedifying spectacle of girls indulging in fisticuffs.'

Kay's first All-Ireland medal came twelve months later. Dublin were held to a draw by Cork in 1942 but won the replay. A year later and Mills won her second O'Duffy Cup in some style – this time beating Cork with Kay scoring a goal from fifty yards in an 8-0 to 1-1 win.

Her collection of All-Ireland medals was halted temporarily at three as the Leinster counties withdrew from the All-Ireland Championship from 1945 to 1947. The CIÉ club had a great team and were given the honour of representing Dublin in 1948 and went on to claim the All-Ireland title.

Dublin won six consecutive Championships, from 1950 to 1955. Apart from Kay, this was a star-laden team, with Idé O'Kiely, Peg Griffin, Doreen Rogers, Eileen O'Mahony, Una O'Connor and Annette Corrigan.

Antrim, perhaps Dublin's main rivals at the time, won the All-Ireland in 1956. Normal service was restored when Dublin retained the All-Ireland in 1957 and went on to win a remarkable ten-in-a-row. Kay added five more to her own collection from 1957 to 1961, captaining the side in 1958. She marked her thirty-eighth birthday by winning her fifteenth All-Ireland medal in 1961. She was carried shoulder high off the pitch by her teammates, and later received a replica of the O'Duffy Cup, the All-Ireland Senior Camogie Championship trophy. This would be her last game for Dublin.

Her collection of camogie medals is displayed in the GAA Museum at Croke Park. She was a history maker – becoming the first camogie player to be named as the 'sports star of the week' in the *Irish Independent*. She won the Cú Chulainn hall of fame award and was an automatic on the Team of the Century. The All-Ireland camogie Premier Junior Championship Cup is named after her. In addition, she also contributed to the economic life of the Fair City, running a number of businesses with her husband George Hill.

42

DOWN BUT NOT OUT

Down 1991–94

To paraphrase the Bee Gees, they shone a light, a glorious kind of light, over us.

When Pete McGrath took over as Down's senior manager in 1989, the wider GAA family were unmoved, notwithstanding the fact that he had guided the county's minor team to All-Ireland success two years earlier. Senior football in the county was in an apparently dismal state, but McGrath changed their fortunes dramatically and, two years later, Down lifted the Sam Maguire Cup for the fourth time in their history, thanks to a 1-16 to 1-14 victory over Seán Boylan's Meath.

Meath had won the All-Ireland in 1987 and '88 and lost in the final to Cork in 1990. They seemed destined for All-Ireland glory in '91 after their epic first-round victory over Dublin. After four games, including two periods of stoppage time, only a David Beggy point separated the sides in the end. In the process, they acquired a reputation as 'the team that couldn't be beaten'. The fact that they had hauled back a big Roscommon lead in the All-Ireland semi-final seemed to confirm this.

On a wet and windy November day in Dublin, Ross Carr shared his memories of Down's '91 All-Ireland with me.

'A lot of people thought Down disappeared after '68. But we had four players – Paddy O'Rourke, Liam Austin, Pat Donnan and Ambrose Rogers – who had won All-Ireland minor ('77) and under-21 titles ('79) and an Ulster Senior Championship ('78) and a couple of National Leagues. So you were going to watch Down as a young fella expecting to win things. A lot of us then won Ulster under-21 medals in '84 and '85, Burren were winning All-Ireland club titles and the Ulster universities were starting to dominate in the Sigerson Cup. At senior level we played without much success and had a succession of managers. But once Pete came in, it became obvious very quickly there would be no compromise. If you wanted to stay on his panel, it was going to be his way.

'In 1991, we played Armagh, who had beaten us the year before, in the first round of the Championship, and neither side had any aspirations beyond having the bragging rights of Newry. It was one of the worst games ever played, but at the same time, we had no fear of Derry in the semi-final, or Donegal in the Ulster final. But what became apparent to me was that we had three of the best forwards in the country – Mickey Linden, Greg Blaney and James McCartan. I felt if we could hold our own defensively and break even in midfield, then if the three of them clicked on the same day, there wasn't a team in the country that could hold them.'

In the same Dublin room with Carr that day was Colm O'Rourke.

'The hallmark of a great team is that when the gun is put to their head on the biggest day in September, they are able to produce a game of quality and skill. Down played better football on the day and they had a very exciting, skilful team. They had great forwards, and they bored holes in us. Pete McGrath had them in the shape of their lives, and the thing that distinguishes any great team is that they peak on the right day. They were worthy winners, a marvellous football team, and they will be remembered as such.'

This final will always be remembered for a number of reasons, not least the fact that Down brought the Sam Maguire Cup back to Ulster for the first time since they themselves won it in 1968. There was a moment when the magnitude of the occasion sunk in for Pete McGrath: 'I always remember seeing wee Dan [McCartan]. He said to me, "Did you see the red and black in the Hogan Stand? A risen people!" There was this sense that Down were back.

'What made them winners was their belief, their ability, their character, their courage. All of those things were required in very large measure to beat Meath that day. We were against a very hardened, experienced and durable team with some marvellous footballers. All the qualities they had as players and as people were tested to the full that day in what was a brilliant game.'

A SECOND TASTE OF GLORY – GREG BLANEY

The darkness would quickly return. Derry took away their crown in 1992 and again in '93, in the 'Massacre at the Marshes', by a crushing eleven points. Pete McGrath was publicly critical of the team, and two of their biggest stars – Greg Blaney and James McCartan – walked away from the panel, though eventually McGrath coaxed them back. Without them, 1994 would not have ended in triumph. It began when Down had their chance to take down the All-Ireland champions, their old 'friends' Derry. Celtic Park was going to be the battleground. And there was no back door. It was winner take all, as McGrath recalled.

'Of all the teams I've managed, no team trained as hard as that team of 1994. God rest Pat O'Hare – he was our trainer, and the physical training was ferocious. These were men on a mission. Reputations were at stake – players' and mine as well. Going down the road to Celtic Park that day, I just knew we were going to win that match despite the fact we were written off. And after the match, I knew we were going to win the All-Ireland. There was nothing there to stop us.'

Not for the first time, the Troubles would cast a long shadow. The night before the Ulster semi-final, in Loughinisland, the home of Down player Gary Mason, two members of the UVF entered The Heights bar and shot six people dead with assault rifles.

The past is thankfully a different country for McGrath. 'Loughinisland happening when it did, we were still in a period where violence was the norm. You look back on it now, we are living in a relatively peaceful society. In those days, we were nearly anaesthetised to violence to an extent.'

McGrath had a few quiet words to Mason. 'He knew these people who were shot dead on a Saturday night. I felt that maybe the less said about it, the better. This was in the context of the 1990s. We couldn't change it.'

Tyrone and Cork were also seen off before playing Dublin in the final. It was very clear to McGrath where the media spotlight lay.

'In the build-up to the final, all you could hear from the media, particularly the southern media, was that for the good of the GAA, Dublin needed to win an All-Ireland to save football in the capital. They had been beaten in the final in 1992. Derry beat them in the semi-final of '93. All those matches with Meath in '91 and so on. If ever a team needed an All-Ireland, it was the Dubs.'

The crucial incident came in the game when Charlie Redmond's penalty was saved by Neil Collins. McGrath is phlegmatic about it: 'People said that if Dublin had scored the penalty? The penalty was saved. That was it. We won the game by two points.'

43

CORKERS

Cork 1975–79

Jurgen Klopp claims that sport is the most important thing of the least important things. Not so in Cork hurling. The memories of the bad defeats, as they have a habit of doing, swarm in and sting.

After the great success of the 1940s and '50s, the '60s proved to be rather lean years in relative terms for the Cork hurlers. In the late 1970s though, the Rebel County would reign supreme again.

In 1975, Cork won the first of five consecutive Munster titles, although defeat to Galway in the semis halted their progress for that year. In 1976 though, they beat Wexford to win the All-Ireland, and the following year they repeated that achievement against the same opposition. The build-up to the 1978 All-Ireland was dominated by talk of three-in-a-row. Cork this time faced familiar foes in Kilkenny and ran out winners by 1-15 to 2-8.

The team were managed by Fr Bertie Troy and featured greats of the games like Martin Coleman, Brian Murphy, Johnny Crowley, Gerald McCarthy, Denis Coughlan, Jimmy Barry-Murphy, Charlie

McCarthy, Ray Cummins and Seánie O'Leary. These nine players lined out in all three finals.

With a fifth consecutive Munster title in 1979, chances of emulating Christy Ring with a four-in-a-row looked possible. However, John Connolly's Galway brought them crashing down to earth, and the defeat marked the end of many great careers.

RINGSIDE SEAT

Jack Lynch told me that he followed that team closely because of their great achievements on the field but also because of the management of the team off it. While he spoke, he was no longer in the moment. He was back in Croke Park decades earlier, watching the force of nature.

'Christy Ring was one of the key mentors for that Cork side. Everybody knows that he was one of the greatest hurlers of all time, and I personally would say the greatest. However, what most people don't know is that he had a razor-sharp intellect. During a match, one opponent shouted at Ring: "I'll open you the next time the ball comes in."

'"If you're still here," said Ring.

'In the 1956 Munster final, he was being held scoreless by Limerick and an opponent stupidly did not let sleeping dogs lie. Instead, he complacently told Ring he was very quiet. Five minutes and three goals later, Ring retorted: "It's not so quiet now, boy."

'So I was waiting knowing that there would be some great stories when he became a selector in the 1970s. Christy brought a lot of firm convictions to the task – for example, he believed that there was no point going on a solo run unless it led to something. Seánie O'Leary broke his nose in the warm-up before the 1977 All-Ireland final. He turned to Ring looking for sympathy. Ring shook his head impatiently and replied, "Get out there, O'Leary – you don't play hurling with your nose."'

Mícheál O'Muircheartaigh once said to me: 'As they say in Kerry, if the player has passed on, they are the dead who shall never die – and while they are alive, they are the living who shall never die. Christy Ring was a hurler who stands apart from other players. He will never die.'

44

A BLUE CHRISTMAS

Dublin 2017–21

Christmas came just a little early for the Dublin ladies in 2020 when, on the Sunday before the festive season, they won their fourth successive TG4 All-Ireland title in Croke. The previous evening, their male counterparts had won their six-in-a-row. Carla Rowe's penalty on thirty-five minutes gave them the decisive score. It was the third successive year that Dublin beat Cork, twice in finals, having lived in their shadows for so many years.

It is surely no coincidence that the transformation in the Jackies' fortunes came with the appointment of Mick Bohan as team manager. Part of his success comes from the care he has for his players, as star forward Nicole Owens acknowledges.

'I wasn't ashamed to be suffering from depression, but when I was struggling to figure out all these feelings in my own head, it was difficult for me to articulate the situation to others.'

Nicole opened up about her depression to two of her teammates initially.

'People sort of see it as like a weakness or something negative. If you break your leg, it's something tangible, and people can see it, whereas this isn't a tangible thing. I would have spoken to my friends about it but it's hard to be in that place and understand it. There's no physical appearance of it, so it's hard to verbalise the feelings.'

There were times though when things crowded in on her.

'It just became too much. I found myself cycling to training, to an environment I absolutely adore, yet thinking, *This is the last place I want to be tonight*. Life away from training and games can weigh heavily on us all. Sometimes you can't leave your troubles behind. It could be the stress of work or an argument with a loved one, or sometimes you're just having a bad day.

'Sport has a lovely way of lifting your mood. The girls rally around you and, unless it's been an awful week, the buzz snaps you out of your own head for a few hours. Exercise in general is hugely important for coping with depressive tendencies. Yet, during that claustrophobic period, I began to dread training. I needed to tell Mick. His support, and that of my family, friends and teammates, was huge in ensuring I remained part of the All-Ireland winning team. Weirdly, 2017 produced this dichotomy, as football-wise I've never had a better season, yet from a mental-health perspective, it felt like I was drowning.

'Mick stuck with me when it really mattered. In an All-Ireland semi-final against Kerry, my performance would have prompted another manager to whip me off, but at half-time there was a quiet word of encouragement. Mick, being fully aware of my problems, had taken me aside on the Friday to see if I was able to start, and in the second half, he gave me a chance. I scored 1-1.'

WITH A LITTLE HELP FROM MY FRIENDS

Nicole also spoke about the friendships that have been forged within the Dublin panel, and her appreciation for her teammates and management who look out for her.

'There were times,' she explains, 'where you'd be at work all day and you'd get through the day and when you're going to training, that's when everything would get in on you and you're a bit run-down.

'A few of them would know at this point if I'm a little upset and they'll drag me off for a chat to get away from the noise. Sometimes if you're not in a good mood and the dressing room is kicking off, it's the last place you want to be. It would have been loads of little things, like even people you wouldn't be as close to would text every so often to check in and little things like that. I suppose when I talked about feeling valued as a person, that's massive because at the end of the day, Mick would have always said that he didn't care how well I was playing so long as I was OK.

'At the end of the day, if we're all unhappy, we're not going to play well either. It's just knowing that the whole team has your back, it's a huge thing mentally. This Dublin team has an incredible bond on and off the field and that is why we have been so successful.'

45

BELFIELD BRILLIANCE

UCD 1970s

In the latter part of his career, Colm O'Rourke had great success with Meath, but at the start he enjoyed good times with Eugene McGee's all-conquering UCD side, who proved their greatness by winning back-to-back All-Irelands in 1974 and '75.

'When I started in UCD in 1975, Eugene was already a legendary figure who had almost single-handedly overseen unprecedented success. Two Dublin Championships were followed by All-Ireland club Championships, and there were three Sigerson Cups in a row already in the bag. The big rivalry in Dublin was with St Vincent's, who had dominated Dublin club football since the 1950s.

'After winning the two previous finals, UCD felt they weren't getting fair play in 1975 when the Dublin final was fixed in the middle of exams. UCD, or Eugene McGee, refused to play. The Championship was awarded to Vincent's after the usual round of meetings and appeals. It really grated with McGee.'

WE NEED TO TALK ABOUT KEVIN

Eugene McGee spoke to me about how his relationship with Kevin Heffernan evolved, after a frosty start while he managed UCD.

'Kevin Heffernan and I had many a run-in on the sideline, first when I was with UCD and he was with Vincent's, then when I was with Offaly and he was with Dublin. We didn't like each other very much back then, because we were both competing for the same titles and we both wanted to win very badly, and he was a huge obstacle to me and I was a threat to him. That said, I always had great regard for Kevin and what he did for the GAA in Dublin. I think it would be fair to say that he was very hostile in football terms to anybody who he regarded as a threat to his ability as a manager. We became closer after we left the inter-county scene and were no longer a threat to each other. I would regard Kevin as one of the greatest GAA people I have ever met, and when he passed away, I felt genuinely very sad but privileged to have fought, and won, many battles against such a warrior down the years.

'Managers feed off the kind of hostility Kevin and I had on the sideline. The exception is Seán Boylan. He genuinely respects opponents and never bases his approach to big matches on personalised animosity. It's impossible to dislike Seán, let alone hate him. I'm glad he wasn't around in my day!'

SUPERMC

Legendary Roscommon footballer Tony McManus had some of his happiest memories in the game during his time in UCD between 1976 and '80 under McGee's stewardship.

'In 1979, I was captain and Colm O'Rourke was vice-captain. We became good friends. He was tremendously witty and sarcastic. Eugene McGee produced a newsletter about the fortunes of the team and he named the player who never shut up as the mouth

THE FOGGY DEW The 2020 All-Ireland semi-final between Mayo and Tipperary was surreal for the foggy conditions and the absence of a crowd. Here Mayo's Diarmuid O'Connor beats team-mate Aidan O'Shea and Colin O'Riordan of Tipperary to the throw-in at the beginning of the second half.

A GRAVE MATTER David Clifford's East Kerry team take a breather at half-time against Feakle Rangers in the 2020 Kerry Championship at Frank Sheehy Park in Listowel. On the other side of the wall, those from past generations rest in peace.

DOWN BUT NOT OUT Carlow's Paul Broderick secures possession in an unorthodox manner as Offaly's Ruairí McNamee and Anton Sullivan await his next move during the 2020 Leinster SFC first-round game in Tullamore.

JEEPERS KEEPERS Waterford keeper Stephen O'Keeffe takes off during the 2020 All-Ireland SHC quarter-final win over Munster rivals, Clare, at Croke Park.

© INPHO/James Crombie

UP AND DOWN At the 2020 Roscommon SFC semi-final between Boyle and St Brigid's, at least one person in this graveyard is on a high.

© INPHO

GLORY DAYS Celebrations for Cavan's Niamh Reilly and Ciara Finnegan in Camogie's 2020 Nancy Murray Cup final with victory over Tyrone at Inniskeen Grattans club in Monaghan.

TROLLEY DASH Extra-time was needed again for the 15 December 2020 Munster MFC clash between old rivals Cork and Kerry in Tralee. Only one parent of each player was allowed into Austin Stack Park, so others had to improvise. The Kingdom won 0-21 to 1-15 having trailed for most of the game.

A STAR IS BORN Aimee Mackin of Armagh in action against Eva Woods of Monaghan during the TG4 Ulster Ladies Senior Football Championship semi-final between Armagh and Monaghan at Páirc Esler in Newry, Down.

© Sportsfile/Matt Browne

EASTERN PROMISE

East Kerry's dominance of football in Kerry continued in 2020. They eased to a 2-15 to 0-9 SFC final win over Mid Kerry. Glenflesk's Darragh Roche celebrates scoring his side's second goal in the decider.

© INPHO/James Crombie

UPSIDES YOURSELF Mayo ended 2020 in an All-Ireland final. Nothing unusual there. But winning a Connacht title against Galway (0-14 to 0-13) – their first since 2015 – was an uplifting experience for Matthew Ruane and Jordan Flynn.

© Sportsfile/Eóin Noonan

CENTENARY CELEBRATIONS A full century after the events of Bloody Sunday in Croke Park, the Tipperary footballers suited up and honoured their fallen comrades with a surprise Munster SFC final victory over Cork, the Premier's first in 85 years. Here captain Conor Sweeney and defender Bill Maher enjoy the Páirc Uí Chaoimh moment.

CHEEK TO CHEEK Conal Keaney of Ballyboden St Enda's is shouldered by Ballymun's John Small during the 2020 Dublin SFC final at Parnell Park in Dublin. Ballymun won with surprising ease, 1-19 to 0-8, for their fourth county title and first since 2012.

THE CLASH OF THE ASH Kevin Foley of Wexford blocks a shot at goal by Adrian Mullen of Kilkenny during the Leinster GAA Hurling Senior Championship final between Kilkenny and Wexford at Croke Park in Dublin, 30 June 2019.

© INPHO/Laszlo Geczo

THAT SINKING FEELING Kerry captain David Clifford feels the pain of the Kingdom's last gasp defeat to rivals Cork in the 2020 Munster SFC semi-final at Páirc Uí Chaoimh. The defeat eliminated one of the favourites for Sam Maguire at the first hurdle.

© INPHO/Bryan Keane

UPLIFTING Corofin players celebrate after completing a hat-trick of All-Ireland Club SFC titles in 2020 with an extra-time win over Down's Kilcoo at Croke Park. The Galway kingpins triumphed 1-12 to 0-7 with the goal coming from Conor Cunningham.

of the team, but he added that Colm was a strong contender! O'Rourke is very confident. The only time I ever saw him nervous was when I met him before the All-Ireland semi-final in 2007 when his son Shane was playing. He was never nervous when he played himself but he was that day.

'From our freshers' year, Eugene had taken Colm and myself under his wing. He was a complex character, but it was very enjoyable working with him. He certainly had a way with him. He commanded respect and had great ideas and was able to communicate them. There were lots of county players around at that time but he had no qualms about dropping them. Reputations meant nothing to him. You never knew what to expect from him. Days you thought you played well, he might lacerate you. Days you thought you didn't play well, he would encourage you and compliment you.

'My lasting memory of him came the day we had to play Queens. The night before was the Veterinary Ball and I had gone. The next morning he heard about it and wasn't happy. He made me travel with him in his car and never said a word to me all the way up to Belfast. In the circumstances I was really keen to do well and I scored 2-3. He said nothing to me after the match. Eventually, when all the lads were gone and I was behind, waiting for him in the dressing room to make the journey home, he turned to the caretaker and said in his typically gruff accent: "Would you have a jackhammer to widen the door a bit more? This fella's head is so big he won't be able to get out through it."'

46

THE HAPPIEST DAYS OF OUR LIVES

St Kieran's College 2009–19

What does Eddie Keher have in common with the Oscar-winning films *Schindler's List* and *The English Patient*?

Like Keher, the star of both of those films, Ralph Fiennes, attended St Kieran's College in Kilkenny, one of Ireland's best-known hurling nurseries. St Kieran's, situated in the heart of the medieval city, first opened its doors in 1782 following the repeal of the Penal Laws. For many years, the boarding school was the only means of providing an academic, spiritual and personal formation for most male students in the diocese.

One of the school's most famous former pupils was former GAA president Nickey Brennan.

'I come from a small country parish (Conahy) with a junior hurling club (Shamrocks), but I got the big break when I went to school in St Kieran's which was a big hurling nursery. To be frank, to survive you had to play hurling morning, noon and night between doing a bit of study. If you get on the teams there it brings you to the notice of the county's underage selectors. I played with Kilkenny from 1973 to 1985 apart from missing out on '76 and '77 because of the small matter of getting married and building a house. I was far from being the greatest hurler ever to play for Kilkenny, but I was a reliable and consistent hurler and that was probably my greatest strength.

'I can't give enough credit to St Kieran's for the assembly line of great teams they produced and for the generations of fine hurlers they have given to Kilkenny but to other counties too. Nicky Rackard really began his hurling career with St Kieran's, and Wexford certainly benefited from that, and more recently Eoin Kelly attended there and he did pretty well for Tipperary.'

Fifteen of the twenty-four players who were involved in Kilkenny's four-in-a-row All-Ireland titles from 2006 to 2009 were graduates of St Kieran's College. St Kieran's gifted Kilkenny hurling with its most influential personality, Brian Cody.

'Kieran's College has a huge presence in Kilkenny. Every time you pass by the building it's so impressive. And when you come in here at different times, there could be matches on or whatever, it's the same. I worked in St Patrick's De La Salle just across the road as well and many of our pupils would have come here too, so you would have had dealings with them from that point of view also.'

Cody captained a star-studded St Kieran's team to an All-Ireland Colleges Final victory over St Finbarr's of Farranferris of Cork in 1971.

'It was a terrific game from the point of view that it was thirteen-a-side,' recalled Cody. 'Fr Michael O'Brien – Canon Michael O'Brien as he became – was the man in charge of Farranferris. We had some serious players on our team as well. Obviously to win a Colleges All-Ireland when you're here is terrific – it's great.

'But hurling was just part and parcel of our everyday life in St Kieran's. And you still come into St Kieran's College and the first thing you see and hear is lads beating a hurling ball around. Everybody more or less with a hurl in their hand.'

His time in St Kieran's brought Cody into contact with the legendary Fr Tommy Maher who coached the Kilkenny senior hurlers to seven All-Ireland titles between 1957 and '75. After leaving school, Cody would then play under Maher with the Kilkenny senior hurlers, as a member of that All-Ireland winning team of '75.

THE HAND OF HISTORY

Winning twenty-three All-Ireland titles, St Kieran's have produced many great teams. However, their run from 2009–19 was exceptional, winning seven of the ten All-Ireland titles over those ten years. Up to that point, the most titles they had won in a single decade before was four, which they managed in the 1990s. Such was the scale of their achievement that with the notable exception of St Flannan's Ennis, Kieran's won more All-Irelands in that decade than any other college has achieved in their history.

47

BLESSED ARE THE PEACEMAKERS

Kerry 1929–32

They were only the second team to win a four-in-a-row. Yet they are more important for what they achieved off the field than their great achievements on it.

The War of Independence ended with the Anglo–Irish Treaty. However, this in turn precipitated a bloody and bitter civil war in Ireland. Gaelic football and hurling were always about more than sport in rural Ireland, and in Kerry in particular. My former teacher Professor Liam Ryan told me that the Kerry four-in-a-row played a greater part in healing the many rifts which have threatened to rupture families and communities throughout Irish history in the last century than the Catholic Church.

'Neighbours who had shot at one another in the Civil War, for example, displayed a greater desire to forgive and forget when gathered around the goalposts than when gathered around the altar. Nowhere was that more apparent than in Kerry.'

The late John B. Keane also spoke to me about the power of the GAA to heal the wounds of the past.

'Football has also been part of our identity here. In Kerry, football was called "caid" as it referred to the type of ball used. The ball was made from dried farm-animal skins with an inflated natural animal bladder inside. We take our football very seriously in Kerry, but we also take politics very seriously. Sometimes our twin passions collide. This was probably most clearly illustrated in 1935 when Kerry refused to take part in the football Championship because of the ongoing detention of prisoners in the Curragh.

'The Civil War didn't just cost a lot of lives. It split families down the middle and left intense bitterness. The one place in Kerry where that was put aside was on the GAA fields, and it did bring old enemies together. Football united what politics divided. It was about our sense of Kerry. If we were playing Dublin in an All-Ireland final, politics was put to one side so we would win the match. So, in that way, the Kerry team helped clear the bad blood from the Civil War.'

A good example was Con Brosnan. He is one of the great legends of Kerry football and that is saying something. He reached out to his enemies from the Civil War on the football field. One of the things he did was to arrange safe passage for wanted IRA men so they could represent Kerry. Just a year after the Civil War ended, Kerry won the All-Ireland final with a team almost roughly divided between pro- and anti-Treaty players. When Con was nearing the end of his playing days, 'one of the other side', Joe Barrett, ensured that he was given the captaincy. It was proof that Con was Kerry's great peacemaker after the Civil War.

That Kerry team won four consecutive All-Irelands, but more importantly they helped heal the bitter wounds and united what had been a deeply divided county.

48

CHRISTY OF THE ROVERS

Glen Rovers 1941–67

'Men who are fathers and grandfathers now will tell their
children and grandchildren that they saw Christy Ring play.
The story will pass from generation to generation, and so it
will live.'

JACK LYNCH

The omens were unfavourable.

In 1941, Christy Ring was on the move.

He had been educated at the local national school in Cloyne. On
one occasion, the school master, Maurice Spillane, offered a prize
of a hurley and sliotar to the boy who attained the highest grade
in the school. Ring applied himself to the fullest, as he would
later throughout his hurling career, and achieved first place from
among forty-eight pupils.

Like so many of his generation, he received no secondary education and left school before the age of fourteen. His first job was
as an apprentice mechanic with the Williams firm in Middleton,

before he later moved to Cork city, where he found work as a lorry driver with Córas Iompair Éireann. In 1953, he became a delivery driver with Shell Oil.

In 1940, Ring left the Cloyne club and remained 'unattached' for over a year before joining the Glen Rovers club in Cork city in the summer of 1941. This was a year when Ireland was in the grips of a health crisis which was particularly devastating for the country's farmers. Because of foot-and-mouth, those farmers had to go through the heartbreak of slaughtering their own animals. To add to the hardship, there were no mechanical diggers. Everything had to be done by manual labour. They would build ramps into the pit and drive the animals down into them. There they shot them in the pit and buried them. At that stage there was no burning.

After making his debut against St Finbarr's in the county senior Championship semi-final, Ring went on to win his first senior Championship winners' medal following a defeat of Ballincollig in the final. 'The Glen' had just captured a record-breaking eighth county title in a row.

RING OF FIRE

After a short barren period, the Glen won back-to-back titles in 1944 and '45 following wins over fierce southside rivals St Finbarr's and divisional side Carrigdhoun respectively.

After a one-year absence from county glory, defeats of Blackrock, Imokilly and St Finbarr's in the respective Championship deciders of 1948, '49 and '50 brought Ring's county Championship winners' medal tally to six.

Glen Rovers contested eight consecutive county finals between 1953 and '60. Following the loss of three county finals in a row, they won back-to-back titles in '53 and '54 and went on to win three in a row in '58, '59 and '60. Another county title came in '62. The latter was Ring's thirteenth county victory and was subsequently converted into a Munster club title. His last game with the Glen came in '67, a county quarter-final against UCC.

Ring's thirteen County medals add to his haul of eight All-Ireland senior hurling medals. He captained Cork in three All-Ireland finals and was the first player to receive the Liam MacCarthy Cup three times, nine Munster titles, four National Leagues and eighteen interprovincial medals with Munster.

While Ring is rightly famous for his genius, his endurance was also hugely impressive. He was top scorer in 1959 when he also became Hurler of the Year once again – at thirty-nine! Ring captained the Glen to another County title in 1964, and two years later he led Glen Rovers to the inaugural Munster club final, scoring 1-1 in that match.

COOL CUSTOMER

Rovers though were not a one-man team. Mícheál O'Muircheartaigh furnishes a telling insight into the other star of the team, Jack Lynch.

'I remember sitting beside a man in the church at Christy Ring's funeral who told me a story. He was captain of the Glen when he was younger and Jack had retired the year before. They were in the county semi-final and he asked Jack to come back for the semi-final and hopefully the final. He pulled the letter Jack wrote back out of his pocket and showed it to me. "Thank you for thinking of me, but I have to reject your kind offer because it would mean dropping a promising young fellow for the sake of an old fellow." That was Jack – always thinking of others. He was an extraordinary man, always very, very cool and casual about everything.'

49

JIMMY'S WINNING MATCHES

Donegal 2011–14

One of the social-media events of 2020 was the sharing of jerky footage, shot from beyond the walls of Tuam Stadium, of the Galway team being instructed in a drill by Jim McGuinness. It was eventually explained away as McGuinness doing a favour for his old college friend, the Galway manager Pádraic Joyce, but for a short period, there was the prospect of McGuinness returning to the game. The sensation it created showcased his unique status in Gaelic football.

He tends to attract strong opinions. He is a cult hero in Donegal. He was part of the Donegal panel that won the county's first-ever All-Ireland title in 1992. He started on the bench in the final against Dublin but came on in the second half. Ger Loughnane claims that in '92, Donegal were the first team to really bring colour to Croke Park and his '95 team would take it a step further. There was a huge emotional release in Donegal after they won their first Sam Maguire Cup.

Then, twenty years later, McGuinness would steer the O'Donnell county to their second All-Ireland when Donegal beat Mayo by 2-11 to 0-13. The Tír Chonaill men got off to the perfect

184

start and went seven points ahead thanks to two quick-fire goals in the opening minutes. Footballer of the Year that season, Karl Lacey took off on a typical run before kicking towards the full-forward position, where Michael Murphy showed his power to hold off Kevin Keane and smash the ball beyond David Clarke. After pointing from a free, Colm McFadden then found the back of the net after twelve minutes. Paddy McBrearty's effort came back off the upright and the St Michael's clubman reacted quickly to pounce on the loose ball and make it 2-01 to 0-00. Those early scores would be crucial.

TACTICAL GENIUS?

McGuinness critics, though, were often unhappy with his tactics. He had no problem defending his players or in calling out pundits who he felt were making unfair comments about his side. Just ask Pat Spillane. There is no doubt that he did change the face of Gaelic football.

One of the great blessings of my life was to work closely with Jimmy Magee for six months. In my last conversation with Jimmy, we spoke about Jim McGuinness.

'I'm not sure if everyone properly appreciates his importance. Donegal were in a bad way when McGuinness took them over. They had some talented individuals but were seen to be more interested in having a good time than committing to the hard slog that would be needed to win the All-Ireland. McGuinness believed that for Donegal to win a second All-Ireland, he would have to get his side to redefine how football was played.

'He frightened the so-called "established counties" in a way they hadn't been rattled since the arrivals of Armagh and Tyrone at the start of the 2000s, and what Donegal did in 2011 and, more particularly, in 2012, forced the big teams to radically revise how they went about their tasks.

'The famous victory of Dublin in the 2014 All-Ireland semi-final was probably more important than winning the 2012 All-Ireland because in the way he reacted to it, Jim Gavin changed the way his Dublin team played the game.

'There were perhaps unintended consequences. Less and less became known about how the big powers of football like Dublin, Kerry and Mayo went about their business, with the leading counties and the people in charge of them determined not to let anything slip that could be of help to their rivals. I suspect that the way Jim famously dropped Kevin Cassidy, one of the county's greatest-ever players, from the panel after he cooperated with a book in 2011 fed into that mindset.'

BEATING THE BLANKET

In 2012, the song 'Jimmy's Winning Matches' was hugely popular in the build-up to All-Ireland final day. Not for the first time, Joe Brolly was singing from a different hymn sheet.

'It is a truism to say we want to be entertained when we commit to an hour and a half of TV viewing or a long trip to Croke Park. The entire point of the game, after all, is entertainment. Entertainment for the players, the supporters and the larger GAA family.

'The bottom line is that Jimmy was single-handedly responsible for bringing Gaelic football to a sorry state, his zonal defensive system spreading like myxomatosis. What can teams do when faced with a thirteen- or fourteen-man defensive system? I can still vividly remember the way he dragged this great game into the mire in the 2011 semi-final. By the way, they managed a total of 0-6 that day, which sounds like a team that didn't particularly care if it scored.

'Or what about his team's nihilistic strategy in the 2014 final, by common acclaim the worst and most boring final ever played? Inevitably, this zonal system created a template for copycat coaches all over the country to spoil the majority of county and club football and deter people who loved the game from going to watch. Jimmy, however, merely washes his hands of responsibility. The good of the game and the wider GAA family are irrelevant, sentimental considerations.

'The essence of the game is a shared journey. For the players, supporters and the wider GAA family. Instead, because of Jimmy and his legacy, the fabric of Gaelic football is being systematically ruined, and we are shedding spectators by the hundreds of thousands. Jimmy said that "there is no denying this will be boring for spectators". He needn't worry. If the game continues to be played his way, soon there won't be any.'

Brolly believes that the 2014 All-Ireland final was a particularly low point. Kerry beat Donegal, with both sides playing very negative styles and making multiple mistakes. Hence one fan's tweet after the match: 'In a game that both sides seemed to want to lose, Donegal seemed to want to lose it more.'

Jimmy Magee saw the Donegal team in more positive terms.

'Donegal's defence was still to the fore in 2012. They conceded just 3-77 across their seven games, with Cork's scoreline of 1-11 in the All-Ireland semi-final the highest total they conceded in a single game. The difference between 2011 and '12 was that Donegal struck the perfect balance between having a steely defence and a formidable attack, led brilliantly by Michael Murphy. They were easily the best team in the land in 2012.

'It has been said that the 1990s were the revolution years in hurling. If that's true, and I'm not fully convinced it is, for a few years, that Donegal team challenged the traditional football status quo. For that I salute them.'

50

HYMN TO HER

Kilkenny 1974–91

The former Aston Villa chairman 'Deadly Doug' Ellis started paying himself a salary in 1983 once the club went public (which got around a Football League rule that prohibited club directors from drawing down salaries) and dismissed critics with the line: 'Only women and horses work for nothing.' A small parable that indicates some of the journey women have had to travel to get a degree of equality in sport. It is a shocking fact that men walked on the moon before women played Gaelic games routinely in Croke Park. When I spoke to Jimmy Magee, he was keen to change that narrative.

'For a long time, women were, in the main, neither seen nor heard in mainstream Irish sport. Thankfully that has changed in recent years. I find that more and more people are asking me who is Ireland's greatest sportswoman. There are so many great candidates. There is a strong case for considering the merits of Angela Downey for that title and, indeed, her sister Ann.'

Angela made the senior county team when she was fifteen and won her first All-Ireland at seventeen. The Kilkenny team were trained by Tom Ryan, who often came to training in his wellingtons.

Not surprisingly, she has been immortalised in folklore. Hurling was in her genes. Her father was the legendary Shem Downey who starred for the black and amber in the 1940s and '50s, with an All-Ireland medal in '47 in Kilkenny's classic triumph over Cork. Shem brought the passion he exhibited in the black and amber onto the sidelines when he watched his daughters on the camogie field.

Angela played in her first senior All-Ireland final with Kilkenny in 1972 against Cork. It was to be a rare reversal for the young player, but all present that day remember their first acquaintance with Angela. Although she would be defeated in '72, she went on to win seven consecutive All-Irelands for Kilkenny from 1985 to 1991. In total, she would win twelve All-Irelands, the first coming after a replay against Cork in 1974. Only Dublin's Una O'Connor with thirteen and the late Dublin star Kathleen Mills with fifteen had surpassed that achievement. She also captained the county to All-Ireland successes in 1977, '88 and '91.

To give a flavour of her own contribution: in 1977, at the tender age of twenty, she scored 6-3 against Tipperary, four goals against Dublin and then 2-3 against Wexford in the All-Ireland final. In 1986, Angela became only the third camogie player to be awarded a Texaco award.

Angela was also keenly appreciative of the importance of the club, in her case St Paul's and later Lisdowney. To add to Angela's medal haul, she won an incredible twenty-two county titles and six All-Ireland club titles.

A lovely bonus for Angela was that all her All-Ireland medals were won with her twin sister, Ann. In 2010, both were jointly presented with the Lifetime Achievement Award in the Irish Times Sportswoman of the Year awards. Jimmy Magee assessed their legacy.

'Angela and Ann Downey of Kilkenny made a fantastic contribution to camogie. Their longevity at the highest level is amazing and I believe will never be equalled, not to mention surpassed. Ann was fiery, strong, tough and was a non-stop runner. Angela was like lightning and skilful beyond belief. Camogie owes a great deal to the Downeys.'

Angela Downey was a great player, but she was more than that. She transcends the sport because she was a stylish genius who had a unique capacity to thrill the crowd by regularly producing jaw-dropping moments. She brought the magical and the mythical. Who is the greatest soccer player of all time: Messi, Maradona, Pelé? Who is the greatest hurler of all time: Christy Ring, Mick Mackey, Henry Shefflin? Who is the greatest camogie player of all time? In every other sport there are a number of candidates, but for most people there is only one answer when it comes to camogie: Angela Downey.

51

SIX OF THE BEST

Crossmaglen 1996–2003

Fīat jūstitia ruat cælum.
Let justice be done though the heavens fall.

In 2021, the Ursuline sisters marked the 250th anniversary of their mission to Ireland. One of the most interesting elements of their history came in 1804 when the Mother Superior in Thurles heard rumours that a barracks for British soldiers was to be established nearby. She was unhappy with the prospect, as she felt that having troops so near the girls would be detrimental to the moral fibre of her school. Conscious that the hand who holds the pen writes the history, she promptly wrote a letter and made her feelings known to the Lord Lieutenant in Dublin Castle. It was a gutsy move given the political climate. How could a note from a Roman Catholic nun who led a community of just four expect to change the plans of the greatest army the world had ever seen from the Empire in which the sun never set? She could rightly be forgiven for responding to anyone who thought the mere suggestion was ludicrous by saying: 'Oh ye of little faith.' The letter of reply stated in language that could only be written by a bureaucrat that her concerns had found a receptive audience.

> A Concern is fitting up at Thurles for the reception of Troops, contiguous to a school established by you for the maintenance and education of young females – that such a measure must involve the dissolution of so useful an establishment, and therefore, praying that the proceedings in fitting up the said Concern may be countermanded. And His excellency, having taken the facts therein set forth into consideration, I am directed to acquaint you, that His Excellency has been pleased to agree that the Scite [sic] of the intended Barrack at Thurles shall be changed, and has issued the necessary orders to the Deputy Barrack Master General accordingly.

> I am, Madam,
> Your obedient humble servant,
> E. B. Littlehales

In sporting parlance, the outcome was: the Ursulines 1, the British Army 0.

Crossmaglen Rangers produced one of the greatest club sides ever seen winning six All-Irelands in sixteen years, but like the Ursuline sisters they have faced down their most difficult opponent, the British Army, and won.

Margaret McConville, the club's officer, became a household name because of her media appearances and famously described her home place as 'the town the army took over'. The club's premises and playing pitches were requisitioned in 1971, and it stood for more than twenty-five years as a potent symbol of the GAA's importance in the community.

On the pitch, the club have provided a who's who of Armagh

legends like Joe Kernan, the McEntees, Francie Bellew and Oisín McConville. Their stats are incredible. In the thirteen years from 1996 to 2008, the club secured thirteen consecutive Armagh Senior Championship titles, seven Ulster Club Championships and four All-Ireland Club titles. Over that period, they played a total of 108 Championship matches, losing only nine times with eighty-nine wins and ten draws to their credit. In 2009, they lost their grip on the Armagh Championship, but four Armagh titles in a row followed, three Ulster titles in a row and two more All-Irelands in a row, bringing the club's tally to forty Armagh Championships in total, ten Ulster titles and six All-Irelands. By the end of 2013, the games tally from 1996 stood at 144 Championship matches played with twelve defeats, fourteen draws and 118 wins.

CELEBRITY FAN

Every great team has their celebrity fans and Crossmaglen are no exception. Joe Brolly has written about going to Berlin for a weekend break only to discover when he arrived that the Crossmaglen match had been fixed for the Saturday night, not the Sunday. So he came home early.

Brolly loves the ethos of the club. He offers a snapshot to illustrate it: 'As John McEntee once said when I remarked that Crossmaglen players never lie down or look for an opponent to be carded, "Why would we embarrass ourselves like that, Joe?"'

PART III
The First Cut is the Deepest

Quidquid recipitur ad modum recipientis recipitur.
We don't see things as they are; we see things as we are.

Today we know this concept as 'confirmation bias'. Long before they had ever heard of confirmation bias, GAA fans were experts in the area. We see things through the lens of our county colours. When I bought my house, the crucial fact that swayed my decision to purchase it was that all the bedrooms were painted in the primrose and blue colours of my beloved Roscommon.

The one time we go beyond our county colours is when a new team emerges on the national stage. Throughout its rich history, the GAA has produced teams who have captured the hearts of the sporting nation by surpassing all expectations and giving their counties and others the delicious opportunity to drink from the keg of glory. This section celebrates some of these teams.

52

THE BOYS IN BLUE

Dublin 2013–21

A former Dublin manager is reputed to have told the team before they played an All-Ireland final, 'Bear in mind, lads, every wide ye kick will be captured on national television.'

Not surprisingly they lost. Jim Gavin would lead Dublin to an unprecedented five-in-a-row All-Ireland titles. His approach would be very different. His favourite film is *The Snapper*, but his favourite book is Homer's *Odyssey*. From sources such as this, Gavin forged a clear philosophy: 'Leaders don't get results. It's the people they lead who do.'

Gavin delegated leadership. His style was less like an orchestra where the conductor is always in charge and more like a jazz band where leadership is passed around, depending on what the music demands at the moment and who feels most moved by the spirit to express the music.

Will Greenwood was asked to sum up the successful Lions coach Sir Ian McGeechan and he did it using just one word: empowerment. Under Gavin, Dublin players were empowered to exercise leadership through influencing others and using their own initiative.

On the pitch, mistakes were tolerated. They took risks. Gavin shared the philosophy of Facebook's Mark Zuckerberg: 'If you please everyone, you aren't making enough progress.'

We live in a world which lays great stress on achievement and 'measurable outcomes'. While it is good to encourage individuals to become the best version of themselves, the problem is that can create a culture of individualism. We exist in two dimensions: as a person in a community but also as a community of persons. The lesson Jim Gavin taught us is that if you want to go fast, go alone. If you want to go far, go together. It is a significant insight into leadership. What do you call a leader with no followers? Somebody out for a walk.

Jim Gavin rang Brian Kerr to recommend a goalkeeper coach and Kerr recommended Josh Moran to him. Gavin also sought his advice about tactics. It showed Gavin's willingness to learn from other sports.

When Gavin stepped away after winning the five-in-a-row, Dessie Farrell took the torch from him and led the Dubs to a unique Christmas All-Ireland in 2020 before an empty Croke Park, because of Covid restrictions. Gavin lost one Championship match, to Donegal in 2014, in seven years as boss, and Dessie Farrell became the only man in GAA history to have managed a team to win the All-Ireland football title at minor, under-21 and senior level, having won a senior title as a player.

Colm Cooper paid this Dubs team the ultimate compliment: 'The most intimidating thing about Dublin is that they completely ignore you. It's as if you weren't even there.'

NOT SO HARD TO BE HUMBLE

Apart from their greatness on the pitch, one of their most attractive qualities is their normal humility off it (though critics would say their breach of Covid guidelines in 2021 undermined their role-model status). A revealing insight into this came in

January 2021 with the retirement of Michael Darragh MacAuley.

Clearly MacAuley ranks among the GAA immortals. Against that background he would have been forgiven for saying good-byes with some fanfare. However, he walked away by using his Twitter account to confirm his departure, simply writing, *'Sin é uaimse. Míle buíochas ó chroí.'*

MacAuley thinks that ethos is key to the success of the Dublin team. He told me: 'I took for granted that I had role models. With my football team we had different people. I had a good family structure around me. When people do not have those things, don't have the family structure I had or don't have the support from different clubs, it's easy for them to stray off the path and go down a more dangerous route. You see it all along.

'I have always been involved with teaching and sports, outside of sports as well. I've been working with special-needs students for years and mainstream teaching, as well as my work now in the inner city. So that is where I get my kicks, seeing people develop and grow. I enjoy that side of it.

'I don't know how teams can function if they have someone who is maybe too egotistical or looking out for their own interests. Sometimes I wonder how the dressing rooms look in the Premier League with all the ego that's involved. It's the opposite with the Dublin dressing room at the moment, so long may it continue. The group is an impressive collection of human beings in that I think people are aware that there is a higher purpose than themselves or the team.

'If individuals came into the team and thought they were bigger for any reason than the team, they'd be quickly weeded out. So I think that's definitely been the cross that they fall on, that we all know that we're playing for something bigger than us. We self-police that at this stage, and that creates a humility around the squad that is badly needed in any team.

'It was definitely sold to me how socially conscious a lot of the Dublin team of the 1970s were. Even from speaking to them, they were aware of that higher purpose with the Dublin team and that there was more to life than football. That kind of stuck with me as well.'

Dublin's dominance was strikingly illustrated when the most talked about footballer of 2021 was a player not kicking a ball. The saga about Stephen Cluxton's future dominated the summer especially after Dublin manager Dessie Farrell said Cluxton had decided to step away from the squad 'for the time being' but insisted he had not retired. Colm O'Rourke claimed that the speculation surrounding the goalkeeper put Dublin manager Dessie Farrell in an 'invidious position'.

The team that Dublin inflicted most heartbreak on was Mayo. It was indeed right and fitting that it should be Mayo that should end their reign as All-Ireland champions after the Westerners trailed by seven points during the first half and were down six at half-time in the 2021 All-Ireland semi-final. In the end it's not the years in a team's life that count. It is the life in the years. What a life this Dublin team had.

53

OFFALY PROUD

Offaly 1980–89

The decision of a third of the Ballyduff hurling team to emigrate in 1958 inspired John B. Keane to write the play *Many Young Men of Twenty*. The shadow of emigration lurked like a vulture hovering over its prey. It was the traditional Irish solution to economic problems. It churned out an assembly line of bodies for the boat to England and America.

Emigration was central to the culture of Ireland. Communities were stripped of their young people in the same way a flock of sheep would demolish a field of fresh grass. It shaped the way people thought and felt, conditioning them to accept the grotesquely abnormal as normal. That was the way it was and that was the way it would always be. Although there were no industries, there was one highly developed export – people.

There were many scenes of families travelling en bloc to the train station. Everyone wore their Sunday best. The mother was blind with tears. The father's eyes were dry, but his heart was breaking. Men did not betray emotion. It would have been seen as a sign of weakness. The young people leaving leaned out of the window, choking with sadness as they saw their parents for perhaps the last time. Younger brothers and sisters raced after the train shouting words of parting. Sometimes, white handkerchiefs were produced and waved until the train went out of sight. Those handkerchiefs gave a ritual, almost sacramental, solemnity to the goodbyes. Their presence was a symbol of defeat, a damning indictment of an economy unable to provide for its brightest and most talented.

In the 1980s, Ireland was in the depths of a prolonged depression. The curse of emigration returned with a vengeance. Hundreds of young and not so young people left every year that decade. The collective tale of woe concealed thousands of individual nightmares. Young people wanted to stay in the country they loved but had no way of making a living. They wanted to be close to family and friends, but they had no other choice than to leave. Many had good skills. Some had excellent examination results. Yet the piece of paper that was most important was the ticket to America.

Offaly was a county badly hit by emigration throughout the 1980s. But there was a glimmer of hope.

LIFTING THE SHADOWS

Before 1980, Offaly had never won a senior Leinster hurling title. By the end of the decade, they had won six, in comparison to Kilkenny's four.

At a time when the country was on its knees, the Offaly hurlers offered light into the darkness. So prevalent was the belief Kilkenny would comfortably win the 1980 Leinster final, only 8,000 witnessed Offaly's historic first success in Croke Park.

Although they lost to Galway in that year's semi-final, the following year, they exacted revenge on Galway in the All-Ireland final. Offaly, managed brilliantly by Kilkenny's Diarmuid Healy, were making their debut in a final and playing the reigning champions. Defeating Kilkenny in the previous year's Leinster final had been momentous, but this was a whole new level. Despite Galway leading by six points at one juncture, the Faithful County staged a comeback, eventually winning 2-12 to 0-15 thanks in no small part to a goal from Johnny Flaherty. To this day in Galway they are still asking if Johnny Flaherty threw the ball into the net. Pádraig Horan became the first Offaly player to lift the Liam MacCarthy Cup.

After the final whistle, the Offaly goalkeeper Damien Martin and the full-forward Pádraig Horan met at the halfway line and embraced.

Horan said: 'Damien, this makes all the sacrifices worthwhile.'

Martin replied: 'They would have been worth it if we never won anything.'

In the centenary year, 1984, Thurles was chosen to host that year's All-Ireland final as a special one-off, but Offaly suffered a heavy beating at the hands of Cork, 3-16 to 1-12. A year later, Offaly were back again and this time they beat Galway by two points to win their second All-Ireland.

54

UP DOWN

Down 1960–68

They were history makers.

In 1960, Down became the first team from the six counties to lift Sam Maguire and bring it across the border amid emotional scenes. Before 1959, they had never even won the Ulster Championship (they lost the All-Ireland semi-final to Galway that year).

In marked contrast, in the 1960 final they were facing a Kerry team seeking a twentieth All-Ireland. Down ran out eight-point winners in front of a then-record 87,768 people at Croke Park. Down's winning margin was the biggest loss Kerry had suffered in a final at that juncture. The following year, Down once again overpowered Kerry, this time in the semi-final by six points. Subsequently, they went on and beat Offaly 3-6 to 2-8 in front of 90,556, a record attendance at Croke Park. In 1968, they once again defeated Kerry in the All-Ireland final, cementing their position with Galway as the joint team of the decade.

THE STAR OF THE COUNTY DOWN

Their star player was Seán O'Neill. Evidence to substantiate that analysis would be O'Neill's selection as Footballer of the Year in 1968 (when he scored twelve goals and sixty-five points for the county that year); his place on the inaugural All-Star team in 1971 and the following year; and above all his inclusion at right half-forward on both the Team of the Century and the Team of the Millennium. He was the first Down man to captain Ulster to Railway Cup victory in 1960.

In conversation with this writer, O'Neill expressed his concerns with the way the game has developed.

'I would like to see the cynical fouls that were so apparent in recent Championships cut out. Gaelic football has such a rich tradition and we can't have that tradition scarred by the cynicism and sometimes nothing less than thuggery that has cast a dark shadow on our games. This is not a new thing, but since I have retired I have been disappointed by what some teams have been prepared to do to win an All-Ireland. I sometimes shake my head when I see some that I can think of fêted as greats of the game when they have done so much to change the culture from playing positive football to one of stopping the opposition. The Down team I was part of played football the way it should be played, and I was glad to see the Down team of the 1990s doing it the same way. John O'Mahony's Galway team did it too, but more recently too many teams have gone down a very different route. We should be able to hand on the game to the next generation in a good state.'

DOWN BELOW

Weeshie Fogarty observed the fortunes of that Down team through Kerry-tinted glasses.

'A new power arrived on the GAA scene in the sixties as Down dominated those early years of the decade. They proved too good for Kerry in the final of 1960, and in the following year's semi-final, they again proved masters of the kingdom. As the decade drew to a close, Kerry had another defeat by Down in the 1968 final. I take my hat off to them. They were one of the best and most stylish sides I have ever seen.'

55

DOYENS OF THE DÉISE

Waterford 1938–48

The ultimate compliment to John Keane came from Nicky Rackard.

After Keane's funeral Mass, in the best tradition of GAA hospitality, generous refreshments were laid on for those in attendance. Keane's club, Mount Sion, were an essential part of his DNA. A club official observed a solitary mourner staying behind to say a final farewell and invited him to the meal. Nicky Rackard responded, 'I came here to bury John Keane, and now all I want to do is go home.'

A HURLING PILGRIM'S PROGRESS

The manner of Keane's dying tells us much about the values by which he lived. Being aware that he was going to meet his maker because of a serious illness, he had been doing a hurling version of the Camino to say a final farewell to the giants of the ash he'd lined out against years earlier when he died on the way to see Limerick great Jackie Power.

Those values were also apparent after Keane retired from playing. He returned to be team trainer when the county won a second All-Ireland in 1959. During one of their games, one Déise player, annoyed at being substituted, bounced his hurley off the ground. Keane pulled him aside and instructed him not to hand the advantage to his opponent by showing his frustration.

Keane's status in the game is such that he prevents the Clare legend Seánie McMahon from being described as the 'prince of centre-backs'. The evidence is compelling: Keane was chosen as centre-back on both the GAA official Team of the Century (in 1984) and Team of the Millennium.

THE PLAYBOY OF THE SOUTHERN WORLD

He had a baptism of fire marking no less than Mick Mackey in a Waterford–Limerick Championship game when he was only twenty. Indeed, Mackey would furnish not just Keane but the entire Waterford team a powerful lesson into the ethos of hurling when Mackey marked another Waterford player, Christy Moylan. The exchanges were hot and heavy, and this prompted Mackey to go looking for an orange from the gallery. An avalanche of fruit pelted onto the field. The 'Playboy of the Southern World' (one of Mackey's nicknames with the 'Laughing Cavalier') picked one up, peeled it and threw half over to Moylan, his marker. His sportsmanship and generosity prompted a spontaneous round of applause from the crowd.

John Keane was central to Waterford's arrival as a hurling power. He was at the heart of their first Munster final win in 1938. They narrowly lost the All-Ireland final to Dublin that year.

Ten years later, Waterford won their first All-Ireland. It was an extraordinary final in that there were more goals than points. Waterford beat Dublin by 6-7 to 4-2. The key moment in the game came when the Déise switched Keane from centre-back to centre-forward. Keane scored three goals and two points.

A FALLEN HERO

In April 2021, a great oak fell in the forest with the loss of Austin Flynn: full-back on that Waterford 1959 side. He also won three Munster medals, a National League and Oireachtas title during an inter-county career that spanned from 1952 to 1967. He marked some of the game's greats such as Christy Ring and Nicky Rackard during his career, and was widely regarded as one of Waterford's greatest hurlers. In a less public way than John Mullane, Austin Flynn and John Keane were men who loved their county.

56

MIGHTY MEATH

Meath 1940–54

In the 1800s, fighting in Afghanistan, British soldiers learned to condense receipt of orders into a simple word: HUA.

Heard, understood, acknowledged.

Their philosophy was: keep it simple.

The mighty Meath team that won two All-Irelands, two League titles and six Leinster triumphs between 1940 and '54 did the same.

It was a different time. Only thirteen Meath men paraded before the 1949 Leinster final. Brian Smyth and his brother-in-law Michael O'Brien from the Skryne club, who were county champions at the time, stayed behind in the dressing room to decide who should be Meath captain. Smyth was chosen and a few months later became the first Meath man to raise the Sam Maguire Cup.

THE MAN IN THE CAP

It was also the era of the most celebrated headgear in the history of the GAA – that of Peter McDermott, famously christened by the voice of Gaelic games Michael O'Hehir as 'the man in the cap'. The cap was to control what Peter modestly described as 'my fabulous head of long hair'. He was the driving force behind a great Meath team. He also has the unique distinction of being the only man to referee an All-Ireland final both before and after winning one as a player.

He also made his mark as an official. He was county secretary when he captained Meath to the All-Ireland in 1954. He was a key advisor to Down when they won their first All-Ireland in 1960. Eight years later, he initiated the link between Ireland and Australia Rules by lining up games for the county's tour of Australia.

The late Mick Dunne was a big admirer of the man in the cap.

'He continues to occupy a hallowed place in the annals of the GAA, as a star of All-Ireland winning teams in 1949 and '54. If I was going into battle, the one player I would choose would probably be Peter. He had the heart of a lion but was a gentleman to his fingertips. When the chips were down, he would always come through for you. His nickname added to his iconic status, particularly as back then the GAA did not have a tradition of exotic nicknames, other than Roscommon's Bill Carlos – "The Lion with the Velvet Paw".'

McDermott's fifty-one Championship appearances was the Meath record until it was surpassed by Colm O'Rourke in 1992. While Meath enjoyed League triumphs, Championship success remained on the distant horizon. 'Although we had great teams and great players, we just couldn't make the big breakthrough at All-Ireland level,' McDermott once recalled to Mick Dunne.

'Meath's luck changed in 1949, largely due to the efforts of new county board chairman Fr Tully. Starting the Championship campaign as no-hopers, the Meath players, including McDermott at left corner-forward, confounded the critics and reached the final. They then won the final, beating Cavan 1-10 to 1-6. Peter remembered the "special aura" of that first All-Ireland win, saying: "We always appreciated the feelings of the supporters." In 1954, Meath faced Kerry in the final and, captained by McDermott, won 1-13 to 1-7. He said of the runners-up: "They were the most magnanimous of losers and showed great sportsmanship."

'Meath became a force again in the 1960s with Peter as coach and Fr Tully as trainer. The team won the 1967 All-Ireland final, beating Cork 1-9 to 0-9.

'As a referee, he was probably as good as we've seen. It was much harder in his day to keep control. That time you couldn't pick a ball off the ground. If you dived on the ball, you had to get up and put your toe under it and lift it. There was little chance of that in a goalmouth. There was way more body contact then, which Peter relished, as it made the game very exciting. Mind you, if you lost possession, you couldn't always use it well because the game was so crowded. So you needed eyes in the back of your head. So you couldn't be a shrinking violet if you were a referee.

'As a naïve young journalist, I found myself standing alone with him on the sideline at a match when a schemazoole broke out that would leave the toughest contest today look like a harmless tiff between two little girls in a playground. Think Mayo versus Meath in 1996 and multiply by four, with the spectators bunched so close together on the centre of the pitch that they could hear each other's inner thoughts. The referee was not having a good day and Peter gently said to me: "The advantage law is the best because it lets you ignore all the others for the good of the game." He was a great referee but I feel is best remembered as a great player and part of a great team that won two All-Irelands.'

57

SHANNONSIDE SENSATIONS

Limerick 1921–23

The 1921–23 Limerick side are perhaps more accurately described as a noteworthy team rather than a great one.

They were captained by Bob McConkey. His fingerprints were all over the 1921 final. He was a carpenter who was born in Killaloe, and he holds the distinction of being the first captain to lift the Liam MacCarthy Cup. McConkey was a tricky and nimble forward, whose party piece was goals scored from whipped groundstrokes.

THE CUP

The Cup itself attracted significant attention among hurling fans and in the media. The newly minted trophy awarded to the All-Ireland winners was described by the *Irish Independent* as being of 'racy and costly design' in a match report of that year's final.

Because of the Civil War, the final wasn't played until 4 March 1923, and Dublin were favourites. But McConkey scored three goals in the first half and a fourth in the second in Limerick's 8-5 to 3-2 win.

That Limerick side epitomised an era when hurling was a game for 'manly men'. For some, hurling has lost out because it no longer has the same physicality. I sought some expert opinion on this issue and spoke with the voice of authority, Mícheál O'Muircheartaigh.

'I think that hurling has changed a lot for the better, and many of the players – and this has amazed me because generally a lot of players hang on to the theory that their own generation was the best – that hurled maybe fifty years ago are admitting that the modern generation of hurlers are better than they were. I think that video evidence would swing you around to that view. There is a greater emphasis on skill now.

'In the past, the man was played more in hurling. Now it was never as bad as football, but there was a lot of holding in the old days, for example full-backs penned into the forwards, they held on to their man when the ball came in and kept their man away from the goalie – that would all be deemed a foul nowadays. The emphasis today is on speed and skill, and I think hurling is better now for that.'

THE CONSTANT

Mícheál believes that although hurling has changed, there is one constant: 'The people make the GAA what it is. I love the support and the commitment that's there to your team, even in failure. To pat them on the back and say, "We'll be there next year," that's what keeps us all going. Hope.

'We have this phrase in the Gaeltacht, "*Go mbeirimid beo ar an am seo arís.*"

'That means, no matter who wins, whether it be everything or nothing, may we all be alive and well on this day next year. *Le cúnamh Dé*, that's all we can ask for.

'We also though have a great store of memories to draw from, and as a young man I was fascinated by the teams of the twenties who made a mark on the hearts of the hurling nation. What a great feat for Limerick to be able to say they were the first team to lift the Liam MacCarthy Cup.'

In March 2021, the Limerick GAA family launched a commemorative jersey to mark the centenary of the county's 1921 All-Ireland win.

58

WITH GOD ON THEIR SIDE

Tyrone 2003–08

Thirty unbroken seasons as Tyrone manager through minor, under-21, and senior teams came to an end for Mickey Harte when he retired from his duties in 2020 before taking the manager's job in Louth. It was an incredibly successful period in Tyrone's history. Harte's great team of the noughties changed the game forever, landing the Sam Maguire three times in 2003, '05 and '08. Even though that would be his last All-Ireland, in subsequent years he still won four Ulster titles and led the county to another All-Ireland final appearance. There is no doubt he is the greatest Tyrone manager of all time.

Harte rewrote the manual for GAA management. He was a very astute, shrewd manager who is most meticulous in his preparation. The great managers are often not easy men. They have to be driven by an endless quest to avoid the inevitable, to minimise risks and to maximise potential. Management is a process of replacing one anxiety with another. Harte was noted for his attention to detail. His record as a manager at minor and under-21 is unrivalled, and the final part of his CV came when he delivered

Sam Maguire to Tyrone. He is a very serious thinker about the tactical side of the game. He is a stickler for statistics.

The Tyrone manager showed himself to be a genius, a tactical master. He innovated a new style of football which nobody had seen before. His towering gifts as a manager – the priceless 'feel' for players and commanding urgency of his voice, the cold nerve and iron determination, the judgement that springs a sub at precisely the right moment to suit their capacities – have never been better exemplified than in his icily patient delivery of the injured Peter Canavan in the 2003 All-Ireland final.

Enda McGinley claims that Mickey Harte was not authoritarian, but you weren't going to win an argument with him. Twice winning All-Ireland manager John O'Mahony is a huge admirer of Harte's achievements as a manager.

'In 2005, Mickey Harte had been working on the team for three years and had a harmonious blend between defence and attack. Although Kerry got off to a great start in the All-Ireland final that year, Tyrone wiped the floor with them and played beautiful football and showed they had some great players. Harte's tactical genius was again showcased in 2008 when, against the odds, he led Tyrone to another All-Ireland at the expense of red-hot favourites Kerry, having earlier crushed the highly fancied Dublin side in the All-Ireland quarter-final. He's one of the best managers we have seen.'

PETER THE GREAT

Of course, Tyrone's three All-Irelands would not have been possible without a number of great players, none more so than Peter Canavan. He is widely considered to be godlike in Tyrone. When one of his children was getting married, the presiding priest said at the start of the wedding ceremony, 'This is the first time I have said Mass in front of my employer.'

59

FIVE OUT OF SIX AIN'T BAD

Tipperary 1999–2004

It is often said, usually by Tipperary people, that Tipperary is the home of hurling. In the noughties, Tipperary became one of the powerhouses of camogie as the county won three consecutive senior camogie All-Irelands between 1999 and 2001 and although they lost to Cork in '02, they won back-to-back All-Irelands in '03 and '04. One of the stars of the team was centre half-back Ciara Gaynor.

'I can't recall when I actually started playing camogie,' she states. 'Back home, my sisters and I would be playing around the yard. My interest developed further when I got to primary school. Our principal, Albert Williams, won an All-Ireland club hurling medal in 1986 and he was a big influence. I went to St Mary's secondary school in Nenagh. We had great success winning junior and senior All-Irelands.'

From the outset though there was one voice whose whisper was worth more than the shouts of most other critics. No one is more attuned to the nuances of the game than her father, Len Gaynor. He won three All-Ireland senior hurling medals and trained both the Clare and Tipperary senior teams and took Tipp to the All-Ireland Senior final in 1997.

'When I was young, Dad was still playing at inter-firms level. When he got into management then with Clare and Tipperary, we'd all head off with him when he was going to training or to matches. As a result, hurling was always talked about back home, and I suppose that was part of the reason why I became so passionate about camogie.'

There is one jewel of memory from the sport's greatest theatre that outshines all others for Ciara. She lurches into nostalgia about a victory that will leave bubbles of pleasure that will never disappear.

'The highlight of my career was winning my first All-Ireland in Croke Park in 1999,' she recalls with a smile. 'The buzz was great in winning each of the All-Irelands, but the first one was really special.

'I suppose it was a bit of a fairy tale really. We'd only been playing at senior level for four years and we quickly won three All-Irelands. The team had been building for many years. A lot of us played together at minor and junior level in the 1990s. The junior team won an All-Ireland in '92. The talent was there, and it was just a question of getting the blend right. Then Michael Cleary, who had been a great hurler with Tipperary, got involved in training us and he was the biggest influence of all. He put the emphasis on the skills.'

For Ciara, the rewards for playing camogie were largely spiritual: its true function was to inspire, absorb and reflect deep emotions. Victory created a personal connection between the players and the fans, and rare moments when worries about medals seem irrelevant.

'The biggest achievement we had was not to win All-Irelands but to play as well as we could. That was the ultimate ambition.

I think the biggest compliment we got is that in Tipperary now, camogie is very strong with young girls and a lot of them are now swinging hurleys for the first time. We know that whatever happens, the future of camogie in the county is secure.'

60

O'ER THE BRIGHT MAY MEADOWS OF SHELMALIER

Wexford 1912–18

Liam Griffin is a man with a very strong sense of Wexford's place in Irish history. He believes that Wexford people carry the DNA of the 1798 Rising in their genes because it was their 'rebel hands' that 'set the heather blazing'. It was they alone who followed the call to 'Arm! Arm!' They were martyrs to the cause: 'For Ireland's freedom we'll fight or die.' It was then that 'Fr Murphy from County Wexford' swept 'o'er the land like a mighty wave'.

Amidst the hotbed of political intrigue and the reams of revolutionary rhetoric that rampaged through the nation, it was Wexford people, and Wexford people alone, who put their pikes where their mouths were 'o'er the bright May meadows of Shelmalier'. Griffin argues, 'We were the only ones who stood up when Ireland needed someone to take on the Empire.' From this perspective, winning the All-Ireland in 1996 was much more than winning a match – it was another instalment in the county's unique tradition of defiance, determination and dignity.

However, on the sporting fields, the first manifestation of this came not in the hurling arena but in the world of Gaelic football. Wexford achieved their success despite a turbulent political landscape. To take one example, in Sackville Street (now O'Connell Street) on the afternoon of Sunday, 31 August 1913, the Dublin Metropolitan Police (DMP) baton-charged crowds attending a banned protest led by Big Jim Larkin. In a five-minute period, between four hundred and six hundred civilians were injured. At a time when politics and religion were so intertwined, it is noteworthy that over eighty per cent of the DMP were Catholic.

In 1914, England found itself at war. A new adage came into play: 'England's difficulty is Ireland's opportunity.'

There is a saying in Swahili which has a powerful parallel for Irish nationalists: *Paka akiondoka, panya hutawala*. This partially translates to the traditional Western saying: 'When the cat's away, the mouse will play.' However, it has an added twist: 'And be themselves.' There was a very colonial connotation to this which gave it additional resonance in an Irish context.

A CUT ABOVE THE REST

It is a matter of fact that during the 1910s, Wexford's footballers were the best team in the country. What they achieved has been emulated just twice, and on both occasions by Kerry, though in recent years Dublin have surpassed them.

Six successive Leinster titles were complemented by four All-Ireland titles on the bounce between 1915 and '18. To add to their status, they lost the previous two All-Ireland finals to Kerry.

In 1918, the Spanish flu was raging across the world; at home, GAA matches themselves were being outlawed by the police. The world burned. Across four deadly waves, that pandemic would infect around 800,000 in Ireland, 23,000 of them fatally. It killed indiscriminately, with a quarter of the deaths coming among those in the twenty-five to thirty-five age bracket.

Unlike Kerry, in 1982, Wexford never got a chance to compete for the five-in-a-row, losing to Dublin in the second round of Leinster in 1919. Seán O'Kennedy, the team's star player and the first man to captain three All-Ireland winning sides, blamed fatigue and a downturn in ambition for the defeat. He claimed players were 'fed up and tired' after winning their fourth All-Ireland.

Until the arrival of the Rackards in the 1950s, Wexford remained a predominantly football-orientated county. However, they won just two subsequent Leinster titles, with their last coming in 1945. Despite a welcome resurgence in the 2000s, driven by the brilliance of Mattie Ford, an All-Ireland final has eluded them ever since.

61

CARLOW'S CROWNING GLORY

Carlow 1941–44

'What a change in the last half did the minutes unroll.
The boys from the Barrow were swarming the goal.
It was blue in an odd spot, but red, gold and green
Were the colours that rallied the Carlow fifteen.'

That verse is taken from 'The Carlow Fifteen'. It may not rank with 'Imagine' as one of the greatest songs of all time; however, it does have an appreciative fan base in Carlow as the county's victory song, which is a hymn of praise to the magnificent rally staged by Carlow in the Leinster football final of 1944.

Since the first meeting of the Gaelic Athletic Association in Carlow was held in the CYMS (Catholic Young Men's Society) Hall on College Street on 2 April 1888, the county has played its part in the GAA. In the 1940s, the senior football team had its most successful era. In 1941, Carlow reached the Leinster final for the first time. The match was due to be played in August against Dublin but had to be postponed due to an outbreak of foot-and-mouth disease. When the match finally took place on 9 November 1941, Dublin had an easy win over Carlow.

The following year Carlow again reached the Leinster final. However, there was a dispute following the match in relation to the eligibility of one player. Dublin were finally awarded the Leinster title. In 1943, Carlow narrowly missed out on a place in the Leinster quarter-final when they were defeated by Laois.

On 15 July 1944, Carlow played Wexford in the Leinster semi-final and beat them emphatically by a score of 5-7 to 3-6. Next stop the Leinster final, and once again the opposing team were Dublin. The Carlow team was trained by Jack Dundon. Long before Babs Keating had the same idea, a training fund was set up by the football supporters' club in the area. The people of Carlow responded generously to the call for subscriptions despite the hard times. The *Nationalist and Leinster Times* of 20 July 1944 predicted that the side had a 'bright prospect of bringing the first Leinster Senior Championship to Carlow'.

The final was played in Geraldine Park, Athy, before what was an enormous crowd in the circumstances. Despite the difficulties posed by 'the Emergency', people made their way to the game to support their team using every possible mode of transport, with bicycles particularly prominent. In the fine weather, the crowd witnessed a thrilling and close game. The Carlow team made history by defeating Dublin 2-6 to 1-6.

LYNCH-ING

A Roscommon great of that time observed the county's progress with interest. The rain hit the window at an angle, carried on a strong north-easterly wind, and the comfort of the fire lapped over us like a wave in his Bray home. We gulped from our mugs of tea like hungry farmers after doing the milking before Brendan Lynch shared his observations.

'I can still remember reading about the "never-ending stream of cyclists and horse-drawn vehicles" travelling to the Leinster final. It would never happen now, but the Carlow supporters outnumbered the Dubs at the game. Carlow trailed 0-5 to 0-1 at half-time but finished very strongly in the second half. Of course, the first one is the sweetest so because it was the first Leinster final they won, the celebrations were very enthusiastic. I heard of one pub in Carlow that ran out of porter that night! Over 40,000 people attended the All-Ireland semi-final between Carlow and Kerry on September, 1944. The Carlow team fought hard, but Kerry beat them by two points. This was a big crowd for the war years. I like to think that Carlow people were very happy when we beat Kerry in the final that year!

'I know today people aren't impressed by moral victories, but it was a fantastic achievement in '44 to win the Leinster final and to push the mighty Kerry so close in the All-Ireland semi-final. In 1945, the backbone of the Leinster team for the Railway Cup were Carlow players and they were all there on merit. They had some fantastic players who would have walked onto any team in the country. The only pity is that the likes of Jimma Rea, who was such a classy forward on that team, are not the household names they would have been had they played for a team like Kerry.'

62

DONEGAL'S DESTINY

Donegal 1989–92

It was the day of days.

In 1992, Donegal claimed their first-ever All-Ireland with a 0-18 to 0-14 triumph over red-hot favourites Dublin.

When I spoke to the late Donegal legend Seamus Bonner, he felt that the foundations for their success had been laid ten years earlier.

'In 1982, Donegal got a massive boost when we won the All-Ireland under-21 title. We picked up a lot of new players like Anthony Molloy and Martin McHugh, and they would be crucial to us winning in 1992.'

THE LIFE OF BRIAN

In 1989, Brian McEniff took charge of training Donegal again, and he invited Bonner to be a selector. The offer was readily accepted despite the fact that it committed him to extensive travelling up and down to Donegal from his Dublin base. McEniff's Midas touch was soon in evidence again as Donegal won the Ulster title the following year. What did Seamus Bonner believe was the secret of McEniff's success and what was he like as a player?

'As a forward, he's the sort of guy I would really hate to have marking me. He was very tough and tenacious. He'd be standing on your toes almost and wouldn't give you much time on the ball.

'His dedication was total. Although he's got his own business, if he heard a Donegal man was playing football in Cork, he'd drop everything and travel down to Cork to see him play and it wouldn't cost him a thought. He never missed a single training session in the 1992 campaign, and this encouraged the players to do the same. His willpower rubbed off on the players. He's also got incredible enthusiasm and that's infectious.'

INSIDER TRADING

McEniff had his finest hour in 1992. Bonner's inside knowledge of the Dublin players was to prove invaluable in the final.

'Having played club football so long in Dublin, I knew the Dublin players better than McEniff did. One of the highlights of my career had been captaining Civil Service to the Dublin Championship in 1980.

'Basically, I was keen that we would do two things in the All-Ireland. Firstly, that we would keep very tight on Vinnie Murphy. I knew he was their target man and if we kept him quiet, the other Dublin forwards would struggle. It was also vital that we curbed the Dublin half-back line because we didn't want the likes of Keith Barr running at our defence with the ball. We took steps to do both, and after we got over their penalty chance, which Charlie Redmond didn't take, we were always holding our own.

'We had been so unimpressive in the All-Ireland semi-final against Mayo that nobody gave us a chance against Dublin. I think that gave the Dublin players a false sense of security. The media really built them up, and I think the Dubs started to believe their own publicity. That's a dangerous game. I think something similar happened to Kildare in 1998. In contrast, there was no hype about us because we hadn't done anything to deserve it. None of our fellas were going on radio shows blowing our own trumpet.'

A HEAVY HEART

Although the excitement was unprecedented, Donegal's marvellous victory came with a price tag attached for Seamus Bonner.

'The hardest part of my time as a selector came in the run-up to the final. Tommy Ryan had played for us in the All-Ireland semi-final, but we felt that Manus Boyle could do a job for us on the day. He scored nine points in the final so our judgement was vindicated, but nobody wants to miss out on the chance to play in an All-Ireland final so it was incredibly tough to have to tell Tommy that he was going to miss out.'

McEniff gave leadership from the sideline but who were the Donegal leaders on the pitch?

'You can't win an All-Ireland without leaders on the pitch and we had four of them in 1992: Anthony Molloy, Martin McHugh at centre-forward, Tony Boyle at full-forward and Martin Gavigan at centre-back were all leaders in different ways. Molloy was a superb leader. He could catch a ball in the clouds and that would lift the team. If you could get past Martin Gavigan, you were doing well, and Tony and Martin could get you a score from nowhere.'

63

COME ON THE ROSSIES

Roscommon 1943–47

The 1940s saw the most glorious era in the history of Roscommon football, with the county's only All-Ireland successes in 1943 and '44, both under the captaincy of Jimmy Murray.

'The first time I lined out in an All-Ireland final in 1943 and an hour before we got to Dublin I was nearly standing up just to get my first glimpse of Croke Park. That was my dream come true.

'One of my most vivid memories of my playing career is my brother Phelim telling me that Paddy Kennedy came over to him in the 1946 All-Ireland final and said: "Phelim, I think it's your All-Ireland." Phelim replied: "You never know – anything can happen. There's still over five minutes to go." Phelim's words were prophetic because Kerry got two goals in the dying minutes to draw the game and they went on to win the replay.'

Brendan Lynch was right half-back on that Roscommon team. He announced his arrival on the national stage in bold print in the All-Ireland semi-final against Louth.

'I was marking Peter Corr, who'd been Player of the Year at that stage. He'd scored thirteen points in the Leinster final. I decided it was his career or mine. I handled him roughly and kept him scoreless. Peter, who was related to the singers the Corrs, went on to play for Everton.

'My lasting memory from the game was when the County Secretary John Joe Fahy came running up to me at the end and said: "Ye'll beat them in the second half if you play like that." I turned to him and said: "We have already." He looked shocked and said: "God, did I miss it?" He was so embroiled in the whole game and the tension it created, he'd lost all track of time.

'We beat Cavan in the All-Ireland final after a replay. I marked Mick Higgins who was very quiet and a very clean and good footballer. What I remember most was the mayhem at the end. First Cavan's Joe Stafford was sent off after having a go at Owensie Hoare. We got a point, but Barney Culley didn't agree and put the umpire into the net with a box. Big Tom O'Reilly, the captain of Cavan, came into remonstrate and threw the referee in the air.'

It was not the medal that mattered to Lynch.

'The euphoria of winning was incredible. I felt like jumping out of my skin. I was on top of the world. I was twenty years of age and the world seemed to be my oyster. I've given away all my medals to my family. I read that Christy Ring had donated one of his All-Ireland medals to the foreign missions and I did the same. It was the sense of achievement that mattered most to me.'

Roscommon had a slice of luck before claiming a second title in 1944.

'Sligo drew with us in the first round of the Connacht Championship in Boyle. They should have beaten us. We were lucky to survive. There were only 2,000 people in attendance when we played Mayo in the Connacht final because of the transport problems during the war. We were worried by Cavan at half-time in the All-Ireland semi-final, but they collapsed completely in the second half and we had an easy win. It was extra sweet to beat Kerry for our second All-Ireland because they were the kings.'

Roscommon were not to recapture the same winning feeling again.

'We were unlucky with illness. Phelim Murray got TB and spent twelve months in a sanatorium. I would consider Phelim to be Roscommon's best-ever footballer. The nearest to him I have seen since was Dermot Earley, who was close to perfect. TB also finished Liam Gilmartin's career. We also lost John Joe Nerney, so we were never the same force again.

'Mayo beat us in the first round of the Championship in 1945. We were suffering from burnout and they were hungry. It was a relief in a way because you had the chance to take holidays. I met Jimmy Murray that summer and he asked me how I was finding the summer without football. When I said I thought it was great, he told me he felt the same.'

SNATCHING DEFEAT FROM THE JAWS OF VICTORY

Roscommon were to come within a whisker of taking another All-Ireland in 1946.

'It was a Mickey Mouse ruling in the GAA that cost us the title. We played Mayo in the Connacht final in Ballinasloe. They had a goal disallowed and then we got a goal that was going to be disallowed. Jimmy Murray grabbed the green flag and waved it and we were awarded the goal. After the game, Mayo lodged an objection. What should have happened was that the referee should have produced his report saying Roscommon won the match and that would have been that. Instead, we had to go into a replay and on top of the heavy collective training we were doing, we didn't need another match. We lost Frank Kinlough with a leaky valve in his heart, and Doc Callaghan our full-back was injured. By the time we faced Kerry in the All-Ireland final replay, they were getting stronger and we were getting weaker. I was never as happy as when the final whistle sounded in that game because the whole year had been absolutely exhausting with the two replays and all the collective training.

'It finished us as a team. We lost to Cavan in the All-Ireland semi-final in 1947 which meant they went on to play in the Polo Grounds instead of us. I didn't begrudge them. It was only right that players like John Joe O'Reilly finally won an All-Ireland.'

64

KILKENNY KINGS

Kilkenny 1931–35

It was a time when the kettle was always on the boil for the obligatory greeting when friend, casual caller or total stranger called: 'Sit down there by the fire. Ah sure you'll have a cup of tea in your hand.' People never seemed to be put out when the stranger called unexpectedly, inevitably at the most awkward times.

The legacy of the Civil War lingered powerfully in Kilkenny. Heated exchanges between neighbours on the merits and demerits of the polices of the two main parties Fianna Fáil and Fine Gael were a regular occurrence. On election day, party activists spent the entire day in the local polling station as observers, ensuring that nobody from the other side would try something underhanded, like voting twice. There was also a more positive purpose to ensure that all the party faithful 'did the right thing'. Everybody in the parish knew how about four-fifths of the parish voted. A good indication was provided at Mass on Sunday when people bought the Sunday papers. The Fine Gaelers bought the *Sunday Independent*, while the Fianna Fáilers took *The Sunday Press*.

Equality of the sexes was not yet a feature of Irish elections.

Although women's rights were being recognised by a series of legislative measures, party activists concentrated their energies on the male voters in the theory that the men would always keep the women in line. This was a very simplistic proposition. Another presumption which sometimes led to inaccurate conclusions was assuming that a particular voter's decision to travel in a party's car indicated support for that party.

Once the voter walked into the polling station, they were watched like hawks. A discreet nod was passed between the voter and 'the party man', to signify that the duty would be discharged in the expected fashion. A telltale sign was when a traditional party supporter was unable to make eye contact with his observer. This meant they had transferred their allegiance to the other side. News of this turncoat's treachery was quickly communicated to party bosses in the area, and within hours, the whole parish knew about it. The people who came up with the idea of the secret ballot would have to devise something far more sophisticated for rural Ireland.

Like the Catholic Church and the GAA, Fianna Fáil occupied a prominent place in Irish life, as they stretch their tentacles into every parish in the country. Those who loved 'The Long Fellow', Éamon de Valera, the towering political figure, in his lifetime, exposed their children to that hero worship to support their instinctive certainty. On the other 'side', people did the exact same for Michael Collins.

In rural Kilkenny, the other two dimensions of men's lives were farming and hurling – though it was hard to be sure which came first. Their social excursions were to go to Kilkenny games, complete with a flask of tea and sandwiches and often a bag of what were called 'beauty bats', which were really sweet apples.

One of his father's enduring legacies to Lorenzo (Lory) Meagher was a passion for the GAA. Hurling's first superstar took to this infatuation with the intensity of a new lover, drinking in every word and gesture. When it came to hurling, Lory became as curious as Galileo gazing at the moon through his telescope. His obsession never wore away.

Hurling at the time was not a game for the faint-hearted. Michael Smith, the former Minister for Defence, often told the story of the 1935 All-Ireland semi-final. After six minutes, the ball ricocheted off the post and went into the stand. The pulling continued relentlessly and it was twenty-two minutes before any of the players noticed the ball was missing!

OVER THE BAR SAID LORY MEAGHER

In contrast, the 'Prince of Hurlers', or 'King Lory', was famed for his overhead striking and for pioneering lifting the ball. The 1931 final between Cork and Kilkenny went to two replays. The reaction to this saga established hurling as a mass spectator sport, nearly doubling the crowds that had been attending hurling finals. Lory Meagher broke three ribs in the first replay, but as there were fears the Kilkenny crowd wouldn't travel if they knew the truth about his injury, he boarded the train for the match with his boots over his shoulder. It is said he wept as Cork won.

A year later though, he was on the winning side as the Cats beat Clare. The following year, Limerick were put to the sword in the All-Ireland final. Two years later Lory captained the 1935 side to beat a Limerick team defending the All-Ireland.

It was a fitting coronation for a man who hooked with the hurley and, more fundamentally, hooked hurling into the soul of the nation.

65

ANTRIM ARRIVE ON THE BIG STAGE

Antrim 1946

The late great Weeshie Fogarty was a big fan of the 1946 Antrim football team. When I spoke to him, he saw the side through the prism of his cherished Kerry.

'People so associate Antrim with hurling today that many forget that in 1946 they had a formidable team – a team that would ask serious question of the Kingdom.

'Kerry began their 1946 campaign in great style when they dethroned their great rivals and reigning All-Ireland champions Cork in Tralee in June of that year 1-8 to 1-4. Waterford was easily defeated in the Munster final. Antrim were then the opponents in the All-Ireland semi-final on a day which rained cats and dogs. These conditions would suit the Kerry men, and the match would prove to be one of the most contentious for many years.

'Antrim got off to a disastrous start. Bill O'Donnell goaled within ten minutes as Jackie Lyne set him up. The Northerners had drawn level by half-time only to go four points down again in the third quarter. The exchanges were rugged, fast and furious, and a player from both sides was sent off. A bottle was thrown from the Cusack Stand at one of the Kerry players – an incident raised by the Kerry delegates, Dan Ryan, J. J. Sheehy and Mícheál Ó Ruairc at the subsequent Central Council meeting. Paddy Burke was in superb form at full-forward and he was involved in a slick passing movement with Jackie Lyne and Bill O'Donnell. The dynamic West Kerry man Batt Garvey was on hand to crack the ball past Harry Vernon in the Antrim goal, and it was all over bar the shouting. Kerry were through to the final, 2-7 to 0-10.

'The Antrim officials were furious with the Kerry tactics and they formally protested to the Central Council and demanded that the result be overturned. However, the Antrim players were totally against the objection and their brilliant attacker Kevin Armstrong was quoted as saying, "It was a mistake to protest, a regrettable mistake. The county board allowed themselves to be influenced by public opinion and I, for one, would not accuse Kerry of been over-robust in that match." Antrim had stormed out of Ulster with their open, weaving handpassing style of play. Cavan had won fourteen of the previous fifteen Ulster titles and it was Antrim's first since 1913. Full-back for Kerry that day was the towering and powerful army man Joe Keohane. Joe later became a selector on many Kerry teams and was one of Mick O'Dwyer's sideline mentors during the glorious era of the seventies.

'As a regular attendee at Kerry training sessions in Fitzgerald Stadium during that period, I would often sit and chat to Joe. A very cordial, soft-spoken gentleman, he had a wonderful memory of events that occurred during his career, and that defeat of Antrim came up for discussion on a number of occasions. He recalled for me as we sat on the Michael O'Connor terrace overlooking the playing pitch one beautiful summer's evening events of that afternoon in Croke Park in 1946.

'"We were Croke Park specialists: they were making their first appearance in an All-Ireland semi-final and were greatly confident that their short, classy handpassing style would be too slick for us. They tried to walk the ball right into our goalmouth and were reluctant to shoot from far out the field. We were ready for this and our motto was, be close to them at all times and be prepared to tackle the man receiving the ball when he immediately took the pass. The tackles were hard but fair. We did not stand on ceremony and when we prevented them playing that basketball style of football, they had no plan B. This is one of the secrets of Kerry – changing tactics whenever the occasion demands."

'Kerry's legendary midfielder Paddy Kennedy began on the forty that day on 18 August 1946. I never had the privilege of meeting this legend of Kerry. I have constantly been told by the older generation that Paddy was equal to Mick O'Connell, the Kingdom's other legendary midfielder. I did visit Paddy's grave in Dublin and spent a memorable afternoon at his home with his wife, sons and daughters. His home is adorned with mementoes of his brilliant career in the green and gold, and his wife had a beautiful bracelet formed of his five All-Ireland medals. The jersey he wore in the Polo Grounds final in New York is also a family heirloom, while his daughters proudly display several of his other medals as brooches.

'Like Joe Keohane, Paddy Kennedy too was adamant that the one way to stop the flying Antrim forwards was to hit them hard and fair. "When you went to tackle an Antrim player, he automatically passed it out to a waiting colleague and moved on for the return pass. The only counter to this was to take the man getting the return pass and put your arms around him and hold him as the ball came to him. If a man was caught in possession five times in a row, you would expect that he would change his tactics. Antrim never did, and when forced to kick the ball in from far out field, our full-back line usually won the duels in the air. We outsmarted them that day."

'In that way, Paddy Kennedy admitted that Kerry did foul their opponent in a concerted plan to stop them and, indeed, even in today's game we see the tactics of swarming, dragging and holding and preventing a player from finding a teammate. Some things never change. Antrim failed that day because when Kerry thwarted their running-short style of play, they failed to adapt and the men on the line did not have an answer to Kerry's tactics.

'So Antrim lodged their objection and for over three hours on Saturday, 31 August 1946, the Central Council debated the Northern objection. The allegations were that members of the Kerry team indulged in rough play and that these tactics before an attendance of over 30,000 people were calculated to bring the GAA into disrepute. The referee, Paddy Ratty of Meath, reported that play was over-robust towards the end and he had to award several frees to Antrim. The objection was declared lost by nineteen votes to ten.

'Kerry advanced to the final, but due to a very "wet harvest", the decider against Roscommon was postponed until October. Two goals in the last seven minutes from Paddy Burke and "Gega" O'Connor brought that dramatic game to a replay. Kerry captain Gus Cremin was dramatically dropped for the second meeting and the legendary midfielder Paddy Kennedy was presented with the Sam Maguire Cup following Kerry's 2-8 to 0-10 win. Kerry had four captains that year as Eddie Dowling and Bill Casey had led the side in earlier rounds. Dan O'Keeffe won his seventh medal to put him top of the winners' list.'

For his part, Roscommon star of the 1940s Brendan Lynch was a big fan of that Antrim team and two players in particular.

'Cavan were the great power in Ulster football in the 1940s and we were the power in Connacht, having won the All-Irelands in 1943 and '44. Kerry were the big threat, but we were also on the lookout for a new threat, and when they won the Ulster title in

1946, we all took notice of Antrim. To take Cavan's scalp, they had to be taken seriously. They were a formidable team and I, for one, was in no way surprised when they put it up to Kerry in the All-Ireland semi-final. Knowing we would be playing the winning team in the All-Ireland final, we watched that game keenly. Probably if they had a bit more experience in Croke Park, Antrim could have come out on top.

'That Antrim team had some superb players. Kevin Armstrong was as good a footballer as I have ever seen and was probably equally good if not better as a hurler. George Watterson was another star on that team. He was my type of player. He had true grit and great determination. He was the sort of player you would want to have by your side when you were going to war. I was very shocked to hear that he died at just forty-nine years of age in 1969.'

George's son Johnny is now an acclaimed sports journalist with *The Irish Times*. The Troubles cast a dark shadow over the family in 1973 when George's son Peter was murdered when he was just fourteen in a drive-by Loyalist shooting as he stood at the front of his mother's corner shop on the Falls Road in west Belfast. The next morning the body of leading UDA man Francis 'Hatchet' Smith was discovered in an alleyway in Rodney Street off the Donegall Road. The IRA said they shot Smith, who was buried with full paramilitary trappings, claiming he had been responsible for killing Peter Watterson.

66

THE LONGFORD LEADERS

Longford 1965–68

Jimmy Flynn was literally at the centre of the most successful period of Longford's history. His towering performances at midfield helped Offaly to beat the mighty Galway in the National League final in 1966. Longford's only previous successes at national level had been the All-Ireland Junior Championship of 1937. In 1968, Flynn helped Longford to take their only Leinster senior title.

In the distance, the yellow sun glimmered on the trees and a creamy haze wrapped itself around the peaks of the Dublin mountains as Flynn recalled his early days. Success quickly came at schoolboys, juvenile and minor level with his club. That trend accelerated when he went to the famous footballing nursery, St Mel's College. In 1961, he helped them reach the All-Ireland Colleges final.

'I was playing at midfield on John Morley. We lost by a point in front of 15,000 in Athlone. Apart from the best from Longford, we had up-and-coming talent from other counties like Mick Ryan from Offaly and Dermot Gannon, who went on to play for Leitrim and Connacht. His father had been the first man to captain Leitrim to win a Connacht final, back in 1927.'

Flynn made his senior debut for Offaly in 1963 as a nineteen-year-old marking Larry Coughlan. A turning point in Longford's fortunes came when three-time All-Ireland winner Mick Higgins of Cavan agreed to become county trainer in 1965. Longford had earlier reached their first Leinster final in 1965, losing out to Dublin by 3-6 to 0-9 after missing a penalty at a crucial stage. That September they won their first senior tournament of note when they defeated Kildare to take the O'Byrne Cup.

'To win the League was a great achievement for a small county like Longford, and although there was a lot of dedication on the part of the players, I think Mick Higgins has to take a lot of the credit for it. He was never a hard taskmaster in training or anything, but he grew into the job with us. There was always great local rivalry between ourselves and Cavan, but Longford people up to then had never much to shout about in comparison with our northern neighbours, though we changed that. He gave us the confidence to do it.

'We should have won the Leinster final in 1965. We were a far better team than Dublin on the day, but we hadn't the experience nor the confidence. We didn't drive home our advantage. I was marking Des Foley that day and I remember talking to him about it later, and he pointed out that they had got two very soft goals from speculative balls that went into the square.'

Flynn points out though that Higgins was not the only one responsible for the upturn in Longford's fortunes.

'We had a great county chairman in Jimmy Flynn (no relation). He had a very cool head and was a very astute man. Another key figure was our manager Fr Phil McGee (brother of Eugene). He had a great love for the game. It was much more a passion than an interest for him, and you need people like that behind you. In 1966 we were invited to go to America. I well remember Fr Phil making a statement which I think he regretted afterwards. He said, "We'll go to America when we're All-Ireland champions." We never got there! There was no such thing as foreign holidays then. You were lucky if you got to stay in a good hotel before a big match.'

Surprisingly, Flynn does not see the victory over Galway as the defining moment in Longford's changing fortunes.

'One of the great memories I have of that League campaign was of playing Sligo, who had a very strong team that year. They were a bit like ourselves in that they could have made the breakthrough, especially as they had Mickey Kearins, who was a fantastic footballer. When Sligo wanted to beat you, they dragged you into Ballymote, which was a fairly remote part of the country. Our sub goalie was the late Michael "Smiler" Fay, but on that day he was doing the sideline. At one stage, John Donlon got the ball towards the end of the game and ballooned it over the line. It was as clear as the nose on your face it was a line ball to Sligo, but Smiler gave it to us. Afterwards, we got a point and stole the match. The Sligo crowd were incensed by that and rightly so. When the game was over, the crowd were baying for Smiler's blood. Smiler saved a fair few goals for Longford in his playing career, but he saved that match for us and I believe that was the day we won the League.'

In the build-up to the League final, Galway looked invincible, but an indication that they did not regard Longford as pushovers came when they flew their outstanding half-back Martin Newell from Frankfurt, where he was attending university. Longford though won by 0-9 to 0-8. Eight of Longford's points came from Bobby Burns, while Seán Murray got the remaining score. Jimmy Flynn's high fielding and work rate earned him the Man of the Match accolade.

'There were hardly 5,000 people left in the county the day of the final. When we got home on the Monday evening, we hopped on a truck. I'll always remember Larry Cunningham, who was at the height of his fame, got up with us and sang a song. Particularly as it was the first time we won a national title, there were ecstatic celebrations in the county. Although we didn't become Longford's answer to the Beatles, at least when any of us went to a dance in Rooskey after that we were recognised!

'The final was one of those days when you are up for it and the game went well for me. The one incident I remember most was Martin Newell coming up the field with the ball and hitting a diagonal pass to Cyril Dunne. I intercepted it and there was nobody between me and the goal – which was about seventy yards away. We were two points up at the time and there was about ten minutes to go and I was very tired. I soloed through and had nobody to beat but the goalie, but I shaved the post and put it wide. I fell on the ground with exhaustion and I can still hear Jackie Devine saying to me, "Why didn't you f**king pass the ball to me?" It made for an agonising finish because Galway were throwing everything at us, but our backs held out well.

'The memory though that stays with me to this day is of the joy on the faces of the Longford crowd. We had a hell of a night in Power's Hotel afterwards and a hell of a day the following day. The party finished on Tuesday – but I'm not saying which Tuesday! We came down to earth with a bang though when we lost in the first round of the Leinster Championship against Louth. I did think it was unfair to us to have to play a Championship match just two weeks after winning the League final though.'

LEINSTER GLORY

Having reached the dizzy heights of success, Longford football soon founded itself shrouded in controversy.

'After we won the League, we had to play a two-header with New York: one in Croke Park and the second game a week later in Longford. The Croke Park match was a fiasco and ended in an absolute shambles. The Longford fans were livid with the referee because they felt that he let the New York lads away with murder. Murder is too strong to describe what they were up to, but they were very, very physical. I talked to journalists after the match and they told me we should refuse to play them in the second game. A lot of the Longford crowd came on to the pitch to try and get at the New York fellas afterwards. When we played them in Longford, it was the first time they had to put barbed wire around the pitch.'

Happy days returned to Longford in 1968, particularly after they beat reigning All-Ireland champions in the Leinster semi-final in Mullingar.

'Winning the Leinster title against Laois was a big thrill, though I got a knee injury and missed out on the All-Ireland semi-final against Kerry. It was a big disappointment to have to miss out, but what really killed me was losing out on the opportunity to mark Mick O'Connell. I was on the sideline and we lost by two points. One of the problems of Longford and weaker counties generally is that we didn't have strength in depth and that told against us in the Kerry game. We had good players when we were all free from injury but couldn't afford to be short of anyone.'

67

FOR NUDIE REASON

Monaghan 1979–88

Monaghan's most famous footballer, Eugene 'Nudie' Hughes, is part of an elite few who won All-Star awards as a forward and a defender. Michael O'Hehir immortalised him with the famous line: 'And here comes Nudie Hughes for Nudie reason.' His team put Monaghan into the national consciousness, winning three Ulster Senior Football Championships in 1979, '85 and '88, as well as a National League title in '85. In recent years, Nudie has shown the same spirit that he displayed on the field in his courageous battle with cancer.

'After it hit me, I said to Gerry McEntee [former Meath great who Nudie would end up consulting in his role as a surgeon] it was like playing against the wind in a game. The wind wasn't always going to go the one way – and I was going to get a chance to play with it too.

'I said to him, "You'll have to take some responsibility for this, Gerry." He looked at me quizzically. I said, "Remember the '84 Centenary Cup final – some of the tackles I got ..." Gerry looked at me for a minute before a smile came to his face. I said to him, "I won't be able to line out for the second half now." But he replied, "Oh, you will be, but you'll not be selling me dummies!"'

Nudie exploded into the national consciousness in 1979, in Monaghan's first Ulster title in forty-one years. They lost the All-Ireland semi-final to Kerry as they did in 1985 – though they took Kerry to a replay that year – in which they also won the National League title. Three years later, it was Cork who beat them in the All-Ireland semi-final.

'We played in the Centenary Cup [in 1984] – we played in five, won four, lost the final to Meath, and that was the inspiration for the team to come forward for the success we had in '85 and '88, in '86 in reaching the League final where we lost to Laois. We played against all the greats on the great Kerry team. We were unfortunate that we always met the Munster champions when we came through – we never met the Leinster or Connacht champions. The only thing I would have loved was for Monaghan to have reached an All-Ireland final, to see how you'd react on the day.'

EVERYBODY NEEDS BAD NEIGHBOURS

Cavan great Stephen King has some fond memories of playing against that Monaghan team.

'In 1987, they were red-hot favourites coming to Breffni Park, but we won it, although they had a very good team with Nudie Hughes and Gene Sherry and those fellas. It was a tough game. Myself and Dick Clerkin's dad, Hugo, were asked to leave the vicinity of the playing area! That was the only time I was ever sent off for Cavan.

'I remember Nudie saying to me, "Cavan only won because you went off and they got you out of the way!"'

'There was something different about those games. The size of the crowd was one thing, and there was a different atmosphere, and both sets of supporters really got into it. It's probably one of the greatest things about the GAA, that honest-to-God rivalry. Both sets of supporters want to win, and both teams want to win, but there's no animosity – it's competitive but good-natured rivalry. I remember someone saying to me once that there's no such thing as a challenge game against Monaghan and they would feel the same way towards Cavan. It's do-or-die.'

68

WESTMEATH'S WONDERLAND

Westmeath 2004

The defining image of Páidí Ó Sé for me is of him knocking Dinny Allen onto the seat of his pants in the 1975 Munster final after Allen had thrown the first punch. Then came a moment of classic comedy when the referee, running in to admonish the two bold boys, slipped on the wet ground. To add to the sense of incredulity, neither player was sent off. Páidí explained the background to me.

'Dinny scored two points early on in the game and my heart sank because I thought: *I'm going to have a bad day at the office.* After he scored the second point, Dinny turned to me and said: "They'll be taking you off soon." I thought, *Well if I'm going down, I'm taking you with me.* Thankfully after I struck him a belt, the ref got so excited that he fell over and forgot to send me off."'

I felt like I'd taken a punch to the stomach from an invisible assailant when I heard Páidí Ó Sé had died. We were bewildered ghosts at his funeral a few days later. We dragged ourselves through the ceremony. The grief had gathered like a grey mist around me, despite the best efforts of those turning on the compassion tap.

My enduring memory of him was the way his eyes would begin to shine, as though he was already formulating the version of the story he would tell me. Then he would smile benignly, as though every word would be a nugget of wisdom. His conversation would play on a loop in my mind for a long time, and I would analyse every syllable he'd uttered. His stories would stretch the truth sometimes. When I challenged him in that once, he merely shrugged and said with a typically mischievous grin, 'Ah sure I would say Mass!'

WONDERWALL

After parting company with Kerry in controversial circumstances, Páidí made his way to Westmeath and within months had led them to their only Leinster title in 2004 when they beat the reigning Leinster champions Laois 0-12 to 0-10. It was the lowest winning score in a Leinster final since Meath beat Dublin by 0-10 to 0-8 in 1996. With Gary Connaughton in goal; a defence containing John Keane, James Davitt and Damien Healy; midfielders Rory O'Connell and David O'Shaughnessy; and with Denis Glennon, Alan Mangan and Dessie Dolan prominent in attack, the team finally reached the mountain top.

Páidí's triumph with Westmeath came as a surprise to Pat Spillane.

'After an inauspicious League campaign, I was sceptical of Westmeath's chances. That April I divided counties into various categories. One of my five no-hopers was Westmeath. I said at the time: "One would not normally expect a team who managed to avoid relegation from Division One to be parked here. But Westmeath's Houdini-like escape from relegation had precious little to do with their own ability and more to do with other counties shooting themselves in the foot, notably Longford, who would have stayed up and put Westmeath down had they managed to beat Fermanagh at home. This is looking like a temporary little management arrangement for Páidí."

'I had no doubts before the Championship that Westmeath were going nowhere. I'm always like that. I may often be wrong but I never have any doubts!'

69

FIELDS OF DREAMS

Armagh 2002

After Armagh lost the 2003 All-Ireland final to Tyrone, Kieran McGeeney stayed on the pitch for Tyrone's celebrations. 'I wanted to be there to feel the hurt.' That hurt would fuel him in the future.

The GAA times are a-changing. One measurement of that is to be found in the All-Stars. In the 1970s and '80s on All-Stars, when players were found early morning in hotel lobbies, it was because they were coming back from a night on the town. Now though it is because they are hitting the gym. The man who set the standard in this respect was Kieran McGeeney. In 2003, McGeeney captained Ireland to victory over Australia in the Compromise Rules Series. The next morning McGeeney was in the gym at 6 a.m. Why? He wanted to be sharp for playing a club game the following Sunday. This is a small snapshot into the intensity that drove the man.

TALK TO JOE

If Hollywood is ever to make a biopic of a GAA figure, it will surely be Joe Kernan. Think of all the ingredients: an All-Star footballer, Armagh, Crossmaglen, the Troubles, coaching with his club and county, before a short spell with Galway. Sadly there were a series of personal tragedies, including the death of his father when he was a child, the death by suicide of his younger brother, the death of his infant son and the experience of bankruptcy.

The high point of his career came in 2002. A stunning second-half display saw Kernan's resilient Armagh side come from four points down to beat pre-match favourites Kerry by 1-12 to 0-14 in the All-Ireland football final. If ever there was a telling example of a game of two halves, this was it, with Kerry completely dominating the opening thirty-five. It looked like curtains for Armagh when Oisín McConville had a thirty-fourth-minute penalty saved by Declan O'Keeffe. Armagh overwhelmed them with a powerful second-half display culminating in Oisín McConville's fifty-fifth-minute goal. Armagh completed the job to ensure the Sam Maguire Cup would be heading to the Orchard County for the first time after disappointments in the 1953 and '77 finals.

A SPEECH FOR ALL SEASONS

Of course, the game has gone into folklore for the most famous half-time speech in the history of Gaelic games. Joe Kernan would bring Armagh to football's top table when he was appointed Armagh manager. Enda McNulty had an eyewitness view of the journey.

'The biggest thing that Joe brought to the table was belief. When Joe walked into the Canal Court Hotel in December 2001 for his first team meeting with us, he had already won All-Irelands with Crossmaglen. So when he sat down with us, you knew you were in the presence of a winner in Croke Park. Allied to that, he had already played for Armagh in an All-Ireland final. Of course, when Joe walks into the room, he brings a great presence because of his physique. All he said was: "Get me to Croke Park and I'll ensure ye'll win." You believed him. We knew we were on the edge of winning an All-Ireland and believed that Joe was the final piece of the jigsaw – and he was.

'We knew we could win if we played to our potential, and most of our team performed but didn't know we would win. We knew our conditioning was better than Kerry's. We knew we were a tougher team than Kerry despite what anybody said. There was a bit of a myth about how good that Kerry team were, and the press had built them up the way they built up Dublin in the noughties. We weren't under any illusions though that it was going to be easy. We knew it would probably go down to one kick of a ball and that's what happened.

'It hadn't gone well in the first half, but what hasn't gone into folklore is that we started off well. Then Kerry had a period of dominance and we sort of went off the rails after that, but we finished well and only went in at half-time tailing by four points. I remember I personally went in at half-time, having slipped a few times on the pitch because I changed to studs rather than blades on my boots before the match, knowing I had to pick my game up. I started on Gooch Cooper and then moved on to Mike Frank Russell. I changed my boots at the break and that made a big difference in the second half.

'I remember looking around the dressing room and thinking the mood in the team wasn't unbelievably spirited and the body language wasn't very strong. Joe came in and he started talking: "Listen, boys, we weren't playing well. I played in the 1977 All-Ireland final and I remember going home on the bus crying and with all the boys crying. Do ye want to be like f**king me?" It wasn't really what he said next but the impact of him physically throwing his loser's medal from that game against the shower and it rattling all over the wall and then shattering into little pieces and the plastic breaking and the coin or whatever it was rolling all over the floor. I again vividly remember looking around and seeing the body language change immediately. There were other games when you'd look into the boys' eyes and you'd see a bit of uncertainty, but there was none at that stage.'

70

FROM SMALL ACORNS

Derry 1993

According to the well-known GAA fan Fyodor Dostoyevsky, 'If you wish to glimpse inside a human soul and get to know the man, don't bother analysing his ways of being silent, of talking, of weeping, or seeing how much he is moved by noble ideas; you'll get better results if you just watch him laugh. If he laughs well, he's a good man ... All I claim to know is that laughter is the most reliable gauge of human nature.'

If that is the case, Eamonn Coleman was the finest man I ever met. On the surface our conversation should not have been so punctuated by his laughter. The GAA banned him twice for a year. Not to mention that he was sacked almost immediately after bringing his county its first senior All-Ireland.

THE YOUNG ONE
Coleman began managing teams when he was just twenty-eight, having acquired an All-Ireland minor and under-21 medal. He took the under-21s in 1985 when nobody wanted them, but this oak-limbed man nurtured an acorn.

'Cork beat us in the under-21 final. Then I went to England. Derry couldn't get a manager in 1991 and the county board flew me home to talk to me. Flew me home. Can you imagine? Then we won forty-three matches out of forty-seven, the National League and the All-Ireland and then they sacked me.' Not for the first or last time, he collapsed into laughter before shaking his head in bewilderment. 'I can laugh about it now but it wasn't funny at the time.'

For all the laughter, I wondered if he had been traumatised by the experience.

'It took me a long time to get over that sacking after 1993. I just lost the appetite for the game. I lost the heart. I went to Derry matches all right – I was always a Derryman – but it didn't bother me. What bothered me badly was that good players like Johnny McGurk and Henry Downey and Anthony Tohill were getting beaten by thirteen Tyrone men that weren't fit to be on the same pitch. The team was wrecked. If it hadn't happened against Tyrone, it was going to happen against somebody else.

'It was going to happen though. That annoyed me. A great team that should have won two All-Irelands, maybe three, only got one. Those players – McGilligan, Downey, Barton, McGurk, Gormley, Brolly, all of them – they don't come along often. It took so long to build them. They are a special breed and to have it all thrown away by the county board, that bothered me. I suppose the low point was that game in Clones with Seamus McCallan and Pascal Canavan sent off when we lost against Tyrone in 1995. We should have been in our prime but we were gone. Auch, it was tragic.'

To add to his frustrations, that Derry team had one great jewel.

"Anthony Tohill is an exceptional fella. He's a great man, a great friend and the best Gaelic footballer I ever saw, and I'm talking about them all. He had everything. You've had the men who could catch the ball and the men who could kick a free and the men who could carry it. Well, Tohill could do everything. He's like Henry Downey. When he speaks, everyone stops and looks and listens. He's held in the highest respect. His back pocket should be bulging with All-Ireland medals.'

While he had great respect for the likes of Seán Boylan, Coleman was scathing about two groups: the Derry county board and GAA pundits. One criticism of his All-Ireland winning team rankled.

'They said that we lacked quality forwards in 1993. We got to Croke Park and scored fifteen points against Dublin and 1-14 against Cork. That's enough to be scoring.'

ONE-IN-A-ROW JOE

Arguably that team's greatest legacy was to bring to the national stage a man who continues to transcend Gaelic football: Joe Brolly. Winning an All-Ireland was a big dream for him.

'My life was Gaelic football for Dungiven and Derry – everything else was secondary. We won a club Championship in 1991 and then Derry, for the first time, were going into high gear. We had some great players: Brian McGilligan and Anthony Tohill in midfield; [Tony] Scullion and Kieran McKeever, probably the two best corner-backs of their generation; Henry Downey at centre-back – the prince of centre-halves. And two superb free takers – left-footed Enda Gormley and right-footed Anthony Tohill. So we had all of the ingredients there. So that became the obsession. We won a couple of Leagues and then we were the All-Ireland champions in '93.'

Typically Joe had an atypical reaction to that win.

'Since I was a wee child, we used to play in the back garden. The oul fella had built a set of goalposts for us and we would always have the national anthem before we would play the matches. All I ever wanted was to win an All-Ireland; you thought it was some type of Holy Grail, but in fact it was just a massive anti-climax. I remember waking up next morning and thinking: *What the f**k was all the fuss about?*

'It was a total anti-climax. It was like "What's next?" I have a very poor memory for games. I know that people make a big fuss about being All-Ireland champions and club champions and all that, and people always recount all of these things, but they mean nothing to me.'

Brolly's late father Francie, himself a former player, who once told me that he 'was a much better player than Joe ever was' passed on a set of values about Gaelic games which his son has clung to. Joe's well-known antipathy to the GPA (Gaelic Players Association) was very evident in January 2021 when it was announced that there was a changing of the guard in the leadership of the organisation: 'World stock markets slumped on Friday with the news that GPA CEO Paul Flynn is stepping down.'

Not even a global pandemic could quell Brolly's irrepressible spirit: 'The GAA has ruled that *no* collective training will take place until after Easter, with the exception of all secret training, which shall continue as normal.'

71

THE OFFALY ROVERS

Offaly 1959–72

Offaly made a breakthrough of sorts in 1959 when they reached the National League football semi-final, although Kerry beat them easily. Laois beat Offaly in a replay in the first round of the Leinster Championship that year and went on to the Leinster final where they lost to Dublin. Offaly were taking shape the following year, but it needed a catalyst to pull the threads together. Their goalkeeper Willie Nolan had no doubt that the decisive influence was a 'blow-in' from Dublin.

'There was no such thing as a manager then. Peter O'Reilly had trained the Dublin team to win the All-Ireland in 1958, but he fell out with Dublin. Some of our boys knew him from playing club football in Dublin and knew he was at a loose end and asked him to take us on. He loved the idea of the chance to get back at Dublin.

'Carlow were leading us by six points at half-time in our first match in the Championship, but we beat them by three points at the finish. That meant we would be playing in the Leinster semi-final against Dublin. I had seen them play in the previous round against Longford and they beat them by seven goals. I thought,

We're rightly bunched. We beat them by 3-9 to 0-9. It was one of the biggest thrills of my life. Peter [who died in 1998] was the figure-head and was a lovely man, so we were really fired up to win the match for him.'

In the Leinster final, Offaly were unable to raise their game to quite the same standard but scraped a one-point victory over Laois. It was an historic occasion as it was the county's first Leinster senior title in either football or hurling. Their opponents in the All-Ireland semi-final were Down, who had the advantage in terms of experience, having contested the All-Ireland semi-final the previous year.

It was a case of so near yet so far for Willie Nolan when he captained Offaly to a place in the 1961 All-Ireland final. In front of a record crowd that exceeded 90,000, his team lost by a solitary point to the reigning champions Down. The game turned on a controversial incident as Nolan recalled in a face that was a map of concentration.

'We were leading by two points with a couple of minutes to go. Jim McCartan got the ball and charged with it towards the goal and some of our fellas went towards him, and the referee gave them a penalty, which Paddy Doherty scored. We got a point to equalise. Mick Dunne was writing for *The Irish Press* at the time, and in his report the next day, he wrote that it shouldn't have been a penalty. It should have been a free out for charging.'

The final score was Down 1-10, Offaly 2-7. Down won the replay by two points and comfortably beat Kerry in the All-Ireland final. In 1961, Carlow were accounted for again in the Leinster Championship, paving the way for a Leinster semi-final clash with Kildare.

'The match was played in Portlaoise. Kildare were supposed to be the coming team that year. Mind you, they've been saying that nearly every year since and they still haven't come! There was a lot of hype about them with the result that the game attracted a massive crowd. Too many people were let into the ground with the result that the crowd had to be let in on the sideline. The referee wouldn't start the match because of the crowds so he got the two captains to speak to them and get them back a bit more. We got going eventually and beat Kildare to qualify for another Leinster final against Dublin.

'A lot of people in Offaly and elsewhere felt that Dublin should not always have home advantage in Leinster finals and that the match should be taken from Croke Park. The powers that be agreed but where did they hold it? Portlaoise. Sure, they couldn't get in or get out with the chaos. All hell broke out after the match. It wasn't too easy during the game either! There wasn't a final played outside Croke Park since and there won't be one either.'

Having accounted for Dublin in the Leinster final, Offaly brushed aside the challenge of Roscommon in the All-Ireland semi-final. Was he nervous captaining the team in an All-Ireland final?

'If you're not nervous before an All-Ireland, there's something wrong with you. It was the thrill of my life, but I was as nervous as a kitten. Basically, all I had to do was keep the backs from roaming up the field.

'I was lucky I had a great full-back line: Greg Hughes, Johnny Egan and Paddy McCormack. Paddy went on to win two All-Irelands in 1971 and '72. He was a hard man and a great footballer. He ended his career at full-back, but he was a better corner-back. You have to remember it was much harder be a goalie then. If you went for the ball then you got five or six lads on top of you in the square. Nowadays goalies get so much protection from referees that no one can even get near them.

'We also had great players up the field. Phil O'Reilly was a great right half-back. Our centre-back was Mick Brady. He was too classy for that position. He was a much better natural footballer than Jim McCartan, but McCartan was a tough man who could push him out of the way.

'Losing that match was effectively the end for that first Offaly team. My great hero Mick Casey had been playing for years and Seán Foran likewise, and we didn't have replacements for them. Offaly won the minor All-Ireland in 1964 and it wasn't until some of those lads came through that Offaly achieved success.

'We were invited to America a while after losing the 1962 Leinster final. We played New York twice. My brother, Peter, was playing for them. I stayed on for a few weeks after the tour was over because I had two brothers over there and came back in November. Offaly had played two matches in the League by that stage. Tommy Furlong, an older brother of Martin, was in goal. The Reverend Chairman of Offaly at the time was very annoyed with me for staying on in America. Although Peter O'Reilly was supposed to be in charge, the Reverend Chairman had the final say and there was no way he was going to let me play again. My heart was broken because I wasn't playing football so I went back to America to stay. I started playing with Offaly and New York.'

Offaly won their first-ever All-Ireland in 1971, beating Galway. Twelve months later, they inflicted Kerry's heaviest-ever defeat in an All-Ireland final (1-19 to 0-13) upon them to successfully retain their All-Ireland title.

Longford's Jimmy Flynn was a big admirer of the star midfielder on that Offaly team.

'If you're talking about great footballers, one of the lads I would have to mention is Willie Bryan. We had some great tussles. I met him a few years after we retired and he said, "I've a great photograph of you and me up in the air catching the ball and we both have our hands around the ball – but I have mine on the inside!" I thought it was a great remark.'

NO PAT ANSWERS

Pat Mangan played for Kildare seniors from 1964 to 1979 when he retired from inter-county football without ever being dropped for a match. While Mangan feels that Kildare were in the main the architects of their own destruction, he also believes there were other contributory factors to explain their failure to make the breakthrough.

'One reason we didn't win was that we played Offaly a few times in Leinster finals, and although they had great players, it's fair to say they exploited the rules to the fullest, to put it as diplomatically as I can. We were a very skilful team and never resorted to the physical. It's not that we weren't able to because we had a lot of big fellas, but we weren't that sort of side.

'Offaly's Paddy McCormack was a great character and had a reputation as the Iron Man of Rhode. Mind you, I saw someone putting it up to him once in a club match and it wasn't so obvious who was the iron man! Another great player on that Offaly team was Willie Bryan. He wouldn't be associated with the type of football I spoke of earlier, a class player who played football as it should be played. He never resorted to dirty play. He didn't need to, but it wasn't his nature to anyway. He always had a great leap when he came in for the ball and had a lovely drop-kick – though he always gave the impression that he wasn't a hundred per cent fit.

'Offaly were a very, very tough, physical team, but at the time refereeing wasn't as strict as it is today and usually they didn't take much notice of what was going on off the ball. The umpires were only there to put up the flags. Offaly were a very, very good team and had a lot of skilful players, but I think everybody knows some of those guys prided themselves on being hard men. Today, people speak about winning at all costs, but even back then that Offaly team had that attitude.'

72

THE WEE COUNTY HIT THE BIG TIME

Louth 1950–57

His eyes glazed with nervous energy, but his force crackled like electricity.

Before Louth won their only All-Ireland in 1957, their full-back Tom Conlon gave a rousing speech when he recalled losing the 1950 final to Mayo that was of epic proportions: 'The way I feel is that if I break a leg today then I will get up on the other one and play on. I expect everyone to do the same.'

The defeat to Mayo in 1950 was most disappointing as the side held a slender lead going to the closing stages, only to be denied by a late Mayo goal. Three years later, Louth would again be on the edge of glory. A famous Louth double was achieved in 1953 in Leinster when the minor and senior footballers won their respective Championships, the minors beating Kildare and the senior side beating Wexford, only to lose out to Kerry at the semi-final stage. Sunday, 22 September 1957 would change everything when Louth became All-Ireland Senior champions for their only time beating Cork by 1-9 to 1-7. The Cork side included Pádraig Harrington's father, Paddy.

That year, Louth were the surprise packet in the Championship, beating Carlow and Wexford before upsetting the odds by beating Dublin and 1956 Leinster champions Kildare on the way to the provincial title, powered by their ace forward Jimmy McDonnell, who scored 5-5 in those two games alone. In the All-Ireland semi-final, they met Tyrone, led by the great Iggy Jones, but Louth won, 0-13 to 0-7. The Rebels were 1-7 to 0-9 up with minutes remaining in the All-Ireland final when Kevin Beahan's sideline kick was sent to the net by Seán Cunningham for the decisive score.

That game was full of fascinating subplots. One of the last Mayo men to have won an All-Ireland title was the late Dan O'Neill. Originally from Castlebar, O'Neill ended up playing for Louth in their All-Ireland win, having been stationed there as a Garda. He lined out for Mayo previous to that, winning a National League medal and the Connacht Championship in 1955.

Ollie Reilly was one of the few players who could contain Kevin Heffernan, one of the finest corner-forwards Dublin ever produced, and with his lifelong friend Patsy Coleman, the pair – who patrolled the right side of the Louth defence – had a great understanding for coping with Heffernan and other dangerous corner-forwards. In the Leinster final against Dublin that year, Ollie broke his nose in a clash with Heffernan. He only learned of Louth's victory over Dublin from Michael O'Hehir's broadcast while he was receiving medical attention in the Mater hospital. Dermot O'Brien, Seán Óg Flood, Dan O'Neill, Stephen White, Kevin Behan and Reilly were the only players to start in the same positions throughout the campaign. A recurring ankle ligament problem meant that former Louth great Eddie Boyle had to strap up Ollie's ankle before the final.

The Louth forward line was powered by Jimmy McDonnell, a senior ESB fitter at the time, and 21-year-old goalkeeper Seán Óg Flood, who was working as an organiser on the Rural Electrification

Scheme. In fact, Flood became something of a poster boy. Shortly before the All-Ireland, he was featured on the cover of a magazine demonstrating washing machines. Another ESB man on the pitch that day, but playing for Cork, was Seán Moore from the ESB station at Marina. (Five players from the 1971 winning All-Ireland Offaly football team worked in ESB.)

LEAVE IT TO MRS O'BRIEN'S BOY
Louth were captained by Dermot O'Brien. He had been having intensive treatment on a shoulder injury and didn't travel with the rest of the panel to Croke Park on the day of the All-Ireland final. Consequently, when O'Brien got to the stadium, he was locked out of the Cusack Stand and had to hurry around to the Hogan Stand side to get in, the PA in the stadium calling for him to go to the Louth dressing room the entire time. Afterwards, O'Brien conceded that it had taken him the entire first half to settle down.

His club mate Patsy Coleman was the original skipper for the 1957 season, but he broke his arm against Dublin. O'Brien went on to become a showbusiness legend and his smash hit 'The Merry Ploughboy' became, with 'The Hucklebuck', one of the anthems of the 1960s.

73

THE GREEN AND RED OF MAYO

Mayo 1936

The first Connacht team to win an All-Ireland was Galway in 1934. Two years later, Mayo won their first All-Ireland. The star of the Mayo team was Henry Kenny, father of former Taoiseach and now television presenter Enda Kenny.

'A mythology developed in the county about the 1936 team, not least because they went fifty-three games without defeat. People thought they could jump over telegraph poles.

'My father went to teacher training college in De La Salle, Waterford. Times were very tough and the food was so scarce there that my father said you needed to have the plates nailed to the tables! After he qualified, he went to teach in Connemara and cycled sixteen miles to train for the club team and sixty miles to Castlebar to play for Mayo. One of his teammates was Paddy Moclair, who was the first bank official to play county football and he cycled from Clare. I've seen telegrams from the time from the Mayo County Board and they were told: "Train yourself – you've been selected to play."

'My father was particularly famous for his fielding of the ball.

He grew up on the same street with Patsy Flannelly, another of the stars of the 1936 team. They had no football as kids so they went to the butcher's shop and got pigs' bladders from him to use instead of footballs. Dad always said: "If you could catch those, you could catch anything."

'The other thing he was noted for was his ability after he caught the ball in the air to turn before his feet touched the ground. When my brothers and I started playing, his advice to us was always: "Be moving before the ball comes." He found a big change in the way the game was played, especially when they started wearing lighter boots like the soccer players. When he saw a pair of them, he said: "These boots are like slippers." He didn't have much time for the solo runs and that's why he called it "the tippy toe". He said he would "beat the solo runner with his cap".

'Dad had great admiration for athletes. That's probably why the player he admired most was Kildare's Larry Stanley, who of course holds a unique distinction of winning All-Irelands with Kildare [1919] and Dublin [1923] and of representing Ireland in the Olympics [in the high jump at the 1924 games in Paris].

'In 1936, Séamus O'Malley captained the Mayo team to the All-Ireland. He travelled to Dublin by train the evening before the match. On the day of the match, he announced that he could not stay for the celebrations and got a lift back to Mayo after the match. The Sam Maguire Cup was put in the boot of the car. He had to go to his work as a teacher the next morning, so he left for work by bicycle with the Sam Maguire Cup strapped on his back! The times have changed!'

MAGIC HANDS

Tom McNicholas was the last survivor of the 1936 Mayo team. At ninety-five years of age, he was still driving his car, and his former career as a teacher was evident in the clarity of his directions to his home. He retained vivid memories of that team and was best equipped to give me an objective assessment of Henry Kenny.

'There wasn't the same cult of personality back then, but there was no question that the star of our team was Henry. He was wonderful at catching balls in the air. He had great duels with the mighty Kerry midfielder Paddy Kennedy and was probably one of the very few players, if not the only footballer, who could hold his own with Kennedy. This was particularly the case in the All-Ireland semi-final in Roscommon when we beat Kerry 1-5 to 0-6 in 1936, when Kennedy was the new star in the game.

'Henry was known as "the man with the magic hands". He had big hands and he could hold the ball in one hand. Now our game has become more like basketball, there is so much handpassing. Back then though, it was a game of catch and kick, and nobody did it better than Henry. I don't think any of our team would believe the way the game has changed, especially the emphasis on stopping teams from playing and above all the number of times people pass the ball backwards. We believed in positive football and playing your own game rather than the opposition's.'

74

THE TRIPLE CROWN

Sleacht Néill 2016

What is right is never impossible.

It has been said that Charles Kickham rose like Slievenamon (he wrote 'Slievenamon', the song most synonymous with County Tipperary) above the men of his time. As the result of an accident in his youth, he had impaired eyesight and was almost totally deaf – yet he wrote *Knocknagow* the most popular Irish novel up to the mid-twentieth century, running to twenty-eight editions between 1873 and 1944. Fellow Fenian John O'Leary wrote of him: 'He knew the Irish people thoroughly ... and from thoroughness of knowledge came thoroughness of sympathy ... and, anyway, what merits or demerits they might have, they were his people.'

Judge William Keogh sentenced him to fourteen years' penal servitude, at least to some extent in retaliation for the articles he had written in the *Irish People* about the 'hanging judge', who sentenced the McCormack brothers to be executed unjustly for the murder of a land steward. *Knocknagow* has provided the anthem for clubs in the GAA. Mat the Thrasher's *cri de coeur* 'for the credit of the little village' continues to resonate deeply in the GAA.

Having played camogie for Derry, Rosanna McAleese is keenly aware of the sociological differentiation of clubs in the county.

'My home club is Eoghan Rua Coleraine, situated on the North Coast in County Derry. I was lucky enough to come into a strong senior panel built on many hard years of struggling by gritty northern women. This set-up of girls went on to win three consecutive Ulster titles, and two consecutive All-Irelands. To play at a senior level in Croke Park at age fifteen in my club jersey was something that I only now realise the significance of, and maybe that fearless approach was an asset I didn't know I had. I have had All-Ireland success playing at different levels for County Derry, but club camogie has also been my passion and priority.

'I remember reading that if you draw a straight line from the Loughshore to the Glenshane Pass and another from there to Derry city, you'll find fifteen of the county's sixteen senior county Derry clubs either on or within a couple of miles of it. Except for my home club Eoghan Rua, sitting on the North Coast. Playing the part of my youth's anchor, Eoghan Rua pitch was the backdrop to some of the most important events in my life.

'However, I feel there is often a reluctance to accept that the experience of GAA in the north and the south can be very different. You have my mum's native, a true collective of like-minded Gaels, agreeing both on the experience of the north's history, and the vision for the north's future. Eoghan Rua is not a Sleacht Néill. My dad as the chairman is a prime example of this – a Royal Portrush golfer whose love of the GAA was ignited long after his own sporting days had passed.

'A club in a town shared by nationalists and unionists, the key figures being largely blow-ins from nationalist areas who have been brought to the North Coast by jobs, loves or a wish to wake up to the waves. But different does not mean less. My club's recent years of unprecedented success stand on the shoulders of men and women who formed and sustained the club since 1958 – the Joe Passmores, the Schira McGoldricks and the Brendan McLernons having enough grit and passion to turn any abandoned soccer field into a place to raise camogs. A memory of my dad scraping sectarian graffiti off the club's mobile changing rooms as we tried to establish our first pitch. Those who laced up their boots to kick a Gaelic football in 1980s Coleraine. Maybe a tested love of the game is as significant as a habitual one.'

AN UNFORGETTABLE YEAR

That tight-knit community was key to the success of Sleacht Néill. In 2016, they achieved a sporting miracle: they became Ulster champions in three codes – football, hurling and camogie. For the club members, their epic journey was not ultimately about silverware – sweet though it was! At its core it was a profound statement of their identity. For the current generation, the club is a sanctuary from the pressures of daily life. For the older members though, it was a bridge over the troubled waters of the Troubles: 'Being a member means being Irish but, when you boil it down, it's about being Sleacht Néill.'

75

TEAM THOMOND

Thomond College 1978

There have been many remarkable university teams like Canon Michael O'Brien's UCC, who won eight consecutive Fitzgibbon Cups in the 1980s. One of the most memorable club teams was the 1978 All-Ireland Club Football Championship winners Thomond College. The team were managed by the late Dave Weldrick. He was one of the first-ever analysts on *The Sunday Game*.

At the time, Thomond College hosted Ireland's training college for PE teachers and, in earlier years, had attracted huge names like Kerry's Jimmy Deenihan, Dublin's Brian Mullins and Fran Ryder, and rugby legend Tony Ward.

Born into a family steeped in Gaelic football history, Pat Spillane played with his local club in Templenoe. His father Tom died when he was just eight years old, leaving his mother Maura to take over the running of the family pub while simultaneously raising four children. Tom had played with Kerry, won a Railway Cup medal with Munster and a Kerry County Championship with the Legion club, and Maura was one of the Lynes of Cleeney,

Killarney, whose brothers had won All-Ireland medals with Kerry in the 1940s and '50s.

Pat attended St Brendan's Seminary in Killarney, that great nursery that has provided the Kingdom with some of its greatest players down through the years. In fact, Spillane made his Croke Park debut as a member of the St Brendan's team who were defeated by St Pats of Cavan in the All-Ireland Colleges final of 1972. He subsequently went to Limerick, where he studied to be a PE teacher at Thomond College of Education (TCE was integrated into the University of Limerick in 1991). He was later joined by his brother, Mick, at Thomond, and both played on the college football team where Pat captained the side to victory in Croke Park in the All-Ireland Senior Club Football Championship in 1978. The 2-14 to 1-3 win over St John's of Antrim gave Spillane his only All-Ireland club winners' medal. It was the start of a memorable year for him. He won his second senior All-Ireland medal with Kerry (start of the three-in-a-row) and won the first of his Texaco Awards for Footballer of the Year (his second came in 1986).

Thomond had faced a much tougher challenge in the All-Ireland semi-final when they beat St Mary's 1-12 to 1-8. The teams were level at the interval, and it was St Mary's who looked the more likely winners as they made most of the running in the early stages of the second half. However, the star-studded Thomond side put in a strong finish, and seven unanswered points helped them to a somewhat flattering four-point winning margin. John Kent led the fight for the Connacht champions. While Pat Spillane was prominent for Thomond, he was no one-man team. Other inter-county players of note on the team included Galway's Brian Talty and Declan Smith, Mayo's Richie Bell and Sligo's Mick Kilcoyne.

Spillane pays tribute to the new president of the GAA Larry McCarthy's role at the time.

'We were students together in the then National College for

Physical Education. I played alongside him on both the college football and hurling teams. Though he wasn't the greatest goalkeeper in the club, he was Mr GAA in the college. Officially, he was club secretary/treasurer – in truth Larry did everything, from booking the buses to travelling to games to washing the jerseys. Such was his influence that we went from being a Division Two team in the higher-education sector to being the top club side in the country when we won the All-Ireland club title in 1978.'

PIONEERING PAT

Thomond's progress in 1978 attracted huge media attention. Spillane attributes the victory largely to the four-game series Thomond (it required three replays to separate the teams, and the second replay went to extra time) had with the reigning All-Ireland champions Austin Stacks, which he contends was perhaps the greatest series of games in the club competition.

'That series of games tuned us in, but they had other advantages. We trained like professionals, we had video analysis, the whole thing. We played Nemo down in Páirc Uí Chaoimh, but I couldn't see us being beaten. The one thing with Nemo was you always knew what to expect. You could beat them for fifty-nine minutes, but they were capable of a winning goal in the last minute. We beat them handy enough that day; I think that as Nemo teams go it might have been a transitional side.

'You have to admire them. They're like Dr Crokes in Kerry – they've a small following and a small population base, and they play a possession game. Nemo live and die for their club. The likes of Billy Morgan, Dinny Allen, Jimmy Kerrigan were hugely involved. The big problem for most GAA clubs is golf, with ex-players taking up golf and putting nothing back. Nemo are the exact opposite; all the former players get back into coaching.

'Some people like to slag them off, but they're the template for every club. Their facilities are second to none; they're one of the finest sides in the history of the club Championship. They're everything a club ought to aspire to.

'Billy Morgan will probably rank as one of the greatest club managers of all time with Nemo Rangers. I have heard it said that he would die for Nemo but would only get wounded for Cork.'

PART IV

Teams for All Seasons

'The Apaches have a great saying:
"We are who we are, but we are who we were, also."'
                                        SEÁN BOYLAN

The famous Dutch soccer team of the 1970s won nothing but are regarded as great for the impact they made, the entertainment they gave and how they changed the sport. Their star player Johan Cruyff claimed: 'Quality without results is pointless. Results without quality is boring.'

The teams who feature in this section were all teams of great quality and were never boring. Some of them may not have won a huge number of trophies, but they were and remain much loved teams.

In their barren years their fans learned that quiet isn't always peace as they suffered a haemorrhage of the soul. We braved the belly of the beast as we watched our rivals take all the silverware. Our team's blunders become our burdens. Then the day of victory comes and changes our children's birthright and we finally find light in this seemingly never-ending shade.

The teams featured in this section brought light into dark moments.

76

MIGHTY MEN

Meath 1996–99

Forti et fideli nihil difficile.
To the brave and faithful nothing is impossible.

One of the great mysteries of Irish life is that I have never under-stood why there has not been a campaign to consider Seán Boylan for the presidency of Ireland. Leaving aside his contribution to the GAA, his role as a healer, his deep connection with Irish history and, above all, his unique ability to connect with old and young; male and female; rich and poor surely make him ideal for the post. Everybody comes away from an encounter with him feeling better about themselves.

Having conquered the football world in the 1980s, Boylan did the same thing in the 1990s. The two teams were very different. The spine of the first team were seasoned veterans. In the immortal words of Colm O'Rourke, they were a group of 'thugs and dirty basta*ds'. O'Rourke was at pains to point out that Boylan never sent them out to intimidate opponents. On the other hand, he directed them never to take a step back from an opponent.

In marked contrast, the 1990s incarnation of the Meath team were driven by young players like Trevor Giles and Graham Geraghty. They were incredibly talented, but meek and mild they were not.

THE QUEST

Boylan has a fascinating background. His father, the man he still calls 'the Boss', was steeped in the Irish War of Independence and the Civil War and was a friend of Michael Collins – though he never spoke about it. The family also have a strong connection with the Hill of Tara.

'My great-great grandparents came from Tara, and for hundreds of years before that my family were herbalists on Tara. There were seven or eight herbs that have been handed down since the thirteenth century. There's a herb called parsley piert – it's been native of Skellig Michael since the tenth century and I take some of that every day. Horsetail, I take some of that as well. There's a herb called ox-eye daisy and it regenerates tissue.

'You can actually go there, and there's people who walk it every day, and you can stand on the hill or any part of it and you can turn towards Slane, over towards Rossnaree. That energy is there and it becomes part of you. It helps to root you and it helps to earth you, and it keeps you from getting too many notions about yourself. Right beside it, on the Dunslaney road from Tara, my great-great grandparents came from there. The house was burned and they came to live in Dunboyne, and they were attacked in Dunboyne as well.

'They were eighty-five when the house was burned to the ground and the house where my grandparents came to, that was burned as well. My great-great-grandmother's people were evicted off a farm the day after they'd paid the rent, and the funny thing about it is that you didn't hold animosity for the people.

'There was a pride of place that was there. That sense of place is a huge thing. There's certain things you can't take out of it, you can't change. You can't take the Boyne Valley out of it, you can't take Slane, you can't take Oldcastle, you can't take Loughcrew. There are centuries of wisdom there. We might not all have been able to absorb it, but at least it was there for us to take the energy in, and I like that about the county. There's so many Dublin people living in Meath now and they're part and parcel of the community, and that's the way it is, and that's the way it should be, and you'd hope that that would continue.'

Boylan imbued his young Meath team with his love for the county and his energy. They fed off his resilience and never-say-die attitude. A late point from a difficult angle by Brendan Reilly sealed a 2-9 to 1-11 victory for Meath over Mayo in the 1996 All-Ireland final replay.

Boylan wanted another All-Ireland to confirm the team's greatness. On 26 September 1999, Meath beat Cork by 1-11 to 1-8 in the All-Ireland final, thus winning their second All-Ireland title in four years and their seventh in all. In the process, they denied Cork the double, the hurlers having claimed the Liam MacCarthy Cup two weeks previously.

77

THE CLARE CHAMPIONS

Clare 1974–78

In 1995, Ger Loughnane and his back-room team assembled a collection of all bachelors whose status as a dream team had more to do with potential than achievement. In a county where hurling has been a painful passion, he wanted the doors of victory to be opened to his team.

The last time Clare had won the Munster final in 1932, Éamon de Valera had just been elected Taoiseach for the first time. The Clare fans had not any success to savour, simply false dawns and shattered expectations, but they waited and hoped, sang and dreamed. That anticipation, togetherness, fervour and love of the county team, even in bad times, was awesome. Even when the county team treated the fans to some dreadful performances, they never wavered in their commitment to the team. Loughnane brought the lessons of his playing career to bear on the task. What is sometimes forgotten is that Loughnane was Clare's first player to win an All-Star (in 1974 at right half-back; a second came three years later). His team won two League titles. He looks back on those years through the prism of missed opportunities.

'Justin McCarthy was brought in to coach the hurling skills and Colum Flynn to do the physical coaching, and Fr Harry Bohan was the manager. With the three of them, the whole scene was transformed. They brought a professionalism that was never there before and everyone responded initially. They tried to eliminate the differences that had been there between parishes. What club you came from didn't matter. All that mattered was ability. They brought in players from intermediate and junior clubs, from all parts of the county. They also looked for certain qualities from the people they brought in. They wanted no player who was going to act the maggot.

'For his time, Justin was a good coach. He was an outsider, had won an All-Ireland with Cork, was very articulate and thorough in his approach. I found him really good, but a lot of players didn't take to him. There was conflict between himself and Colum as to how much physical training would be done. The mix wasn't right between the back-room personnel and this led to many conflicts.

'Justin was very professional. He would always be first to training. He always presented himself very well. There wouldn't even be a hair out of place. Even though he had a great knowledge of hurling, he lacked the ability to get inside players' heads. He wasn't able to make that vital link which would enable us to get out of the old ways of thinking. He did great work. Sometimes you've got to drive the horse over the fence. Bringing him up to the fence and asking him to jump it wasn't enough. If he's forced over the first fence, he'll jump all the others. We didn't have anyone to force us over the fence.

'Harry was badly treated by the county board. There was a massive conflict between what he wanted and the county board officers, who were stuck in a time warp. They weren't prepared to come forward with things like meals after training, proper facilities, proper gear and proper travelling expenses. There was a constant battle between Harry and the Clare County Board.

'We didn't have the harmony that we needed. We had a coach who was out of sync with the trainer and both were pulling out of the manager. The manager was also being dragged by the county board. Harry should have said: "Colum, you do this. Justin, you do that." It was a great lesson for me. I wasn't going to fall between two stools. It's much better to prevent problems arising before they develop. It's better to create a situation where everybody gravitates towards you and asks, "What'll we do next?"'

REGRETS

Hanging up on a wall in Loughnane's home is the following quote from Calvin Coolidge: 'Nothing in the world can take the place of persistence. Talent will not; nothing is more common than unsuccessful men with talent. Genius will not; unrewarded genius is almost a proverb. Education will not; the world is full of educated derelicts. Persistence and determination alone are not omnipotent. The slogan "press on" has solved and always will solve the problems of the human race.'

Loughnane's playing career is a testimony to the value of persistence. Most of his stories about his playing days are distinguished by wry self-deprecation.

'I was an average player, but I was able to play at my best in the big games. So many players play way below their best when big games come around. The bigger the reputation of the player I was marking, the better I played. I made the most of what I had. I had a very poor left-hand side. I wasn't great in the air, but I was able to disguise my faults and to make the most of what I had. As time went on, I developed very good skill by consistent practice. Whenever we went into training, I played as if it was a Championship game. A lot of players would be pucking around, but I believed in doing everything at the maximum pace.'

As Clare manager, Loughnane always encouraged his players to air their views in part because it strengthened the collective mindset, the sense of 'we'. As a Clare player, that had not been his experience.

'I first played for Clare, with Enda O'Connor, against Tipperary in 1972. What struck me most when I first went into the dressing room was that the Newmarket-on-Fergus players were on one side and the Clarecastle players on the other and there was no communication between them. I made myself as small as I could in the middle and said nothing!'

If a school report had been written on the Clare team Loughnane starred on, it would have read 'good potential but underachieving'.

'I played on a really terrific team. It was very similar to the team that won two All-Irelands. The half-back line was particularly well known. Seán Stack was centre-back, I was on one wing and Seán Hehir on the other. We understood each other's play very well. For its time we were a terrific half-back line, but I wouldn't compare us with the team we had in the 1990s. Liam Doyle was better than me, Seánie [McMahon] was a better player than Seán Stack, and Dalo [Anthony Daly] was a better player than Seán Hehir. Seán Stack was the most talented of the three of us. He had fantastic stick work; Seán Hehir and I were more of a manufactured talent. Seán Hehir had a real hardness about him. He was a man who would get the job done and wouldn't let his man past him.

'Séamus Durack was a great character. He was the very same as Fitzie [Davy Fitzgerald] – totally self-centred, which you have to be if you're a goalkeeper. He's had fantastic success in business and I've terrific regard for him.

'The best character of all on the team was Noel Casey. He was known as "The Case". He'd turn up for training and he'd belt a few balls into the net from the 21-yard line. He hardly ever did any serious training, but he got vital scores for Clare in big matches. He had this charismatic personality that drew people to him. Harry and himself got on great. If it was another person in charge, he'd be dumped out the gate and never get another chance, but he was a character everyone really, really liked.

'Jackie O'Gorman was an inspirational figure. He was the first Clare player I ever met who was always totally confident. He would talk down an opponent's strengths, to the degree that you'd think you were playing a Junior B player of forty-four.

'Most of the rest of us were the one age, like the two O'Connors and John Callinan. John had lightning pace and was a great man to score a point. He played a lot of great matches for Clare, but although he was terrifically talented, he had the same hang-ups as your normal Clare hurler had at the time. He didn't have the inner arrogance you need. He's a brilliant person, with the highest ability, and he is an exceptional administrator.

'When we were in Dublin, John Callinan and myself would have to pay our train fare home and then try to get it back from the county board. That was a really tough battle. We learned to wait 'til the treasurer had five or six pints in him to ask him for the money! It was absolutely terrible. They wanted you down to play but they didn't want to pay for it!'

In Loughnane's playing days, the story of Clare hurling in Championship games alternated between the admirable and exasperating: a mixture of sometimes honourable failure and Sunday afternoons on which the supporters could find nothing to praise but the weather. On one of those days, Loughnane learned a lesson he would never forget.

'In the League final replay in 1976 against Kilkenny, I was marking Billy Fitzpatrick. At one stage the ball was in the far corner with Mick Brennan. Billy took off down the wing. I said to myself, "I'll let him off; I'll chance it." Billy caught the ball coming across the square and stuck it in the net! The lesson stays firmly in my mind to this day. You can never take a chance against a good team. One moment of laziness can be the losing of a match.'

78

THE WICKLOW WAY

Wicklow 1952–55

Jimmy Magee always lived up to his nickname 'the memory man' as he trawled through the history of the GAA in the corridors of his mind.

'Wicklow have always produced great footballers though never enough at the one time, like the county's first All-Star in 1990, Kevin O'Brien. Of course he was the star of a great Baltinglass team that famously won the All-Ireland club title that year. It was great that he won that All-Star, but if someone of his talent played for Dublin or Kerry then he would have won many more.

'In more recent years, Kevin went on to be part of Mick O'Dwyer's background team when Micko managed the Garden County. He won eight All-Irelands with Kerry, two Leinster finals with Kildare and a Leinster final with Laois. In 2007, he sprinkled his magic dust again and took them from being ranked the second-worst team in the country to the dizzy heights of a place in the top twelve in 2009. He led them to a Tommy Murphy Cup. It was a remarkable achievement, but think what he would have done if he had a player like Kevin O'Brien in his prime.'

The trouble we brew today we drink tomorrow.

'I sometimes wonder though what would have happened if Micko could have got a time machine and had the finest Wicklow team I have ever seen, the team of the mid-1950s, then he would have taken the county to great heights. What did that '50s team have that Wicklow teams generally lacked? Some genuinely outstanding players. What were they missing? With all due respect to those involved, they hadn't the people in management or in administration to harness the talent they had. I have huge respect for the many volunteers who give so much of their time to the GAA in either coaching or administration. But equally I understand why some people will say that teams succeed not because of the county boards but in spite of them. However, there are teams that don't flourish the way they should because they don't get the leadership they need either on the sideline or on the county board. I think that Wicklow team of the 1950s are the perfect illustration of that. If they'd had a Mick O'Dwyer over them, they would have won things.

'Among not only Wicklow's finest but one of Ireland's greatest was the late Gerry O'Reilly in the 1950s. He was right half-back on the Team of the Century for players who never won All-Ireland medals, and he was one of the nominees for the Team of the Millennium. He was a sensational wing-back, but the only time you'd see him play was on St Patrick's Day in Croke Park, playing for Leinster. That evening, people would be saying what a marvellous player Gerry O'Reilly was and how they'd have to wait for another year to see him perform again. He was tenacious, a good kicker, worked hard and never seemed to play badly. He is at the top or close to the top of any list of great players who never won an All-Ireland medal.

'In more recent times, the player who reminded me most of Gerry was Kerry's Páidí Ó Sé. They even looked a bit like each other. They both knew that the first job of a back is to stop a forward from scoring. Jim Rogers was another star not only of Wicklow but of Gaelic football at that time. He was on the Leinster team that recorded the famous four-in-a-row Railway Cup wins in 1952, '53, '54 and '55.'

Mícheál O'Muircheartaigh shares the high opinion of O'Reilly.

'You know the difference straight away between the casual fan and the real thing. The casual fan will ask: "Who will win on Sunday?" The serious fan will ask: "Who was the greatest player you ever saw?" Or even more tellingly: "Who is the greatest player never to win an All-Ireland?"

'There's Gerry O'Reilly, Jim Rogers and Andy Phillips of Wicklow, and if you moved north, you would have Iggy Jones of Tyrone, P. T. Treacy of Fermanagh, and if you go west you have the great Gerry O'Malley of Roscommon and of course Dermot Earley, who played so well for Roscommon for so long.'

O'Reilly believed passionately that the 1940s and 1950s were a vintage era for Gaelic football and was not too impressed by the changes that have taken place in the game. On a visit home from his residence in Wales some years ago, Gerry told me about the many characters who he lined out with.

'The standard is nowhere near as high now as it was in our time. In fact, it's a different game now with so much handpassing. The other huge change is that positional play means nothing. Players now can turn up anywhere. A right half-back can pop up to score a goal.'

O'Reilly attributed the failure of the Wicklow team in the 1950s to the inadequacies of the county board.

'We had a great team from 1953 to '55, with players like Andy Phillips. While we had players to match anybody, our problem was that we had the worst county board in Ireland. The training was terrible. They had the slowest player on the team out in front when we were running laps. I would always have the fastest guy out in front. Is it any wonder we never won anything?'

79

OUT OF THE WEST

Sligo 1997–2007

The memories of years of defeats were obliterated like a downpour after a long drought.

For an entire generation, the defining image of Sligo football was the penetrating runs of Eamonn O'Hara. In full flight, he lit up the pitch like a flash of forked lightning, flashing brilliantly, thrilling and, from the opposition's point of view, frightening.

In 2007, he produced the defining image of the Football Championship in the Connacht final against Galway. He took a pass from David Kelly fifty yards from the Galway goal. With the defence trailing desperately in his wake, he made over thirty yards before unleashing a rocket of a shot to the roof of the net. A thirty-two-year famine had come to an end for Sligo. In the words of Eamonn O'Hara:

'We said before the game, it's not about heroes today, it's not about a fella getting ten or twelve points on the board or about personal vendettas. It's all about working as hard for the Sligo team, putting your neck on the line. Fellas did that and it's what it took. We hadn't done that completely in thirty-two years.'

The arrival of Mickey Moran was a catalyst in the upturn in the county's fortunes.

'We started to do well in the League in 1997, '98 and '99. We beat Kerry in the League in '97 in Kerry, and we also beat Dublin in Markievicz Park, which was great. We were always capable of creating a shock. The bigger the team, the more we liked it and the better we played.'

The year 2000 was a turning point for O'Hara and the team as a whole.

'We beat Mayo in the Connacht Championship by three points in Markievicz Park. It was a huge relief to finally beat one of the big teams in Connacht. We kind of lost the run of ourselves before playing Galway in the Connacht semi-final, thinking we were about to make a breakthrough. Galway were on fire that day and we failed to get a single score in the first half. Everything they tried, even the most outlandish, came off. Niall Finnegan got a point from such an acute angle that it defied the laws of physics. We lost the game in the end by eighteen points. A lot of fingers were pointed at me after the game. I learned a valuable lesson that day though. After the game against Mayo, I had been treated like a hero so I discovered that there's only six inches between a pat on the back and a kick in the ass.'

A summer in Chicago playing with St Brendan's refreshed O'Hara and his return coincided with Peter Ford's arrival as Sligo manager.

'Peter brought that arrogance that Sligo had never had before and his attitude, his level of preparation and his organisation were eye-openers to us all. Sometimes he trained with us and he wouldn't ask us to do anything that he wouldn't do himself. We did really well in a lot of games in the qualifiers. Beating Kildare in a thriller in Croke Park was the start of it. Looking back now, while those wins – like defeating Tyrone – were great, we won nothing. While we played well at times, we have nothing to show for it. We had the beating of Armagh in both games, but we missed vital chances.

'I suppose for most people it was a story of "should have beens" and "what ifs", and people say we should have got a penalty. In fact, what happened was that I was one of four players to miss scoring chances and that's what cost us the game. Most Sligo people saw it as a good year because we reached an All-Ireland quarter-final, but when I saw Kieran McGeeney lifting the Sam Maguire Cup in 2002 six weeks after they beat us, I was thinking it was a bad year because we had won nothing.'

O'Hara used his time playing for Ireland in the International Rules series as a personal research project.

'I was mixing and sharing rooms with players who had won All-Irelands or experienced great success. I saw myself as a messenger who would relay what I learned to the Sligo team. The big players on the Irish team were all winners. In Sligo we went out to play games in hope. These guys went out in expectation. Our mentality was that we were happy with a good performance. This attitude came from the county board, from managers, from the general public and from friends and did seep into our conscious-ness which led to "Ah well, sure we never expected too much" syndrome. It was because of our attitude that we had never been good enough to win anything. What was different about Sligo in 2007 was that our attitude was no longer about doing well but about winning and doing whatever it took to get a title at last.'

O'Hara plays down the significance of his own goal in the Connacht final.

'If we had taken all the chances we had in the game, my goal would have had no importance. It wasn't about me; it was about winning the Nestor Cup at last.'

80

THE SCRIPT OF HURT

Mayo 2012–21

'I have loved the beauty in all things.'
JOHN KEATS

People pay tribute in interesting ways.

In 1821, 25-year-old poet John Keats died from tuberculosis and was buried in Rome the following day. Only after his death was his poetry appreciated. Twenty months later the famed Romantic poet Percy B. Shelley was drowned in Rome and is buried in the same cemetery. A copy of Keats' poetry was found in his pocket. Oscar Wilde visited Keats' grave and said it was the holiest place in Rome. He wrote a beautiful poem in tribute called 'The Grave of Keats'.

Other tributes are more startling. It did come as a surprise that in 2020 Pat Gilroy claimed on national television that the current Mayo team were 'the second greatest team of all time'.

Nonetheless, Mayo's consistency has to be admired. In 2012 and '20, they contested All-Ireland finals; in 2013, '16 and '17 they lost All-Ireland finals to Jim Gavin's much vaunted five-in-a-row team by a single point each time, and in 2014, they only lost to Kerry in the All-Ireland semi-final after extra time in a replay.

On the way there have been many moments of brilliance. Think of Mayo v Tipperary in the 2020 All-Ireland semi-final. By half-time, Cillian O'Connor had already scored 3-6. He would finish with 4-9. With charming modesty, he played down his performance, saying it fell far short of the 6-12 that he hit in an under-12 game for Ballintubber against Davitts.

MIXED REACTION

The Irish soccer team did not win Italia '90 but has there ever been a more loved team on this island? Maybe there is a lesson there. Could it be that it's the love a team generates, not always the results, that makes them great?

When asked to define the difference between prose and poetry, the author Brendan Behan is reported as saying:

> There was a young fellah named Rollocks
> Who worked for Ferrier Pollocks
> As he walked on the strand
> With his girl by the hand
> The tide came up to his knees.

'Now that's prose,' says Behan. 'If the tide had been in, it would have been poetry.'

There is no metric we can refer to objectively to say what makes a great team. However, Joe Brolly is not a fan of the Mayo team. He describes them as 'celebrity losers'. Joe even delved into the realms of theology to highlight his point.

'The Six Sorrowful Mysteries: *The Agony in the Garden. The Scourging at the Pillar. The Crowning with Thorns. The Carrying of the Cross. The Crucifixion. Mayo's Croke Park Torture.*

'In the second half of the drawn game against Kerry [in 2014], they gave the greatest exhibition of hard-running football I have ever seen. Then blew it all by allowing Kerry to score a last-minute goal. In the same way that [Bernard] Brogan and Danny Cummins were unmarked on the edge of the square, so Mayo left James O'Donoghue alone to blast the killer goal. James Bloody O'Donoghue, the most dangerous predator of his era.

'After the sorrowful mysteries comes the resurrection. There's no curse. Just sh*t defending.'

81

THE CATS ARE BACK

Kilkenny 2011–15

The romantics seek magic. He brings cold calculation.

After the bitter disappointment of missing out on 'the drive for five' against Tipperary in 2010, normal service was resumed for Kilkenny with four more All-Irelands over the next five years. What was the secret of their success? Brian Cody was sharing none of them. Monks with vows of silence were more revealing.

It was such a fascinating experience then to listen to former Kilkenny goalkeeper David Herity talking about Cody to Anthony Daly. Herity won no less than five All-Ireland medals under Cody. Herity suggested that to sum Cody up: he's every-thing to anyone. He claimed that: 'Whatever you think he is, he is. You think he's the most generous guy in the world and the most charitable lad – he is, and I've heard amazing stories about him. If you think he's the most ruthless man in the world, he is, absolutely. I can pay testimony to that. If you think he rules like a tyrant, so be it, some people think he's a great man-manager. No matter what you do in life, once you win, everyone forgets about everything else.'

Cody gave Herity the number-one jersey in 2011 after the Cats conceded four goals in the 2010 final defeat by Tipperary.

'He just asked me how many of those goals in the final would you have stopped? I panicked and went "three". And he just nodded and that was enough for him. If I had said, "Oh, I don't know, I probably wouldn't have stopped anything," he'd have went, "Where is this lad at?"

'The final was a turning point in my own head, career wise. I let in a goal. The difference with the great players is they are able to mentally put it behind them. That's one of the great things about Eoin [Murphy].

'But I got kind of caught up. It started in the dressing room afterwards. It would be a harsh enough environment, but I remember (county secretary) Ned Quinn coming over to me – he was shaking hands with the boys around me, and then he came over to me and said, "I don't know if I should shake hands with you – you nearly cost us." So that was the start of it.'

Herity compounded the problem when he was called on stage at the celebrations in the Citywest Hotel alongside Eddie Brennan, for a *Sunday Game* interview with Michael Lyster, who quizzed him about Cody's tactics.

'I went, sarcastically, "Brian is an absolute genius; if there's ever a wonderful tactician, it's Brian. Win your own ball, win your 50/50 battles." Eddie Brennan was beside me and I could see him going "cut the mic" but the crowd were laughing and everything was going happy enough in my head.

'I sat down and then Mick Dempsey and Martin [Fogarty] called me over and it was a case of, "Do you realise you nearly cost us this All-Ireland today? Have you any cop on? All the work everyone has put in all year could have been gone because of you." I'm sure the two of them were unleashed to sort out this lad fairly quick – he's getting a bit ahead of himself.'

Herity heeded the warnings and retained the number-one shirt the following year.

'I became psychotic in my training in 2012. I became the most extreme person in everything I did, getting my body fat down to five per cent. I thought, *Nothing will ever get in the way and make me cost the team again*. But then I had a moment of stupidity in the 2012 semi-final. I should have flicked the ball away, went to rise it and Lar [Corbett] bumped into me and Pa Bourke stuck it in the net.

'At the very next training session, Brian came over to me. "What do you think?" And I said, "Yeah, made a mistake there." And he just said casually, "What's Eoin [then sub keeper Eoin Murphy] like?"'

Herity held off Murphy until the start of the next League campaign. The manner of his demotion was instructive.

'It was the very first training session in Nowlan Park and I was called into the doctor's room with Brian and Martin Fogarty. It was just like, "Change happens, David." And I was oblivious. I got the hint after a few League games that meant you're not in goal and Eoin is. That was it. Change happens. I still remember joking about it down in Langton's. This "change happens" – no clue what he was on about but I soon realised.'

THE HERITY (SHORT-LIVED) REDEMPTION

Herity was anxious to stress he saw the other side of Cody too when he got back in the team in 2014, after Murphy was injured in the Leinster final.

'Before the semi-final, at the training camp at Carton House, he said, "Don't think for a second you won't play against Limerick." And when Brian Cody says that to you, you feel amazing. I felt amazing going into that match. And then the heavens opened, the most bizarre game I've ever in my life played. And I pulled down one going over the bar and the carnage around the square was mayhem.

'And I had this on my mind going into the next training session. And you're looking at Brian out of the corner of your eye. And you start reading in things that aren't remotely there. And Brian came over and said, "Are you nervous?" And I said, "I'm not nervous." And he said, "You look nervous though, you seem nervous, why are you nervous?" He'd try and nick away at you.'

82

THE EDGE OF GLORY

Laois 2003–05

Ireland's first sporting civil war was not between Roy Keane and Mick McCarthy in Saipan but in 1979 when the country was split between whether Tony Ward or Ollie Campbell should be the Irish rugby number ten. While he was the European Player of the Year, the Irish selectors caused a sensation when they dropped Ward on the tour to Australia. Campbell stepped up to the plate brilliantly, but the Ward supporters were not placated.

A few months later, Leinster travelled to play Munster in the interprovincial series. Leinster were captained by the former Irish scrum-half John Robbie. This was the time when the captain really called the shots. Robbie was determined to beat Munster but knew that their hosts planned to bully and intimidate them. Robbie was the last to speak before the Leinster team took the field. Before doing so, he pulled Campbell aside and told him to ignore what he was about to say.

After giving, in the GAA vernacular a 'tyranny of speech' and telling each of the players individually what he expected of them, he finally turned to Campbell and said, 'Ollie Campbell, you are the best number ten in Ireland. There's no question about that. But are you a winner? I'm not sure.' He left it like that. Those words were like an electric shock to Campbell. He played like a man possessed and guided Leinster to victory. It was a brilliant example of player management on Robbie's part.

People use different techniques to motivate players. At Italia '90, Ireland were facing Romania in a penalty shoot-out. Tony Cascarino was wavering about taking a penalty until Ray Houghton went up to him and said: 'Are you a man or a mouse?' Then Andy Townsend shouted at him: 'Pass the cheese.' Cascarino laughed. He agreed to take the penalty and, critically, he scored it.

In the world of Gaelic games, nobody motivated players better than Mick O'Dwyer. It was no great surprise that when he became manager of Laois, he would bring success to the county. Micko managed the Laois team from 2003 until 2006, reaching three consecutive Leinster finals in a period he describes as 'three really enjoyable, great years'.

'We got to three Leinster finals and we won one in 2003 and we should have won the other two as well. Dublin [2005] beat us by two points, and Westmeath beat us by two points [2004]. You have a huge club there in Portlaoise too. Just the one club there in the town – that makes a big difference – and they bring through a lot of good players.'

In the summer of 2002, Meath trounced Laois by eleven points in an All-Ireland qualifier at O'Moore Park. It was a low point for the home team, prompting O'Dwyer, who attended the match, to ask: 'Do Laois people not buy flags?' At the time, Laois fans were generally not even attending games, let alone buying flags. Dwyer was just finishing his time with Kildare and the Laois county board came knocking on his door.

Before O'Dwyer's appointment in 2003, Laois had not won a

provincial title in fifty-seven years – so how did he manage to sprinkle his gold dust yet again?

'It was a friend of mine actually, Declan O'Loughlin, who wasn't involved at the time but himself and his brother down there persuaded me to come to Laois and I was kind of free at the time and I said OK.'

Laois's glory cannot be attributed to Micko alone. The team had some great players: Brian 'Beano' McDonald, Damien Delaney, Ian Fitzgerald, Tom Kelly, Fergal Byron and the gifted and ever-green Ross Munnelly.

ODDS ON

Micko's tenure with Laois produced drama on and off the pitch. After a poorly attended training session in October 2004, he either resigned or threatened to resign, depending on which version of events is to be believed. In subsequent days, chaos and confusion took over. The rumour mill went into overdrive. Boylesports cut O'Dwyer's odds on taking over as Dublin manager from 6/1 to 5/6, with reports of a tsunami of money flooding in. A players' meeting was called and O'Dwyer walked in. Incredibly, the gathering took place as the large media presence watched the discussion unfold through the windows. O'Dwyer was driven away after it finished.

O'Loughlin stopped just short of confirming that O'Dwyer was to continue, but it was fairly clear the harmony had been restored. Next day, Micko was back talking about winning more Leinster titles with Laois.

83

FERMANAGH FLY SKY HIGH

Fermanagh 2004

It seemed an impermissible thought.

He wanted to reshape the GAA world and Fermanagh's place in it. He was working with the team for only a short time when he observed a shift in their mood and ambitions that contained the faint but constant note, almost beyond hearing, of determination. He knew though that the unravelling of the old routines would have to be swift. He knew that he would need to be the surgeon's knife that would cut deeper, sharper and with a twist. He knew that the players knew too. He achieved a near imperceptible recalibration where those tornadoes of emotion were formed.

Fermanagh experienced a sudden change of management ahead of the 2004 season when Dom Corrigan stepped down and was replaced by Charlie Mulgrew. A number of players then opted out for various reasons, so none of the pundits were predicting Fermanagh would reach the dizzy heights of the All-Ireland semi-final. The GAA world really sat up and took notice when they dramatically beat Armagh in the All-Ireland SFC quarter-final.

Armagh were favourites to win the All-Ireland title, having hammered Donegal in the Ulster final.

Things did not look promising for Fermanagh when they lost to Tyrone in the first round of the Ulster Championship. They got a walk-over in the first round of the qualifiers from Tipperary, and then in the next round had a great win over Meath. Colm Bradley got a wonderful point to bring the game to extra time, and then the Ernesiders emerged on top. Marty McGrath was one of Fermanagh's heroes in 2004 and would finish the year with a richly merited All-Star award. Stephen Maguire at full-forward, James Sherry at centre-forward, Stephen McDermott at centre-back, and Barry Owens at full-back formed a good spine of the team. Mark Little, Eamon Maguire, and Niall Bogue would become household names that season.

Cork were outrun in the next round. Donegal were then dispatched after extra time. Then came the never-to-be-forgotten victory over Armagh.

Jimmy Magee saw the historical significance of the game.

'It mightn't mean a lot to other counties like Kerry, but Fermanagh had never even won an Ulster title. However, that game was a defining moment in Fermanagh's history. It will stand out as their finest hour 'til they break their hoodoo and win the Ulster title. The reaction of their fans after the final whistle was as if they had reached the Promised Land. It's not that common to see a pitch invasion after an All-Ireland quarter-final! The Tyrone–Mayo game had to be put back a few minutes. Fermanagh were entitled to have their moment in the sun. Mayo beat them narrowly in the All-Ireland semi-final but only after a replay. Those games were probably Trevor Mortimer's finest in the Mayo jersey, and Fermanagh did not get the breaks they got in previous games, but the story of the GAA is the story of great teams performing great deeds, and certainly Fermanagh had a great team who performed great deeds in 2004.'

84

FROM CLARE TO HERE

Clare 1992

The story of Mayo football over the last fifty years has been written on the script of hurt. Few people are more intimately acquainted with its dark corners than John Maughan.

Injury cut his playing career tragically short. When he retired at twenty-six, he had acquired an All-Ireland College medal with Carmelite College Moate, an All-Ireland under-21 medal, a Connacht senior medal and had been an All-Star replacement.

'I had been having trouble for a while with my cruciate ligament and I suggested to the manager of the Mayo team, John O'Mahony, that I might have a procedure. John thought I had peaked too soon and thought it would be a good time for me to have it done. Things were more serious than I realised and after five operations I knew it was over. It was devastating. From the first time I had tasted the unique smell of a county jersey, I felt very comfortable playing for Mayo, and working in the army allowed me the opportunity to maximise my potential. In UCG, one of my contemporaries was Tom Carr and we trained twice a day, so football was a massive thing in my life and for it to be taken away like that was very tough on me, especially as Mayo were developing into a fine team and I felt we had the potential to win an All-Ireland.'

Not a man to stand still, Maughan threw himself into coaching with various army teams. In 1990, to his great surprise, he found himself at the age of twenty-eight being offered the opportunity to manage the Clare senior football team. He famously coached them to an historic Munster final over mighty Kerry in 1992.

'It was a magical experience, but I didn't fully appreciate it at the time. Clare hadn't won a Munster title since 1917, and for many people the "Milltown Massacre" [in 1979] was fresh in people's minds when Kerry clocked up a score of 9-21. When I first took the job, no one suggested anything about winning a Munster Championship to me. I was brought up with a very positive outlook and my main priority was to set about giving an improved performance. The Meath game in the quarter-final of the League in 1992, when we nearly beat them even though we had two men sent off, gave me an inkling as to how good we were. The one thing I emphasised very strongly afterwards was that I did not want to see any celebrations for running Meath so close. Our time with being satisfied with moral victories was over.

'After that game we thought we were ready to take a Munster title. We got twenty-six players together and we got a great spirit going. I wasn't worried when we missed a penalty in the Munster final – a penalty miss so early in the game has little significance. It was almost a unique performance, in the sense that all our fifteen players played to the maximum of their potential. I felt for the Kerry trainer, Mickey "Ned" Sullivan. I was afraid he would be made a scapegoat for Kerry's performance – which he was.

'The next morning, I got a phone call at seven o'clock. I spent the next four hours sitting at the bottom of the stairs answering one call after another. Then it started to sink in how big a deal it was. I got a call from the county board and was summonsed down to Clare for a tour of the county with the team and the cup.'

85

THE TRIP TO TIPP

Tipperary 2010–19

Hurling had never known such hype.

In the run-up to the 2010 All-Ireland, Kilkenny were having crowds of 10,000 watching them in training as they prepared to take their fifth consecutive All-Ireland. They were fêted as the greatest team of all time. Tipperary were still hurting from the 2009 All-Ireland final when they had narrowly and controversially lost out to a late Kilkenny flourish.

There was another subplot. There was huge interest in whether Henry Shefflin would play or not having torn his cruciate in the previous match against Cork.

Ace Kilkenny forward Eddie Brennan was unhappy with the build-up to the game.

'With the whole Henry thing, I think historically that when you don't have a smooth run-in and not everything is good in terms of injuries and stuff, you will get caught out. That Henry situation created a monster. The whole hype around it became a big deal. Meanwhile, up in Thurles, things were tipping along nicely and smoothly. They were a very driven and hungry bunch of players.

Tipp had honed in on their touch going into that final, and their touch on the day was perfect.'

Shefflin would hobble off early in the game, but the key figure that day was Lar Corbett.

'The only pressure on us was from ourselves after the disappointment of 2009, whereas all the talk was this team being the greatest of all time and on the verge of doing something that had never been done.'

Lar's three goals that day were crucial. He joined an elite club like Tommy O'Connell (Kilkenny), Séamus Power (Waterford), Donie Nealon (Tipperary), Colm Sheehan and Eddie O'Brien (both Cork) who all scored three goals on hurling's showcase day between 1959 and '70.

Six years later, Brian Cody conceded that his side were 'comprehensively' outplayed by Tipperary as the Premier County outgunned Kilkenny with a tremendous second-half performance to regain the Liam MacCarthy Cup at Croke Park. It was Tipp's twenty-seventh All-Ireland and was fashioned with a dominant display after the break that saw them outscore Cody's side by 2-15 to 2-8. Tipp got goals to beat the stubborn resistance from John 'Bubbles' O'Dwyer and John McGrath, while Séamus Callanan was their top scorer with thirteen points. It was a sweet success at the first attempt for Michael Ryan, who took over as Tipp boss that season. Tipperary had lost seven of their previous nine Championship encounters against Kilkenny.

Ryan stated afterwards: 'It felt like a phenomenal second half, and the intensity levels were really high. Our guys showed great skill and great composure throughout. There's nothing revolutionary about forwards working hard – every team in the country sets out to do it, but we seemed to really get it right.'

Three years later, Tipperary were in their version of Disneyland when what began as a dogfight of a final turned into a hammering as Tipperary went on a scoring spree in the second half to crush fourteen-man Kilkenny and win their third All-Ireland of the decade.

The Cats had the better of a tight opening period, leading by five points after twenty-one minutes, but a goal from Niall O'Meara turned the tide. Then came a gamechanger. Just before half-time, former Hurler of the Year Richie Hogan was dismissed for a high challenge on Tipperary's corner-back Cathal Barrett. Tipperary led by a point at the interval, 1-9 to 0-11 but, like their old rivals have so often done to them, they came storming out in the third quarter. Back in the hot seat, Liam Sheedy, nine years after stopping Kilkenny's 'drive for five', led Tipperary back to the Liam MacCarthy Cup in a style nobody could have conceived of. His team racked up their biggest final win over their biggest rivals since 1964, with a score of 3-25 to 0-20.

RYAN'S SON

Donal Ryan watched Tipperary's triumphs with great appreciation.

'When Tipperary prevented an unprecedented five All-Irelands in a row for the seemingly unstoppable titans Kilkenny in 2010, all the pain of the preceding years was washed away; all seemed right with the world.

'When Bubbles O'Dwyer charged towards the Kilkenny goal from the left wing in 2016, I was three rows from the goalmouth in the Davin Stand. I saw the truth in Bubbles' eyes of what was about to happen. I saw the net shaking before he even struck the ball. John McGrath shook the net again shortly afterwards. "Lord save us, Do," my father roared beside me, "I think we're going to do it!" And we did do it, and my father put his arms around me just as he had in that same stadium nearly three decades previously, and we laughed as we walked towards Jones's Road.

'I'm sure we embraced again before he died, but that's the last one I remember. I have one of the great GAA moments of all time to thank for that memory of a perfect moment shared with my father at his last All-Ireland final.'

86

LOVELY LEITRIM

Leitrim 1990–96

One of the iconic images of 1994 was when Declan Darcy, as captain of the Connacht champions, held the Nestor Cup with Tom Gannon, who captained Leitrim to their only previous Connacht title in 1927. Darcy believes that things moved up another gear when John O'Mahony became county manager.

'The first thing was that he came. Before he did so, he'd seen us play when he was Mayo boss and we beat them out the gate in Carrick-on-Shannon, so he knew what we could do. When he agreed to manage us, we knew that he was coming because he believed something was going to happen.

'My abiding memory of the whole thing came that day in Ballinamore after we won the Connacht final. When my father was asked where he was from, he had always said, "West of the Shannon" rather than Leitrim. We did a tour of the county and it was very special. All the players went to their own clubs. The emotion was unbelievable but as someone who grew up in Dublin 4, I didn't have that local base. I found myself on the stage in Ballinamore not sure what to do when my father ran on, grabbed the cup and threw it in the air like a mad lunatic! It was raw and real. It was about passion and pride. It meant so much to him. It is an unbelievable memory that will stay with me forever.'

Although Leitrim were to lose the All-Ireland semi-final to Dublin, Darcy was literally to leave his mark.

'As captain, when I shook hands with John O'Leary, as the photo shows, I was so fired up I nearly squashed John's hand. He told me afterwards that I nearly broke two or three of his fingers and that he thought I had done it deliberately, but it was just because I was pumped up.

'It was a fantastic achievement for the team, and when I led them out onto Croke Park, and although it meant a lot to the county, I was really thinking about all those training sessions we had suffered in Strand Hill. This was the reward for the sacrifices, the endless travel to training sessions and the blood, sweat and tears.

'For Leitrim people just to be in Croke Park one day in their lives was such a proud moment for them. That's the magic of the GAA. It is so much more than football.

'We didn't do ourselves justice in the semi-final, and the next year we left the game against Galway behind us in the Connacht Championship. If we had won, I believe we would have retained the Connacht final and given a much better showing in the All-Ireland semi-final. I know Armagh's Enda McNulty, and he often says that they should have won more than one All-Ireland. I tell him that they were lucky to win one because it is so hard to make a breakthrough when you have no tradition of winning.'

When John O'Mahony stepped down as Leitrim manager in 1996, it was obvious that things were on a downward spiral. What was it about O'Mahony that made him achieve success with Leitrim?

'One thing is his man management and the belief that he gives you. I remember a very tight game against Galway in Carrick-on-Shannon and we got a potentially decisive free about forty yards out. Two or three of our lads ran over to take it, but John came running to the sideline and roared at the top of his voice: "Dec, I want you to take it." He believed in me to score this vital kick, and because he believed in me, I had confidence that I would. To an outsider it looked a pressure kick, but I felt totally calm because of what Johno had said.'

87

THE KINGDOM'S DECADE?

Kerry 2000–11

Once upon a time the then-cabinet Minister Micheál Martin was favoured by a visit of then-Taoiseach Bertie Ahern to his Cork South Central constituency. They went on a door-to-door canvass. Bertie was in his favourite 'man of the people' mode.

They came to the house of a man with impaired vision, who told a story of appalling bureaucratic incompetence at the Department of Social Protection that had seen him lose his blind pension. Ahern shook his head sadly and with that familiar empathetic expression said to the man: 'I don't believe that they could do that to you Mr . . . . That's a disgrace.' And slowly Bertie's head turned accusingly towards Micheál, as did the old man's, before he hung out his colleague to dry: 'Ah Jaysus, Micheál, what are yous after doing to this poor man. You'll have to get it sorted.' Martin manfully took the blame – although government failures in that area was much more Bertie's fault than his.

Páidí Ó Sé once told me how much he admired Bertie Ahern because of his ability to deflect blame away from himself. Páidí learned well from his hero. He basked in the glory when he led

Kerry to the 2000 All-Ireland after a replay. He deflected the blame away from himself when Kerry were hammered by Meath in the 2001 All-Ireland semi-final and then in 2002 when they squandered what looked like a commanding lead against Armagh in the All-Ireland final. What was all the more impressive about his performance was that he did so escaping a public execution by failing to play the most talented player of his generation, Maurice Fitzgerald.

Kieran Donaghy tells a revealing story about Fitzgerald. He was doing some extra work with Bryan Sheehan on his kicking at goal when Fitzgerald joined Donaghy in front of the square. 'Maurice came up to put manners on me,' he said. 'I didn't win a ball for a while – he was pulling me, bumping me as I took off for a ball. I was getting half thick, but he is a selector, so I couldn't do much.' Fitzgerald had steel as well as the style he was famous for. The mystery was why Páidí used him so sparingly in the noughties.

But just as the economic crash after the 2007 general election left Bertie Ahern with no more opportunities for deflection, Kerry's defeat to Tyrone in the 2003 All-Ireland semi-final left Páidí on the ropes. His attempt to deflect months later by describing the Kerry fans as 'the worse kind of f**king animals' would lead him to take the exit door. Discretion prevents me from naming the Kerry legend that told me that Páidí should have learned from Clint Eastwood in *The Outlaw Josey Wales*: 'Don't pi*s down my back and tell me it's raining.'

IMPRESSIVE STATS

It is sometimes forgotten, despite the best efforts of Pat Spillane to claim that Kerry were the team of the noughties, that the Kingdom contested nine All-Ireland finals between 2000 and '11. Perhaps their failure to beat Tyrone in three crunch meetings has meant their achievements are often overlooked. It is noteworthy that between 2004 and '09, Kerry featured in every All-Ireland final. That's six finals on the trot – a feat not even Mick O'Dwyer's fêted side managed. Mayo were hammered in '04 and '06, while Cork were twice defeated in '07 and '09.

This was a team dripping with star power. During the first half of the noughties there was Dara Ó Cinnéide, Liam Hassett and Séamus Moynihan. As Father Time started to catch up on them, Kerry simply replaced them with the likes of Colm 'Gooch' Cooper, Kieran Donaghy and Aidan O'Mahony. Hardy perennials throughout the decade were the nephews of the legendary Páidí Ó Sé: Darragh, Marc and Tomás.

Three of those All-Irelands were won under the management of Jack O'Connor. O'Connor was not afraid to go outside the county for wisdom. Ger Loughnane was one of the people he spoke with. O'Connor has gone public about his disappointment that his achievements did not get the respect he feels he deserves from the greats of the Mick O'Dwyer era.

88

THE TREATY'S TITLE

Limerick 1973–74

It was a time when the now disgraced Gary Glitter's anthemic 'The Leader of the Gang' was replaced at the top of the charts by the more cherubic and wholesome Donny Osmond and his heartfelt tribute to young love.

When Limerick won the All-Ireland in 1973, it was the Treaty County's first final since 1940, when Mick Mackey secured the third of his Celtic Crosses. They were a coming side. In 1971, Tipperary hijacked them in Killarney and won by a point. In 1973, Limerick got revenge when Richie 'cool as an iceberg, sharpshooter' Bennis (in the words of Michael O'Hehir's immortal commentary) scored the last puck of the game in a 6-7 to 2-18 shootout. It was the county's first provincial title in eighteen years.

London had shocked Galway in the All-Ireland quarter-final and were captained by Gerry Rea. By an astonishing coincidence, he found himself marking his brother Ned in the semi-final that Limerick won by 1-15 to 0-7.

In the All-Ireland final, they faced holders Kilkenny, for whom a nineteen-year-old Brian Cody was starting his first final. He found himself marking the youngest player on the Limerick team – Mungret's 21-year-old Liam O'Donoghue. After forty minutes (it was during the eighty-minute match experiment), Limerick led by 0-12 to 1-7, despite a Pat Delaney goal. The team had star power, notably Pat Hartigan at full-back, Éamonn Cregan at centre-back and Joe McKenna at full-forward.

Their goalkeeper Séamus Horgan had been mysteriously dropped for the semi-final and replaced by Jim Hogan, who had been the goalkeeper for years. Horgan was back though for the All-Ireland final, and his brilliant save from Mick Crotty in the second half was the pivotal moment in the game, which Limerick won 1-21 to 1-14. An abiding image from that game came about a minute or two before the final whistle, when the crowd were on the sideline ready to invade the pitch. It was a very wet day, and as it was only paper hats that time, all the green dye was down around their faces.

SECOND ACT

Twelve months later, Paul Anka was sharing the news with his loved one that she was having his baby (one hopes she knew already) at the top of the charts. The same two teams were back again, but this time Kilkenny won 3-19 to 1-13.

Limerick's preparation was not ideal for the final. Two of their prominent players were not on time for the train journey and had to be picked up at Limerick Junction. When the train left the station, the squad were only a few minutes gone when it had to reverse all the way back into the station, because one of the county board officials had left a huge sum of money in the boot of a car. When they got the bus out to their hotel in Dublin, the bus broke down.

Mícheál O'Muircheartaigh was a keen admirer of both teams.

'Limerick had a great side in 1973 and had a great captain in

Éamonn Grimes. They had to be great to beat that wonderful Kilkenny team. Of course, they pulled off a masterstroke deciding out of the blue to play Éamonn Cregan, possibly the greatest forward Limerick ever had, at centre half-back, to counter Pat Delaney. Without that switch, that Kilkenny team would probably have another All-Ireland.

'Kilkenny got their revenge over Limerick in 1974. Not for the first time, the opposition raced into a big lead, this time twelve points. Kilkenny braved the storm and ended up defeating Limerick by that margin. Kilkenny, again, came from behind to successfully retain their crown against an emerging Galway side in 1975.'

89

BRAIN AND BAWN

Kerry 1940–46

Kerry won All-Irelands in 1940, '41 and '46. They also contested the '44 All-Ireland, only to lose to Jimmy Murray's Roscommon. That team were captained by Paddy Bawn Brosnan. One player who never forgot his encounter with 'the Bawn' that day was Roscommon's Brendan Lynch.

'You have to remember it was a very different time because of the war years. Some people listened to the news on the battery-set radio, which was the only programme we were allowed to listen to because of the Emergency, but they kept it on to hear Seán Óg Ó Ceallacháin reading the sports news. Most people heard that either Roscommon had won or Kerry had lost on radio. The belief then was that you hadn't really won an All-Ireland until you beat Kerry in a final so we were all keen to do that. I was marking the famous Paddy Bawn Brosnan.

'He told me once that he was a fairly nifty sprinter. He gave up drinking once, for a fortnight, before the Dingle sports. He came last. He had a fine feed of pints that night and challenged the lads to another contest the next day. He won. From that day, he never gave up the drink before a match. The team trainer Dr Eamon O'Sullivan allowed him three pints a night during serious training. He knew what he was at.'

For his part, the Bawn believed that the pivotal incident in the 1944 All-Ireland final was when Lynch had a head collision with Kerry's great midfielder Paddy Kennedy, who had to be stretchered off. Kennedy asked Lynch: 'Jaysus what did you do to me?'

Brosnan was a massive admirer of Kennedy, one of the greatest midfielders of all time, and endorsed the sentiment they wrote on his tombstone when Kennedy died:

> God rest you, Paddy Kennedy,
> Your reward you've surely won,
> When duty called, you gave your all
> Both off the field and on.

One of the stars of Mayo's All-Ireland winning teams of the 1950s, Paddy Prendergast went to work as a garda in Kerry where he formed a close friendship with one of the icons of Kerry football.

'Kerry had such wonderful players. I always felt that Paddy Kennedy was the prince of footballers. He was majestic, but Paddy Bawn Brosnan was something else – a great player and an exceptional man. He was a lovely human being and at that stage had a pub in Dingle. He had a great feeling for Mayo, and I spent a lot of time with him. One time Seán Flanagan came down to visit me, I brought him to see the Bawn. We went into a quiet nook of the pub and chatted for hours. What I most remember about it though was over the course of the evening thirty people must have peered into the nook just to get a glimpse of Paddy Bawn, such was his legendary status. It was like going to Lourdes.'

DESIGNER GENES?

Mícheál O'Muircheartaigh is perfectly placed to answer the question of whether Kerry's elite status in Gaelic football for the last hundred years is because of some kind of genetic aberration.

'You have to remember that Gaelic football is completely different now than back then. If it was possible to watch the great games of the 1940s, I'm sure we'd be dazzled by their spectacular high-fielding and kicking, but now football is a passing game – five passes for every kick. The other change is now the scores in games are much higher. If you look back at the scores in 1930s All-Ireland finals, you might find a score like five points to four. Of course the answer that old-timers would give is that the backs were good in those times as well. I'll let you work out the implication for yourself!'

90

THE MEN BEHIND THE WIRE

Burke's Brigade 1916

While the focus of this book is firmly on inter-county teams, I did at least want to acknowledge that there are other great teams who have adorned the hallowed history of the GAA. One of the most interesting was born out of a turbulent time in Irish history.

In 1916, Tom Burke answered the 'call to arms' and was interned in Frongoch internment camp (North Wales) where he met Michael Collins. Following the 1916 Rising, 1,800 Irish rebels were arrested and interned at that prisoner of war camp. In the aftermath of the insurrection, 3,000 Irish rebels were arrested in all, and were marched to Dublin Port to board boats destined for internment camps in Britain. Over the next six months, the internees included leading lights of the struggle for independence – like Michael Collins, Richard Mulcahy, Terence MacSwiney and Sam Maguire – who formed deep bonds of friendship while sharing their knowledge and skills. The lessons of the Rising had been learned and Republican networks were strengthened within Frongoch's north and south camps, located at a former Welsh whisky distillery.

The testimony of one of those men arrested, Johnny Flynn, exists today.

'We were lined up at Richmond barracks, marched down along the quays, and along the north wall. There were two rows of soldiers either side of us, with a lorry behind us with a machine gun mounted upon it.

'We certainly weren't very popular as we were marched down to the boat. But for the soldiers either side of us, we might have fared very badly with the women of Dublin. Many of them were shouting, "Shoot the basta*ds."

'The rebels were brought to Britain on cattle ships, many of them thrown into pens alongside the cattle. Of the 3,000 aboard, 1,800 were interned at Frongoch in Wales: an old, disused distillery which had been used as a prisoner of war camp for German soldiers during the World War I. Living conditions were atrocious, with many of the German prisoners at the camp dying of TB.

'In spite of the poor conditions, the proximity of so many Irishmen with similar Republican ideals led to a community atmosphere among Michael Collins and the other detainees, and the prison became known as Ollscoil Na Réabhlóide, or the University of Revolution.'

THE ALL-IRELAND FINAL WITH A DIFFERENCE

At the time, the Wolfe Tone tournament was the secondary competition in the GAA. Louth – captained by Tom Burke – and Kerry had qualified for the final, which was postponed owing to the Rising. Tom's granddaughter Sarah MacDonald takes up the story.

'Such was the volume of players from both teams interned at Frongoch, it was decided that the Wolfe Tone final would be played on the barbed-wire-enclosed field the inmates had deemed Croke Park. It has become known as the "All-Ireland Behind Barbed Wire".

Attendance at the game was made compulsory, so a crowd of about 1,800 watched a game that has been described as extremely tough and competitive. Perhaps apocryphally, one British officer was recorded as having said: "If that's what they are like at play, they must be bloody awful in a fight!"

'The game was recorded by prisoner Joe Stanley, who was a Louth-based publisher of Republican literature. His report of the game itself is sadly rather vague. All that is known is the game lasted forty minutes (comprising two twenty-minute halves) and that Kerry won by a point. The Proclamation was read out by piper Cormac Bowell during the interval. After the game each player placed a piece of grass from "Croke Park" into the box with their medals as a tribute to the men interned there in 1916.'

There was an unusual marketing strategy for the game. Posters advertising the Wolfe Tone Tournament final match in Frongoch between old rivals Kerry and Louth informed fans that 'admission was five shillings and wives and sweethearts should be left at home'!

Today, the barbed wire has been removed from the field, and now it is grazed by sheep. Locals in the Welsh village still refer to the field as 'Croke Park'. There is a small monument to the memory of the game and the men involved, which was erected by a Liverpool branch of the Gaelic League.

91

THE PURPLE AND GOLD

Wexford 1970–77

He speaks silent lines in a requiem to missed opportunities.

In 1970, Martin Quigley made his senior debut for Wexford, and he played his last game for the county in 1989. In the course of his career, he won four consecutive All-Stars from 1973–76 and was chosen at centre half-forward on the Centenary team of greatest players never to have won an All-Ireland. In 1970, he was part of a unique piece of family history in the first eighty-minute All-Ireland final when, with his brothers Pat and John, he was part of an all-Quigley half-forward line as Wexford lost to Cork. To add to the family connection, another brother, 'Big Dan', was selected at centre-back. An injury-stricken Wexford amassed a highly creditable 5-10, but Cork ran up a massive 6-21.

That Wexford team would contest two further All-Ireland finals. The following year they reached the final. Although they found themselves 2-2 down inside the first six minutes to a great Wexford side with exceptional players like Tony Doran, Cork staged a thrilling comeback, driven by Pat Moylan. They won 2-21 to 4-11 in an all-time classic.

In 1977, the same two teams again contested the All-Ireland final. In another exciting contest, Cork prevailed, despite conceding three goals, 1-17 to 3-8.

THE SWEETEST FEELING

Asked about the greatest moment of his career, Martin Quigley's answer comes with lightning speed.

'Our Leinster final win of 1976. Kilkenny had beaten us in the previous five finals, but we beat them by seventeen points that year. I remember looking at the clock with about ten minutes to go and we were leading by fifteen or sixteen points and I thought, *There's nothing they can do to us now*, though with Kilkenny you can never know. It was such an unusual feeling for me to be so confident against them – that's why I remember the incident so well. The game went reasonably well for me but nothing exceptional. It was one day though when it was all about the team.'

That year also saw his greatest disappointment.

'We really should have won the All-Ireland that year, having been eight points up against Cork after ten minutes. We had really good teams in Wexford those years and we were very unfortunate not to have won at least one All-Ireland in the seventies.'

The downside of a career of Quigley's longevity is that he literally wears the scars of his escapades.

'In a League match against Offaly, I was hit on the back of my head as I went for a dropping ball. At half-time our medics examined it and I had nine stitches inserted without any anaesthetic. I just clenched my teeth and braced myself. When the question was raised if I was fit to continue, it was said, "He's a hardy young fellow and he'll be all right." Out I went for the second half when it was the last place I should have gone.'

92

SIMPLY THE BEST

Mayo 1999–2003

Is she the greatest of all time?

Cora Staunton was the star of the four-time All-Ireland senior football Mayo team (1999, 2000, '02 and '03).

She learned at a young age the folly of Bill Shankly's observation that football is more important than life or death.

'I'm from a country family. My dad was a farmer, and my mom didn't work until we got bigger because there are eight of us. They were very supportive – they just let us off to play and get involved in whatever we wanted to be involved in. It was very much a community thing. Whoever was your football coach at the time was probably your neighbour and they used to bring us to a lot of the games. It was how it worked in rural Ireland.

'I really struggled in the first year of secondary school because I didn't really know anyone. I went from a primary school of about a hundred kids into a school of 850 and none of my primary-school friends went there. I found that change all very difficult at the time, but I was so engrossed in sports I was playing on every team I could play on.

'Between first year and transition year, my mother got sick with cancer and she died when I was sixteen. That was the only time I stepped away from sport for a very short period of a couple of months. Not that I didn't love sport – I was going through a grieving process and I was quite angry at the time. My thoughts were because I was playing so much sport and I was so talented, I was on probably ten or twelve teams, so I kind of got a bit angry at sport that it had robbed me of a lot of time at home and with my mom when she was sick.

'At this stage, I was sixteen. I had started to play on the Mayo senior team as a thirteen-year-old, so, in hindsight, I was probably a little bit burned out as well. I was probably trying to keep every side going, and then obviously the turmoil of what was going on at home made it difficult.

'People kept calling to the house. They'd call to collect me for training and, even if I wouldn't go, they kept turning up. And I suppose the more time I spent with them and the more time I spent watching the game, I started to get my mojo back and have the *grá* for it again. That was the reason I got back to sport, the people that were involved in the teams and my friends. Since I went back, I haven't stopped.'

SCORING SUPREMO

What sets Cora Staunton apart from everybody else in the hall of fame is the longevity of her career and the enormity of her scores. Four examples serve to illustrate. How about the 4-13 she scored for Mayo against Leitrim in the 2009 Connacht semifinal? Or the 2-14 against Galway in the 2016 Connacht final? Maybe the 3-11 against Tyrone in a qualifier in 2012? But the pièce de résistance was the 9-12 she scored for Carnacon in a club game against Westport in 2015. She has also made her mark Down Under. In 2021, she was chosen on the AFLW Team of the Year after an impressive campaign with the Greater Western Sydney Giants.

To misquote Bob Dylan, in ladies football, the times are a-changing. Gaelic football is the fastest-growing female sport in Ireland. There are hundreds of girls down at the nursery in clubs all around the country every weekend. The coaching today is generally way more advanced than when Cora began her career. The skills gap remains with their male counterparts, but that is slowly changing.

Nobody has done more than Cora Staunton to change this. She is the benchmark by which new stars of the game, like Armagh's Aimee Mackin, will be judged.

93

LORD OF THE RINGS

Munster 1940–63

Some competitions make enemies of friends. This one makes friends of enemies.

In 1927, a new interprovincial competition was born called the Railway Cup because of its sponsorship by Irish Rail. The first finals, played in Croke Park on St Patrick's Day, were won by Munster (football) and Leinster (hurling). Initially, there was huge public interest in it. The all-time attendance record was set in 1954 when 49,023 saw Leinster complete a hurling-football double. Having played an astonishing twenty-three consecutive years for the province in 1963, Christy Ring won his eighteenth Railway Cup medal with Munster.

He saw it as a way to make friendships with old foes. To take one example, he had some tasty encounters with Tipperary. In the 1961 Munster final, Ring and John Doyle became embroiled in a punch-up while Tom Moloughney was knocked to the ground, allegedly after being struck by Ring. In the aftermath, Ring was wrongly named in some national newspapers as having hit both

Doyle and Moloughney. The National Union of Journalists subsequently issued an apology to him.

HELL'S KITCHEN

That Tipp team gave the GAA perhaps its most famous unit – the famous Tipperary backline known as 'Hell's Kitchen' of John Doyle, Mick Maher and Kieran Carey. Ring said of their full-back, 'You could go through other full-backs but you had to go around Maher.' In addition, Ring once briefed a Cork team about the Tipp players on the eve of a big match. His analysis of one player was short and sweet: 'There'll be no change out of Maher.'

Maher once grabbed Ring's hurley and threw it into the sideline crowd, only for Ring to dart into the goalmouth and pick up the keeper's spare hurley. Ring broke his wrist after a clash with Maher in 1957. The incident produced one of the most famous photos in the history of the GAA when Ring walked off the pitch and exchanged words with Mick Mackey, who was the umpire, and over sixty years later fans still speculate on what exactly was said between them. The next day Maher sent the Cork icon a get-well card in hospital, and this was the basis for an enduring friendship between the two great exponents of the warrior game.

Maher went on to contest for the presidency of the GAA but lost out to Jack Boothman. The no-nonsense approach which Maher brought to the hurling field was also evident when he served on the Munster Council. When late-arriving Kerry members of the group sought to raise an item, Maher noted that if they were on time, they could have engaged fully in the earlier discussion. Suffice to say they were very punctual afterwards.

The Railway Cup provided the platform for players like Ring and Maher to cement the bonds of friendship off the field. Ring once said, 'Without Tipperary, hurling is only half-dressed.' One of Maher's teammates, Jimmy Doyle, had a photo of Ring in his wallet when he died. Another Tipp legend, Mickey the 'Rattler' Byrne, had a photo of Ring on his mantlepiece.

On the pitch, the Railway Cup added an additional layer to the Ring mythology, and his lengthy catalogue of epic performances in the Munster jersey helped cement his iconic status.

TIME TO SAY GOODBYE

As Ring was walking past the Cork College of Commerce on Morrisson's Island on 2 March 1979, he suffered a massive heart attack and collapsed. He was taken by ambulance to the South Infirmary Hospital but was pronounced dead on arrival. He was fifty-eight years old. 'We carried him at last,' was former team-mate Paddy Barry's remark, in reference to Ring often saving the Cork hurlers from almost certain defeat. Many former Munster teammates including Jimmy Doyle, Micky Byrne, Tommy Doyle (from Tipperary) and Mick Mackey (from Limerick) attended the funeral.

Ring's graveside oration in Cloyne was delivered by a former Cork and Munster teammate – the then Taoiseach, Jack Lynch. Lynch's last words were: 'As long as young men will match their hurling skills against each other on Ireland's green fields, as long as young boys swing their camans for the sheer thrill of the feel and the tingle in their fingers of the impact of ash on leather, as long as hurling is played, the story of Christy Ring will be told. And that will be forever.'

94

OBSERVE THE SONS OF ULSTER

Ulster 1984

Deep in the stillness I can still hear him speaking.

In 2008, I had my fourth meeting with Packy McGarty, the Leitrim player selected on the GAA's greatest team of footballers never to have won an All-Ireland medal. He was seventy-five at the time, and as we were chatting beside a football pitch, he picked up a ball and soloed from one end of the pitch to the other. I recalled that incident in April 2021 when the sad news emerged that he had left us. It was the Railway Cup that brought him on to the national stage.

'l will always remember sitting in the back of the car on the way to my first match with Connacht beside Mayo's Pádraig Carney, "The Flying Doctor", who was the greatest footballer I ever saw. I was only a young lad from Leitrim and I was going to be marking the Munster captain Jas Murphy, who captained Kerry to win the All-Ireland in 1953. He was six foot three and I was only a small lad in comparison. I was thinking about this and looking at

Pádraig's massive legs when he said, "Junior, don't be afraid." It gave me great confidence.

'The only problem was that as we were getting ready to go out on the pitch, Tull Dunne from Ballinasloe, who was in charge of the team, said, "Anyone that's not doing his stuff, we have good subs and we'll take him off." With respect to Tull, that wasn't giving me much confidence. I was thinking, *I shouldn't be on this team.* As I looked around all these great players with great reputations, all I could think was, *Here I am a nobody from Leitrim.* Our captain, Mayo's Seán Flanagan stepped in at that stage and said, "Stop. Ye had a night to pick the team and anybody who was good enough to be chosen that night is good enough to play unless they get injured." I grew in confidence again.

'A few days before the match, I'd got a splinter in my hand and I had a bandage on it and was wearing gloves. The first ball that came into me I caught it and it fell out of my hand and I caught it again and kicked it over the bar. I got rid of my gloves and bandage straight away, and as I was doing that, Pádraig Carney clapped me on the back and said, "Well done, Junior." I got a goal and four points and had one of my best games ever. Those few words from Carney though were critical because I looked up to him so much and they gave me the confidence to take my place among some of the greats of the game.'

In the 1950s, Derry player Jim McKeever's reputation soared.

'The Railway Cup was a big thing at the time. It attracted massive attendances. There were crowds of 25,000–30,000 in every game I played. The emphasis was on playing the best football. It was great for footballers in the weaker counties to play against the very best. Everybody wanted to win. I think it's a great pity that the competition went into such decline. In the first Railway Cup match I played in, I was marking the great Mayo captain

Seán Flanagan. In the second year I marked the legendary Paddy Bawn Brosnan of Kerry. The reputation of players like that tended to emphasise their toughness or hardness but I found nothing untoward happened.'

For seventeen years Stephen King's career progressed without any success with Cavan at inter-county level. He had the consolation though of winning four Railway Cup medals.

'The Railway Cup was hugely important to me, particularly in the 1980s. At the time Ulster football was in the doldrums. The Railway Cup allowed us to rub shoulders with players from the great Kerry team and match ourselves with many of the greatest players of all time. Ulster, probably more so than the other provinces, always took the competition very seriously and it paid off with the success we had.'

MONAGHAN'S FINEST

Monaghan's most famous footballer Nudie Hughes was a big fan of one Ulster team.

'I was lucky to play for a Monaghan team that enjoyed success. We just were a bit thin on the ground for quality players and that stopped us from getting over the line. The door was open for us to beat what at the time was said to be the greatest-ever team, Kerry, in the All-Ireland semi-final in 1985. We drew, but they put us away in the replay.

'It meant a lot to me to win three Railway Cup medals because there were so many great players in Ulster at the time. I have heard a lot of talk about the greatest team of all time. For me, the Ulster team in 1984 is my dream team. Any of the great teams of the past or present would have struggled to beat us.'

That team in full was:

1. Brian McAlinden
(*Armagh*)

2. Joey Donnelly   **3. Gerry McCarville**   **4. Tony Scullion**
(*Armagh*)   (*Monaghan*)   (*Derry*)

5. Ciarán Murray   **6. Paddy Moriarty**   **7. Jim Reilly**
(*Monaghan*)   (*Armagh*)   (*Cavan*)

8. Joe Kernan   **9. Brian McGilligan**
(*Armagh*)   (*Derry*)

10. Greg Blaney   **11. Eugene McKenna**   **12. Peter McGinnity**
(*Down*)   (*Tyrone*)   (*Fermanagh*)

13. Martin McHugh   **14. Frank McGuigan**   **15. Nudie Hughes**
(*Donegal*)   (*Tyrone*)   (*Monaghan*)

95

SO FAR AWAY. SO CLOSE

Mayo 1996–2006

John Maughan's appointment as Mayo manager would usher in a new era for Mayo football.

Shortly after his retirement from playing, Peter Ford soon found himself back in Mayo football when Maughan made him one of his selectors. The big chance of glory came in the 1996 All-Ireland final.

'With fifteen minutes to go I could only see one result. Mayo had a comfortable lead, but we tried to defend it and pushed back too far and allowed Meath to pick off their points.'

It is very evident that Ford feels a strong grievance about the replay.

'The sendings-off were a complete mismatch. Liam McHale was our best player and while Colm Coyle was a fine player, his loss to Meath in no way compared with the loss of Liam to us. I've heard it back since from informed sources, shall we say, that the referee had intended to send off one of the Meath midfielders, but the umpire intervened and told him he had to send Coyle off because of his role in the melee. When we played against the breeze, Liam would have been ideal for that. Nonetheless, we struggled on and only lost by a point.'

BITTER PILL

John Maughan still feels the pain of the two games in 1996.

'There is no doubt the worst moment came when we surrendered a lead to allow Meath to draw with us in the 1996 All-Ireland final. I had been absolutely convinced we were going to win. I told punters that they were safe to back us against the bookies. So that game really hurt. I was physically sick after it. I rushed to empty myself in the cubicle and then I had to go pick the team up for the replay two weeks later. I think we did that very well.'

Mayo's All-Star defender Dermot Flanagan remembers a great display that year: 'We played some super football in 1996 and were tremendous when we beat Kerry in the semi-final.'

A fine lobbed goal by James Horan was the highlight of their 2-13 to 1-10 win.

ON THE SIDELINE

In 1996, when Mayo lost the All-Ireland, it was the referee who was in the firing line. In 1997, when Mayo lost the All-Ireland, it was Mayo manager John Maughan himself who was in the firing line.

'I took a lot of flak after the game for the way we didn't replace Dermot Flanagan directly but made a series of switches and, above all, for leaving Pat Holmes on Maurice Fitzgerald. The best man to have marked Maurice would have been Kenneth Mortimer, but we needed him up in the forwards. With the benefit of hindsight, we maybe should have put someone else on Maurice with ten or fifteen minutes to go, but we felt then it was best to stick to our guns.'

The door was open for Mayo in 1996 and '97, but they were

comprehensively beaten by Kerry in the All-Ireland finals in 2004 and '06. I asked John Maughan what his proudest moment in football was.

'My greatest day was when we beat Galway, who were All-Ireland champions at the time, in Tuam in the Connacht final in 1999. Tuam had always been a bogey ground for us. Every year is sweeter in Mayo when we beat Galway because the tradition of rivalry with our old enemy is so embedded into the Mayo psyche.'

96

PAT ON THE BACK

Dublin 2011

It was written in the stars.

Bernard Brogan offers two revealing snapshots as to how Jim Gavin built on the firm foundations laid by his predecessor Pat Gilroy, in particular the lengths he went to as Dublin manager to ensure the team were not 'emotionally hijacked' again like they had been against Kerry in 2009. Gilroy's response to that infamous 'startled earwigs' seventeen-point defeat in the All-Ireland quarter-final was to recruit a performance and business consultant, Bart McEnroe, who Brogan says, 'tore into Pat, saying he'd brought shame on his county for overseeing that disaster in Croker. "You're only a novice! Bluffer! Choker! Your team can't tackle. You can't coach! You can't manage!" McEnroe kept on abusing Gilroy and his team right until they were nose to nose and the Dublin manager eventually snapped and pinned him against the wall. The consultant just smiled and retorted, "Pat, look at yourself! You've allowed yourself to be emotionally hijacked again!"'

Before the squad boarded the bus to head to Croker on All-Ireland final day in 2011, Gilroy furnished them with a couple of stats. The first was their tackle count from the opening game of the season against Monaghan. It was double what it had been in that loss to Kerry. Then he highlighted their tackle count against Donegal in the All-Ireland semi-final a few weeks earlier: 120. More than double what they'd managed against Monaghan. Further words were superfluous. The message was sent and received. Dublin were a transformed team. The result confirmed that.

THESE BOOTS WERE MADE FOR ...

Joe Brolly believes that Michael Darragh MacAuley was crucial to Gilroy's success. He shares an anecdote from just before the 2011 All-Ireland final. Gilroy was standing in the middle of the changing room, watching. The boys were now togged out, in their boots, ready to go. Suddenly, Michael Darragh MacAuley, who was still in his trainers, caught Pat's eye and nodded him towards the toilets. Pat followed him in.

'What is it?'

'I've forgotten my boots.'

'F**k off, Michael.'

'Seriously, I have.'

'Jesus Christ, Michael. What size are you?'

'Twelve?'

'I'm thirteen,' said Pat. 'They'll have to do you.'

Pat squeezed into the trainers as Michael Darragh put on his boots. 'Do not say a word to anyone,' said Gilroy. The midfielder went on to put in a monumental performance at midfield as Dublin won their first All-Ireland in sixteen years. As Gilroy later joked, 'It made no difference to him anyway because in those days he never kicked the ball.'

'Gilroy first came across him in the Dublin club Championship, when MacAuley marked him. Gilroy said it was "a nightmare. He never stopped. He was as strong as a horse. He tackled so hard, he left me with bruises." When he became Dublin manager, he called him into the squad and, as Gilroy said, "He was the key man. He changed everything. His attitude was the spearhead of the transformation from losers to winners. He was unbreakable. He ran out every bleep test. He trained like he played. He destroyed his markers with his stamina, his tackling, his quick hands, his heart."'

Brolly was also a keen admirer of MacAuley's courage: 'He would put his head where you wouldn't put up a crowbar.'

The dynamic midfielder arrived on the scene in 2009 but didn't make his Championship debut until a year later, when he appeared as a sub in a win over Wexford. After Meath hit five goals past Dublin, MacAuley became an integral part of Pat Gilroy's new-look boys in blue, and by the end of that year he was a regular, as Dublin recovered to reach the All-Ireland semis. In 2011, he won the first of his eight All-Ireland medals, but the summit of his career came in 2013, when he was named Footballer of the Year. Apart from his success with the Dubs, MacAuley also helped his club, Ballyboden St Enda's, win three county Championships, two Leinster titles and the 2016 All-Ireland club title. He won All-Stars in 2011 and '13.

Gilroy's Dubs won only one All-Ireland, but he put the building blocks in place for Jim Gavin to take the reins from him and sweep all before them.

97

THE DARKEST DAY

Tipperary 1920–22

The first flinty hint of winter's breath on the breeze fell on a nice November day. The unseasonal weather was completely at odds with the political temperature. After the countryside, the city's waves of noise and movement seemed clamorous to the visiting Tipp fans who travelled up by train in the shadow of delight.

That morning, like so many Dubs, Jane Boyle walked to Sunday Mass in the chapel where she was due to be married a mere five days later. There was little drama about her, no apparent depths of intensity or unfulfilled longings that were evident on the surface at least. That afternoon she would travel with her fiancé with indefatigable enthusiasm to watch Tipperary and Dublin play a Gaelic football match at Croke Park. She had no idea that at that very moment, nine men lay dead in their beds after a synchronised IRA attack designed to cripple British intelligence services in Ireland. She had no intimations of her own mortality. She had no conception that instead of her wedding, her next visit to the church would be in her coffin.

British intelligence was on a good run and getting closer and

347

closer to nabbing Ireland's answer to the Scarlet Pimpernel, Michael Collins – the mastermind who 'would win the war for Ireland'. Recognising that the tide was turning firmly against him, Collins decided that desperate measures were called for. A storm was approaching. It could not be any darker than his thoughts.

Members of the infamous 'squad', one of Collins' killing machines, were in action. Among their number was nineteen-year-old Vinny Byrne. He killed two men, Lieutenant Ames and Lieutenant Bennett, with an amalgam of mercy and mayhem. Before he shot his victims, he whispered into their ears: 'The Lord have mercy on your soul.' However, the autopsies confirm that his victims were riddled with bullets. Standing beside Vinny was Johnny McDonnell. Just a few hours later, Johnny would line out in goal for Dublin in the big game at Croke Park. His presence in both venues is a reminder not to accept that the distance between them is unbridgeable.

Today we think automatically of Tipp as a hurling superpower. But in 1920 they were a footballing force. Tipperary had lined out in the All-Ireland final twenty months earlier, only to be beaten by a Wexford side that was winning its fourth title on the trot. Although Dublin were not the force they were under Kevin Heffernan or Jim Gavin, they were nonetheless a major power too. That's why so many people flocked to Croke Park that day, despite the mutterings there could be trouble after word spread of the killings that Collins' warriors had inflicted.

They all arrived with their Arcadian dreams of escape from the complexities of the world within the limitation of their resources. A natural passion diverted into tributaries. There was to be no slow fade through the amber mutation of autumn for them; the lilting lightness of anticipation in their voices as the game began simmering in its own juices, a sealed cauldron of electrified, motorised and human sweat.

CARNAGE

Collins' special units had taken out fourteen British intelligence and security servicemen and somebody was going to have to pay a heavy price with their blood. Trucks of police and military sped through the city streets as hundreds of people sought sanctuary in Dublin Castle. Some of the military vehicles were headed for Croke Park. Their mission was supposed to simply be 'a scoping exercise' to gather intelligence, but the military leadership was akin to a man wielding someone else's power and as a result being overgenerous with it. Seeing the military arrive, the crowd panicked and ran. The British forces opened fire on them. Bullets were flying, and people caught up in a tempest were running.

In this tyranny of terror, to die in your bed became the unspoken dream. For a seeming eternity, like a modern-day tower of Babel reigning only confusion and chaos, the attendance were held captive by a cold entanglement of fear in their stomachs – until eventually silence settled and there was only the unsteady beating of hearts. A few sat silently and gave no clue as to whether they had understood what had happened or not.

Some of the wounded sought refuge in nearby homes and were laid out on kitchen tables as inexpert medical care was provided. The corners of the room were folded into shadows and all the light seemed pulled into the centre about the table. Strange thoughts troubled everybody present. Rooted in the inescapable vulnerability of the time, it was difficult not to succumb to a maudlin mix of nostalgia and self-pity.

A vigil of sorrow was praying at the spot where the Tipperary player Michael Hogan had gone to meet his God. The light had faded from his eyes, as if he saw nothing but a trembling darkness.

Having beaten Dublin in the 1920 All-Ireland final (played, confusingly, in 1922), Tipperary would never win the competition again.

98

WHAT THE DOCTOR ORDERED

Kerry 1953–59

Joy unspeakable.

It erupts when you least expect it, when the burden is greatest, when the hope is nearly gone. It rises on the crest of impossibility; it sways to the rhythm of steadfast hearts, and celebrates what we cannot see coming.

Kerry fans are genetically programmed to win All-Ireland finals. They expect to win every final they contest, though 1955 was an exception.

My guide to all things Kerry football was the late Weeshie Fogarty. He believed that 'the most underrated great Kerry team' was the side of the 1950s. They won three All-Irelands in '53, '55 and '59.

'Little did any Kerry follower believe that following the success of 1946 it would be seven long years before All-Ireland honours would again be captured. In the intervening seven years, many of the greatest-ever Kerry players retired. Dan O'Keeffe, Joe Keohane, "Gega" O'Connor, Eddie Walsh, Batt Garvey, Paddy Kennedy, Dan Kavanagh and numerous others faded from the scene. There was a sensational loss to Clare in Ennis in 1949, 3-7 to 1-8. Three years later, in 1952, Cork demolished their great rivals in the Munster final 0-11 to 0-2. This game was remembered for the marvellous display of full-back Paddy Bawn Brosnan and goalie Donal Marcus O'Neill.

'With Jackie Lyne – the only remaining link with the 1946 winning side – lining out at corner-forward, Kerry had a magnificent win over Armagh in 1953. It was the golden jubilee year of Kerry's first All-Ireland success. A record attendance of over 86,000 spectators were present to see Bill McCorry miss a vital late penalty for Armagh as Jas Murphy led his county to a 0-13 to 1-6 victory. Paudie Sheehy, captain in the semi-final, had been sensationally dropped for the final. New stars shone in the green and gold: Tadghie Lyne, Ned Roche, Jim Brosnan, Mixi Palmer, Johnny Foley, Tom Ash and others received a rapturous home-coming to the Kingdom. The team had stayed in the Park Place Hotel, Killarney, for two weeks before the final, and Dr Eamon O'Sullivan and Paul Russell were the joint trainers of the side. Collective training was banned the following year and Meath proved far too good as Kerry attempted to retain their crown. The Royal County won 1-13 to 1-7.'

There was no question for Weeshie which of their titles in the 1950s was the sweetest.

'The year 1955 will forever be remembered fondly by all Kerry supporters as the year Kerry defeated the so-called unbeatable Dublin machine in what was a magnificent final, 0-12 to 1-6. The great-hearted John Dowling captained the side. Johnny Culloty made his senior final debut. Seán Murphy, Mick Murphy, Garry O'Mahony, John Joe Sheehan, Tom Costello, Ned Roche, and John Cronin wrote themselves into the glorious history of Kerry football that never-to-be-forgotten day. Dr Eamon O'Sullivan was once again the man behind the victory. He guided Kerry to nine finals, winning on eight occasions. A magnificent record.

'Waterford stunned the GAA world in 1957 when they defeated Kerry in Dungarvan, and it was reported the team officials delayed the return to the Kingdom until darkness had fallen. In torrential rain, Derry got a late goal to stop Kerry's advance in 1958. The following year, however, saw the county capture their nineteenth title with an easy win over Galway, 3-7 to 1-4. Dave Geaney, Garry McMahon and Dan McAuliffe were the Kerry goalscorers. Dr Seán Murphy gave a superb display at wing-back and was Man of the Match. Mick O'Connell captained the side, and the fifties had seen the emergence of such greats of O'Connell, Mick O'Dwyer, Tom Long, Johnny Culloty, Seamus Murphy, Jerome O'Shea, Niall Sheehy and Tadghie Lyne.'

DOCTOR'S ORDERS

Mícheál O'Muircheartaigh believes that the combination of Dr Eamon O'Sullivan and Kerry's tradition were crucial to Kerry's success.

'Players are much fitter and more mobile now. You could never imagine a player like Pat Spillane staying in the one position in his glory days. The famous Dr Eamon trained Kerry on and off from the 1920s to the 1960s. He was a firm believer in all players keeping their positions. He actually wrote a book about his ideas. I think the name of it was *The Art and Science of Gaelic Football*. He pointed out that for Gaelic football to be seen at its very best, all players should keep to their positions and that every tussle for the ball should be just between two players. He also said that good kicking and fielding would win out in the end. In the book you'll find sentences like, "There is no justification for finding a right-handed midfielder over on the left." He took it to an extreme, but he did win a lot of All-Irelands with Kerry. His theory would be perfect if every player was the ideal and perfect player, but of course they're not. It's now a running and supporting game, as they say.

'Certainly Kerry have a great tradition. As a result of that, almost every young boy in Kerry dreams of playing for the county in Croke Park. I suppose it would be fair to say that a lot of Kerry people believe that winning All-Irelands is their birthright. It's hard to quantify how much that tradition means in concrete terms, but it's fair to say it contributes to the assembly line of talented players that have emerged from Kerry.'

99

THE BOXERS

Ireland 2006–08

Seán Boylan was fuming. It is a rare occurrence, and to see him getting so publicly angry was a sign that something extraordinary had happened.

His former captain, Meath captain Graham Geraghty, lined out for the second test of the infamous 2006 International Rules Series. Boylan managed the Irish team.

Geraghty had been cited for a knee to the head of Australian Lindsay Gilbee in a first test that Ireland won by eight points. The match in Galway was a relatively tame affair by the standards of what was to come. Some of the Australian players took some tough shots on the pitch and planned to settle some scores at the Croke Park decider, one week later.

Geraghty was knocked out by Danyle Pearce and the match descended into what Boylan described as 'thuggery'.

EARLEY DAYS

Like his father before him, Dermot Earley Jnr won two All-Star awards (his sister Noelle and his uncle Paul also won All-Stars) and his displays in the Kildare jersey and in the Compromise Rules for Ireland were a source of immense pride for his father. There was one time though when Dermot Snr was not happy to see his son wearing the green jersey, as his brother Paul witnessed at first hand.

'Dermot was irate about what happened in 2006 in the second test because he considered what the Aussies did to be nothing less than savagery. Many people will remember Kieran McGeeney's comments after the match: "If you wanna box, say you wanna box and we'll box. If you wanna play football, say you wanna play football and we'll play football."

'There was a dinner afterwards and Dermot was one of the guests. I was talking to one of the most high-profile members of the Aussie delegation and he was trying to tell me what happened was no big deal – despite the fact that Graham Geraghty was left unconscious and required hospitalisation. I told him to stop talking through his arse.

'The atmosphere was very tense. Then Nickey Brennan, who was GAA president at the time, stood up to speak. He pointedly said before he started he wanted to wish Graham Geraghty well because he was in hospital. You could feel the tension go up another notch immediately,' he remembers.

'The Aussies' coach that year was Kevin Sheedy and he came over to our table and was trying to be placatory and said that it would be very different the next time and said there would be a dinner for both teams first and that would sort everything out. It was so out of character for Dermot, who was always so diplomatic, but he asked him: "Will you have the fight before, during or after the dinner?" Talk about an awkward silence afterwards.'

Given the fallout from the controversy, the series was postponed the following year. Boylan would lead the Irish side to Australia in 2008. This time there was no controversy about violence and the series was simply a footballing contest. Ireland emerged on top.

100

THE PRIDE OF THE PARISH

Feakle 1987–88

Muideanna chun mise.
We before me.

This book focuses on inter-county teams. However, as clubs are at the heart of the GAA, I wanted to close the book with a club team. This presented a selection dilemma: which club to select? There were a number of contenders in terms of titles won with great stories: Birr, Portumna, Caltra, Newtownshandrum, Donie Shine's Clann na nGael, Baltinglass, Ballyhale Shamrocks, Dr Crokes, Ballygunner, Thurles Sarsfields, Carnacon, Buffers Alley, Castlebar Mitchels, Ballymun Kickhams?

However, I decided to offer a more inclusive approach and to select a less well-known club whose greatness comes from the hold it has on its members. I chose Ger Loughnane to be my guide as he took me on a tour of his home parish. He may have been voted the Manager of the Millennium but in the Feakle roll of honour, he trails in a distant third.

'Not alone am I not Feakle's most famous person. I am at best only the townland of Kilbarron's third most famous person. Its most famous resident was Biddy Early, and its second most famous person was Johnny Patterson, who lived down the road. He wrote a lot of famous songs like "The Stone Outside Dan Murphy's Door" and "Goodbye Johnny Dear". He was also a world-famous circus performer who performed political sketches on stage. He made it really big in America in the nineteenth century before he came to Ireland. He was killed after a performance in Tralee where he did a sketch in which he brought an orange and green flag together on stage and put them together to signify the unification of the two traditions on the island. This caused uproar in the audience. A massive row took place and he was hit on the head with a hammer and died as a result of his injuries.'

A Seamus Durack puckout away from the family home is Kilbarron Lake, where Biddy Early's famous blue bottle now resides. The 'witch of Feakle' put a curse on the hurlers of Clare and over a hundred years later the wizard from Feakle would undo her curse. Nice story but it might be more plausible if Biddy Early hadn't died well before the GAA was founded.

Loughnane's late father, John James, won four national cross-country titles. Although Ger is most likely to be found listening to the dulcet tones of Eva Cassidy, his father's fiddle has pride of place in the Feakle family home. Every morning Ger hand-milked four cows before going to school. The farm was divided in two parts. The smaller part, around the house, and the other a mile and a half away.

'I had the luckiest childhood of all time. I came at a bridge between the old and the new. Having experienced the old but having lived with the comforts of the new, I've had the best of both worlds. It was a great grounding for life, and the value system that was passed on was wonderful. It's great to have the memories of the old but you wouldn't like to still live in them.

'The back-breaking work farmers did then was unbelievable. There were no tractors nor machinery, so everything had to be done by hand. People had such a great work ethic back then. There were so many skills a farmer had to have. He had to be a butcher to kill his own pigs, a carpenter, a vet and a weather forecaster. People never spoke of stress, but my father had seven children and the guillotine was always just over his head. It was hardest of all on the farmer's wife. My mother had to look after seven children as well as the geese, chickens and the calves. She also cycled for Mass at 8.30 every morning, winter and summer.'

HOMEWARD BOUND

We stand around in circles that we never truly leave. One of the proudest moments of Loughnane's life came in the Feakle colours in 1988.

'Having been born and reared in Feakle, and having started hurling with Feakle, and above all having listened for years to all the stories about hurling in Feakle, I wanted to play my part in bringing glory to the parish on the hurling field. Feakle had a great team in the 1930s and won four county titles, but there was a massive gap until we won the next one. We had a great team that won the Clare Cup, a League competition, in the 1960s. They got to the county final but lost. They were just not able to get over the final hurdle. It was a replica of the Clare team.

'We won an Intermediate Championship when I was twenty. When you're an inter-county player, you feel a huge sense of responsibility of delivering a county title to your club, especially when they haven't won for a long time. Coming to the end of my inter-county career, I was living in Shannon so I played for Wolfe Tones in Shannon for two years. Feakle won four under-21 Championships in a row. Those players were coming on to the senior team, and although they had a great team potentially, there was something missing. One night in the West County hotel, Fr Harry Bohan asked me if I'd go back to Feakle. I said I'd go back for a year because I was thinking about retiring at that stage. When I went back, there was a new spirit and a new set-up.

'A new man, Tony Hayes, was in charge. He was the parish equivalent of an excellent county manager. He was so well organised and such a sound man. He had no insecurity about taking advice from outside. We had great inter-county players like Michael and Tommy Guilfoyle and Val Donnellan. We won the Clare Cup and got to the county final. We had a puckout before the match, and afterwards I said to the team, "I've been gone from Feakle for a few years but I'm going to have the game of my life to make sure that Feakle wins today." We were playing Clarecastle, but something punctured the whole team. It was like one of the Munster finals I played with Clare. They just couldn't get going and do themselves justice. It so happened I did play the game of my life, but we lost by a few points.

'It had everything a good county final should have, including a massive row in the tunnel at half-time! I was in the dressing room when it happened, but I knew the row would cause our young players to lose their concentration. Clarecastle were like the Meath footballers of the 1980s! They are a brilliant club, but a row suited them down to the ground!

'Afterwards everyone said we'd give it one more go for the following year. That year, we won the Clare Cup again and had a fantastic game to beat Éire Óg in the semi-final. The young players were playing with great confidence. I played corner-back. Our full-back was Seamus McGrath who was an outstanding player. He had a brilliant brain and we had a telepathic understanding. We beat Ruan easily in the county final, but like the Munster final in 1995, we didn't believe we had won until the final whistle went. If we hadn't won, there would have been a massive gap in my career. It was so near the endline for me that if we didn't deliver that day, there was going to be no other opportunity. It was on a par with winning the Munster final in 1995 for me. It really meant that much. It was just a wonderful feeling to deliver for your parish.'

THE FINAL WHISTLE

Time changes everything. But one truth will always stay the same.

Our teams are part of who we are.

Through the darkness, the great teams are our light that will always shine.

When we stumble in the night, when pain sweeps over us, when our dreams are stolen, through tears and the turbulent years when our lonely hearts break, the great teams are the ones that we can never forsake.

They are the fires that roar to fill the holes in our souls.

While we are gently sleeping, they are in our dreams.

We cherish all they give us because they are our forever love.

The vast majority of teams are simply footnotes. The great GAA teams though constitute one of the most distinctive, dramatic and dazzling chapters in the book of life.

101

GRACED BY MICHAEL COLLINS

Dublin 1921

He was the most famous name in Irish life at the time.

He had taken on the greatest empire the world had ever known in the War of Independence and his innovative tactics had brought them to the negotiating table. It was he who was ultimately responsible for the Truce, and later Treaty, between Ireland and the old enemy. For years he had been the 'Scarlet Pimpernel' of Irish history as he was on the run from the forces of the crown.

The Truce gave him permission to enter the public space. There was no place more public than the hallowed ground of Croke Park. It was indicative of the speed of change in those tumultuous years that only ten months earlier, on a tragic Sunday in November, fourteen civilians were murdered on Jones Road by the hated Black and Tans.

It was time to publicly usher in a new era. As Dublin and Kilkenny went head-to-head in the Leinster Hurling Championship final Michael Collins appeared publicly in Croke Park to throw in the sliotar. In fact, he went further and treated the crowd to an exhibition of his skills with the hurley as he 'took a few pucks' in the company of his great friend Harry Boland. As 15,000 people flocked to the GAA's theatre of dreams to view the contest, they roared Collins on like a hurling star and a war hero.

Before he came to public attention in the 1916 rising and drawn by images like Percy French's of people digging gold in the streets, Collins spent time in London. There he had shown his love of the GAA by becoming secretary of the local club. In 1921 his flicks and tricks with the sliotar in Croke Park allowed him to play out his childhood fantasies.

However, like most politicians, he had another agenda. Although he had no training in public relations Collins was keenly attuned to his perception by the population as a whole. Of course, he was not the only Irish politician to use sport shamelessly to advance their political popularity. Think Charlie Haughey when Stephen Roche won the Tour de France or after Italia '90. More recently consider Shane Ross when he was Minister for Sport. Collins knew that being seen to display his skills with the small ball would do him no harm with sports fans in the political arena. If he was going to appear in public, it was no accident that he did so when there were plenty of photographers present. The sporting theatre was overshadowed by the political performance.

Dublin won the match on a score-line of 4-4 to 1-5, but the day was not primarily a hurling spectacle. That era was the zenith for Dublin hurling. Four of the county's six All-Ireland hurling titles were won between 1917 and 1927.

ACKNOWLEDGEMENTS

I am greatly honoured by the fact that the legendary Anthony Daly agreed to write the foreword for this book.

My deepest thanks to Rena Buckley, Kieran Donaghy, Maura Duffy, Séamus Hickey, Micheál Martin, Oisín McConville, Con O'Callaghan, Diarmuid O'Donovan, Donal Ryan, Ray Silke and Jackie Tyrrell, for their invaluable assistance.

My gratitude to Brendan Coffey for sharing some of his many riches with me.

Special thanks to my former star student Rosanna McAleese for her insights.

Thanks also to Seán Boylan, Joe Brolly, Ross Carr, Joe Connolly, Kevin Doyle, Bernard Flynn, Eddie Keher, Brian Lohan, Ger Loughnane, Michael Darragh MacAuley, Jamesie O'Connor, Pat Spillane and the many others who gave me assistance.

Thanks to Simon Hess, Campbell Brown, and all at Black & White Publishing for their help.

This year, injury forced Donie Shine's premature retirement from football. He is one of the giants of Roscommon football and, like his late father before him, leaves a treasure trove of great memories behind him.

Mary Mahon leaves behind generations of students greatly in her debt as she retires from teaching. Her brilliance as a teacher is matched by her rich vein of humanity.

After a life of dedication and service, Catherine McCarthy stepped off the playing fields this year. May she always know joy and contentment.

Fionn Hickey was born this year. May he inherit the goodness of his mother Sarah and his family's sporting genes.

I am very grateful to a great Fermanagh fan Fr Brian D'Arcy for his generous support of my most recent book, *Inspiration for all Seasons*. He is a man and a GAA fan for all seasons.

Last October, we bid a final farewell to Maurice Flanagan. Maurice was a gentleman in every sense of the term. He was also a man of books and wisdom. *Requiem aeternam dona eis. Domine et lux perpetua luceat eis. Requiescant in pace.*

In January we lost the much-loved Theresa Greene. She left us better than she found us. She left the world better than she found it. *Go ndéana Dia trócaire ar a n-anamacha dílse.* May God have mercy on all we have loved and lost.

Another loving family lost a beautiful woman in Gretta Daly. She remains a bridge of love across both time and space. May the stars shine all around her.

My good friend Fr Tony Draper was much in my thoughts as this book was being written. I wish him every happiness. Former Cork GAA star Brian O'Driscoll has fanned the flames of friendship.

Roscommon hurling lost one of its greatest servants this year in Ray Fallon. May he rest in peace.

I must conclude by celebrating the feat of my own club Saint Brigids who won consecutive Roscommon county finals in 1958

ACKNOWLEDGEMENTS

and 1959. Nothing extraordinary in that you might think. However, what makes this double remarkable is that they featured the exact same team lining out in each game (with no positional switches) and by not introducing a single sub over the two campaigns.